To

Alice e Sally

Thanks for all your

support.

Dave

Dad

xxx

Conny H. Antoni, Xavier Baeten, Rosemary Lucas,
Stephen Perkins, Matti Vartiainen (Eds.)

Pay and Reward Systems in Organizations –
Theoretical Approaches and
Empirical Outcomes

PABST SCIENCE PUBLISHERS
Lengerich, Berlin, Bremen, Miami, Riga, Viernheim, Wien, Zagreb

Bibliographic information published by Die Deutsche Nationalbibliothek
Die Deutsche Nationalbibliothek lists this publication in the Deutsche Nationalbibliografie; detailed bibliographic data is available in the Internet at <http://dnb.ddb.de>.

© 2011 Pabst Science Publishers, D-49525 Lengerich

Typesetting: Claudia Döring
Cover photo: © Franz Pfluegl – Fotolia.com
Printing: KM Druck, D-64823 Groß-Umstadt

ISBN 978-3-89967-725-6

Contents

Preface 7

Reward Mix Conceptualisation and Determination: A Review of the Literature
Jonathan Chapman, Clare Kelliher 9

Expatriate Compensation: A Theoretical Approach
Christelle Tornikoski 38

Talent vs Performance-Based Managerial Pay
Marco Celentani, Rosa Loveira 68

Introducing Performance-based Reward Systems within Collectivistic
National Cultures
Biljana Bogićević Milikić 85

Motivation to Knowledge Transfer: Self-Determination Theory
Laurent Sié, Ali Yakhlef 118

Work-life Balance Accounts and Total Compensation –
An Analysis of the Regulation of Work-life Balance Accounts in Collective
Agreements in Germany
Lars W. Mitlacher 140

List of Contributors 165

Preface

This book is a selection of papers presented at the second European Reward Management Conference (RCM) in 2009 that passed sucessfully a review process by two anonymous reviewers. It consists of six chapters, three of them discussing theoretical approaches to reward management, and three are case studies providing a theory-based analysis of prototypical topics in reward system design with implications for both theory and management.

In Chapter 1 Jonathan Chapman and Clare Kelliher give a review of the literature on reward mix conceptualisation and determination. They focus their review on employee pay and consider theories that treat rewards as the dependent variable, such as contingency, agency, institutional and resource dependency theory. Based on this analysis they develop a conceptual framework for the study of reward mix decisions within a total rewards framework. They suggest to combine different theoretical aporaches and to do more qualitative research particularly on employee level in order to better understand the issues decision-makers consider when determining the reward mix.

Chapter 2 by Christelle Tornikoski discusses theoretical approaches to expatriate compensation. This paper analyses expatriate compensation from the perspective of three different groups of actors, which are embedded in different contexts, and uses different theories for these perspectives. The first one is the perspective of human resources specialists, who supposedly try to guarantee that organizational interests are considered by the design of expatriate compensation packages. Agency theory is used to analyse this perspective. The second one is the perspective of supervisors, who lead and motivate expatriates. The third one is the perspective of expatriates themselves, who manage their careers. Social exchange theory, the concepts of psychological and idiosyncratic contracts, and total rewards are used to discuss the later two perspectives. Finally, environmental or country context factors, influencing both human and organizational behaviours, are discussed using institutional theory. Based on these different perspectives and theories five propositions are developed to guide further research practice and implications for managerial practice are discussed.

In Chapter 3 Marco Celentani and Rosa Loveira discuss critically the notion of „The War for Talent" and provide arguments that it does not make sense to pay „talent" independent of performance. In particular, they analyse the question, whether in markets for managerial services, where information about managerial talent is not publicly observable, information about managerial talent is used in equilibrium contracts, compared to situations, where information about managerial talent is publicly observable. They show that when information on managers' talent is publicly available, it is used in the equilibrium contract. However, if this information is not publicly available, it is not used, because of the competition of companies for talented managers and the existence of information asymmetries with respect to managers' abilities to forecast the realisation of investment projects.

Chapter 4 by Biljana Bogićević Milikić analyses the interdependence between culture and reward systems using a case study of a company that implemented a performance-based reward system within a collectivistic national culture. Based on interviews with managers and employees, as well as secondary analysis of questionnaire data the implementation process of a new reward system and its effects are analysed. It is shown that collectivist values strongly influence employees' equity perceptions and go along with critical views regarding large ranges in base pay, but not necessarily with respect to pay for performance. Based on these results hypotheses for further studies are proposed and implications derived to guide managerial practice.

In Chapter 5 Laurent Sié and Ali Yakhlef analyse the motivation of experts to transfer their knowledge to novices. Based on self-determination theory they assume that in the context of tacit knowledge transfer feelings of competence, autonomy and social ties encourage experts more to transfer their knowledge to younger colleagues than extrinsic rewards. The latter might even lead to crowding out effects. They test these assumptions in a case study of a multi-national oil company, whose success depends to a great extent on the ability of its experts to discover new reserves in an as efficient manner as possible. They had interviewed experts to find out what motivates them to transfer their knowledge to younger colleagues, how they experience the transfer process, and what they perceive as requirements for an effective knowledge transfer process. Furthermore, they compare these assessments with the view of novices in this company. Their results give important guidelines for management, how tacit knowledge transfer can be supported.

Chapter 6 by Lars W. Mitlacher provides an analysis of work-life balance accounts as an element of a total compensation approach. The goals of employer associations, trade unions and government are compared based on two collective agreements on work-life balance accounts in Germany. A strategic choice approach is used as a theoretical framework differentiating goals and activities of these actors on three levels: strategic, collective bargaining and workplace levels. This analysis shows how work-life balance accounts can be used as an element of a total compensation approach. Furthermore, interesting questions for further research are developed.

To sum up, the papers in this book give interesting insights in current issues of reward management. They develop promising avenues for further research in this field and offer valuable implications for managerial practice.

Conny H. Antoni, Xavier Baeten, Rosemary Lucas, Stephen Perkins, Matti Vartiainen

Reward Mix Conceptualisation and Determination: A Review of the Literature

Jonathan Chapman, Clare Kelliher

This presents a summary of the findings from a detailed review of the literature on reward mix conceptualisation and determination. The main purposes of this review are twofold. First, examining the issue of reward mix policy decisions from multiple perspectives, will enable a more complete understanding of both our current knowledge on the determinants of reward mix policy and how we come to know this. Second, building on this understanding, to identify specific research gaps for further empirical work.

The review identifies that the conceptualisation of reward mix, and empirical research in the area has typically examined cash compensation, but neglected benefit provision and non-financial rewards which employers are increasingly emphasising under the banner of a 'Total Reward' approach. In addition, a myriad of factors have been shown to determine reward mix and as such suggests that we in reality know little about why reward mix policy decisions are taken. No dominating paradigm has emerged from the research, which adequately explains the process. Finally, the review shows that the research on reward mix determination has been conducted almost exclusively by statistical review with little time being spent with the reward policy decision makers themselves, in order to understand what issues they consider when determining reward mix. Research from different theoretical orientations could add insight to the area through revised theory generation and potentially contribute to simplifying the field.

Introduction

Employee reward can come in a variety of forms (Dreher et al., 1988). The focus of the reward literature has largely been on pay, both fixed, in the form of salaries and wages, or variable through a range of schemes such as incentives, bonuses and stock related schemes (Gerhart & Rynes, 2003). The interest in pay is unsurprising given the amount that organisations spend on pay as a proportion of their overall costs (Lawler, 1971) and its importance to individuals (Milkovich & Newman, 2008). However, this focus neglects the wider approach to reward management choices that practitioners are increasingly taking in the area of total reward (Milkovich & Newman, 2008; Armstrong & Murlis, 2007).

This has led to a call for academic research to incorporate non wage compensation elements and look at the determinants of aspects other than pay (Gomez-Mejia & Welbourne, 1988; Heneman et al., 2000; Milkovich, 1988).

Gerhart and Rynes (2003) note that there is potential for variance in how organisations allocate compensation across the various forms of reward and therefore construct their reward mix. This is in contrast to what (i.e. the amount) they pay, where there appears to be less discretion due to the perceived need to stay broadly in line with competitors for attraction, retention and overall economic competitiveness reasons (Gerhart & Milkovich, 1990). Significant quantitative research has been carried out analysing the relationships between a range of both firm and environmental items and reward decisions including reward mix (e.g. Eisenhardt, 1988; Boyd & Salamin, 2001; Tremblay et al., 2003). Whilst helpful, this research does not give an insight into the relative importance of these factors in the actual reward mix decisions taken (Perkins & White, 2008).

Baeten (2008) identified thirty-four different theories that have been used in reward research (at Executive level), a number of which examine reward mix determination. In this context convergence around a smaller number of theoretical perspectives might prove helpful in closing a perceived gap around the lack of strong theoretical models to aid in understanding the determinants of reward mix and which would direct future research (Pfeffer, 1993).

After setting out the focus of the literature review and outlining the method taken to conduct the review, this chapter defines key reward mix terms and examines how reward mix has been conceptualised in the literature to date. Following this, four explanations of reward mix determination are reviewed. First, contingency and agency theories are discussed as the base for understanding what is driving reward mix decisions in organisations, as the current dominant paradigms in reward mix research. This base view is then critiqued and accompanied by alternative explanations of reward mix decisions. Resource dependency and institutional theory are offered as both competing and complementary explanations for reward mix policy decisions. Second, the theoretical approaches are then drawn together in a review of research, which combines their insights to examine reward mix policy decisions. Finally, the epistemological positions taken by researchers into reward mix are examined and critiqued. From this a conceptual framework of reward mix determination is presented and a number of research gaps proposed for further empirical research.

Review Question

Gerhart and Rynes identified that although reward strategy is a matter of various choices, "surprisingly little is known empirically about how such choices are made in the first place" (2003: 7). It is in this context that this review is intended to explore what we know about how reward mix is determined and from this to build a conceptual framework to be used in future research. This will be carried out not only with respect to singular theories of reward mix determination, but also how they have been integrated.

The scope of the review is limited to employees, not executives. This focus has been selected in the context of criticism of the concentration of analysis at the reward level of the top executives and in particular CEOs (Gerhart & Rynes, 2003) . Focussing solely on the CEO attributes all the success of the organisation on that one compensation decision and the effect it has on one individual. This creates the impression that the remainder of employees make little contribution to the overall company success. Hambrick and Mason (1984; Hambrick, 2007) showed that the success of an organisation depends on all contributions. This led them to propose that reward research should extend its reach across lower levels of the organisation.

Reward Theories

Bloom and Milkovich (1996) identified two types of reward theories. First, those that treat reward as the dependent variable and help us understand reward determination. Other studies treat reward as the independent variable assessing the effect that different reward policies have on individual and organisational outcomes. For example, motivation theories (e.g. expectancy, goal setting, equity) and pay satisfaction theory, all examine the transmission mechanism between reward and specific outcomes (Bloom & Milkovich, 1996). Reward theories can be categorised further between organisational level reward policies and those that consider individual level reward decision[1] (Werner & Ward, 2004). Reward mix determination is an organisational process; therefore, the correct unit of analysis is the organisation (Barringer & Milkovich, 1996) and individual level reward determinations have been excluded from this review (although it is recognised that these may influence reward mix determination). Within these bounds, the review of the literature indicates five theoretical perspectives that have been applied to reward mix determination at organisational level: agency, contingency, transaction cost, institutional and resource dependency[2]. However, evidence for the transaction cost perspective is relatively weak with agency theory suggested as a more effective explanatory framework (Tremblay et al., 2003; Andersen, 1985; John & Weitz, 1989). Consequently, the transaction cost approach is not considered further in this review.

Method

A systematic review was undertaken of the literature on reward mix determination based on the four perspectives identified. The systematic review was intended to provide a detailed and methodologically rigorous review of the reward literature. The search strategy

---

[1] Individual level theories include human capital theory and justice based theories.
[2] A number of other theoretical perspectives have been used to examine reward policy decisions, for example efficiency wage theory or labour market theories. However, these other perspectives were not selected for review as they typically focus on reward level rather than reward mix.

adopted had two streams. First, utilising the power of electronic databases a systematic search was conducted – ABI Inform and EBSCO. These were chosen as their coverage aligned with the 2004 literature review by Werner and Ward that identified 20 top management journals relevant for all reward related research. This list was established from that developed by Gomez-Mejia and Balkin (1992) and reviewed in Werner (2002) and has since been cited by others as a good guide to journal quality in the reward area (Van Fleet et al., 2000). Second, a range of search strings were developed covering a wide range of terms used in examining reward research from the theoretical perspectives examined. An initial filter of the results was carried out removing any obviously unrelated topics (for example during preliminary searches several hundred articles on compensation were related to other subject areas such as consumer compensation, mathematical modelling and legal redress). Following that abstracts were read for relevance and ultimately selection. Data was then extracted from the articles as shown below.

– citation information: author, journal, year;
– descriptive information: country, sector;
– reward mix choice examined e.g. fixed/variable, pay/benefits etc
– methodological information: empirical/theoretical, quantitative/qualitative, case study/survey;
– theoretical perspective(s) taken;
– objective of research: short description;
– data collected: method, sample size etc;
– tests carried out;
– key findings;
– quality assessment: see below; and
– notes and quotes: likely to form main material for literature review write up.

In addition, research quality was assessed with reference to the guidelines for the Academy of Management Journal Guidelines for Reviewers (2007-2010) (http://journals.aomonline.org/amj/reviewer_guidelines.html).

In addition to the systematic review other literature was examined arising from the reading of these journals and suggestions from an advisory panel that was established to ensure that other potentially good sources (such as books and practitioner material) was not missed.

Reward Mix Defined

There is no consensus in the literature around the conceptualisation of reward mix (Yanadori et al., 2002). A summary of reward mix measures used in extant research is given in table 1.

Table 1: Summary of reward mix measures used in employee level reward mix research

Study	Reward mix conceptualisation	Theoretical perspective
Darmon 1982	Relative proportion of salary, commission and bonus	n/a
Ippolito 1987	Proportion of reward in pension as measured by capital loss	n/a
Balkin & Gomez-Mejia 1987	Relative importance of fixed (salary and fringe benefits) and variable (incentive) components of reward	Contingency
Eisenhardt 1988	Proportion of salary relative to sales commission payments	Agency, institutional
Gomez-Mejia & Balkin 1989	Merit pay as a percentage of base salary. Bonus as a percentage of base salary. Aggregate incentive pay as a percentage of base salary	Strategic compensation
Gerhart & Milkovich 1990	Extent of variable pay, in terms of relative amounts of short term bonuses, long term incentives and base salary in individuals pay	Agency, expectancy
Conlon & Parks 1990	Proportion of contingent versus non contingent pay	Agency, institutional
Gomez-Mejia 1992	Proportion of incentives relative to fixed pay	Strategic compensation
Balkin & Bannister 1993a	Proportion of earnings coming from each pay form	Resource dependency
Werner and Tosi 1995	Bonus to bonus and base ratio	Agency
Umanath et al. 1996	Proportion of salary in total compensation	Agency
Gerhart & Trevor 1996	Average ratio of bonus pay to base pay	Agency
Roth and O-Donnell 1996	Proportion of compensation as incentives (short term bonus, long term bonus, short term equity plan, long term equity plan)	Agency
Stroh et al. 1996	Bonus divided by total cash	Agency
Bloom & Mikovich 1998	Ratio of base pay to bonus	Agency
Demougin & Fluet 2001	Strength of incentives in mix relative	Agency
Boyd & Salamin 2001	Ratio of bonus to base pay	Strategic compensation
Miller et al. 2001	Weighted mean of productivity bonus	National culture
Tremblay et al. 2003	Proportion of salary component as a percentage of total average sales compensation	Agency, resource dependency, transaction cost
Kuhn & Yockey 2003	Salary component relative to bonus	No theoretical perspective
Van der Stede 2003	Percentage of compensation that is performance dependent	Institutional, Hofstede, contingency
Datta et al. 2004	Mix of wage payment between cash and kind payments	No theoretical perspective
Yanadori & Marler 2006	Ratio of long-term pay to short-term pay	Strategic compensation, agency, resource dependency
Burke & Hseih 2006	Balance of fixed and variable compensation	n/a
Pappas & Flaherty 2006	Percentage of total pay in incentives	Expectancy
Segalla et al. 2006	Fixed versus incentive compensation	Agency, expectancy, Hofstede
Ittner et al. 2007	Salary to cash bonus ratio	Agency
Festing et al. 2007	Fixed pay compared to variable pay	Resource dependency, institutional, Hofstede.
Abbot & De Cieri 2008	Extent to which work-life benefits are included in reward mix	Strategic choice, stakeholder, resource based view

The conceptualisation of reward mix is dominated by the examination of cash compensation, albeit defined in a range of different ways. Benefits and relational returns are generally excluded. Festing et al justified this focus as "the decision about variable and/or fixed pay is the starting point which guides all the other decisions" (2007: 122). Some papers included benefits and relational elements in theoretical discussions of reward mix, but the use of these in empirical research has been more limited. For example, Werner and Tosi defined reward mix as "the way that firms orchestrate different components of pay, such as base pay, bonuses and incentives, and benefits" (1995: 1672). However, they then measured mix as the ratio of bonus to total cash compensation. These narrow definitions may be because of the relative ease in measuring cash compensation, or alternatively, given that none of the studies record having spent significant time with practitioners themselves to understand what reward mix means to them, an inaccurate specification of the term.

Scholars have called for the conceptualisation of reward mix to be more widely defined. Gerhart and Milkovich stated that "in structuring monetary compensation, decisions concerning the mix between direct pay and benefits are important. But, at an even more general level, organizations face a choice between allocating resources to pay versus other potential rewards/returns, such as improved supervision, participation, working conditions, advancement opportunities, job design, training and so forth" (1992:551). They add that, given the increase in the proportion of compensation provided through benefits, it is less and less correct to equate direct pay with total monetary compensation (1992:484).

This wider definition is in line with practitioner interest in an extended reward definition often termed total reward (Perkins & White, 2008; World at Work, 2007). This approach has been heavily supported by professional bodies such as the CIPD and World at Work and a range of reward consultancies who have published total reward frameworks.

Reward Mix Research

A Contingency Perspective

Contingency theory contends that one variable's effect on another will depend on a third factor (Donaldson, 2001). These contingency factors will therefore need to be considered when reward choices are being taken, in order to examine the question as to whether there are "general best practices in compensation or do appropriate compensation practices depend on a variety of contextual conditions?" (Gerhart & Rynes 2003 p257).

A number of contingencies have been studied. Gerhart and Milkovich (1992) developed a contingency based model of compensation decisions, which described how they believed employers took decisions about reward mix (amongst other things). This contingency model included a number of both environmental and organisational factors including business strategy, HR strategy, product market and firm size which were said to influence the type of compensation system an organisation pursued. Since then a number of scholars have examined statistically the relationship between some of these factors and reward mix. For example, Gomez-Mejia and Balkin (1992) identified two different pay strategies that were adopted dependant on whether organisations were defenders (i.e. firms staying in the same industry and product line and protecting market share through continual refinement and cost efficiencies), or prospectors (i.e. firms that tended to be first to market with new products and innovations hoping to gain an early advantage in the new market). They showed that defenders typically choose a mix which focuses on base pay and benefits, compared to prospectors who place greater emphasis on longer term incentives. Rajagopalan supported the conclusions of Gomez-Mejia and Balkin that the effects of the pay strategy depend on its alignment with the business strategy and, in addition, discovered that prospectors perform better with long term stock plans (Rajagopalan, 1996). Montemayor, applying a different measure of business strategy based on Porter's Generic Strategies (Johnson et al., 2008), found that the incentive to base pay ratio varied according to business strategies based on cost leadership, differentiation and innovation (Montemayor, 1996). Furthermore Gomez-Mejia (1992) and Kerr (1995) identified that product diversification was significant and Chen and Hseih (2005) highlighted the importance of company life stage.

Other elements of strategy have also been considered including firm size (Artz, 2008; Ang et al., 2002; Russell & Callanan, 2001; Krashinsky, 2002); ownership structure (Blasi et al., 1996) and unionization (Abraham et al., 2008; Colvin et al., 2001; Batt, 2001; Kaufman, 2002; Raphael, 2000). In addition studies have covered a range of factors that could be said to affect business certainty, including economic variables (Olson & Schwab, 2000; Christofides & Laporte, 2002); technological changes (Brown & Campbell, 2001; 2002); environmental uncertainty (Umanath et al., 1996) and legal factors (Addison & Blackburn, 1999; Friesen, 1996; Kaestner & Simon, 2002).

Widely cited research by Bloom and Milkovich (1998) examined the role of business risk as a key determinant of base pay and bonus policies. They found that firms in higher risk environments (measured by volatility in stock returns) will have lower shareholder returns where they adopt more aggressive performance related incentive programs. In addition, Stroh et al. (1996) noted that the use of increased variable pay was about transferring risk to employees, using variable reward strategies to manage the additional variability in revenue and profitability that they are facing at this point in their history.

There has been less work on the influence of organisational culture on reward mix determination. Chiang and Birtsch (2006; 2007; Chiang, 2005) examined the effect of national culture (not organisational) on reward preferences of employees (not reward choices by organisations) using Hofstede's cultural framework (Hofstede, 2001). They found limited predictive capability of Hofstede's approach and therefore speculated that employee preferences may in part be influenced by variables other than national culture, for example organisational and environmental factors. Organisational culture could however be hypothesised to be significant given the view that culture is a key element in creating competitive advantage, the difficultly in imitating it and the effort organisations put into developing it (Barney, 1986; Collins & Porras, 1994).

Agency Theory

Agency theory examines the relationship between owners or principals and employees or agents. It proposes that both parties look to achieve the most favourable employment exchange possible for their interests and will act accordingly (Jensen & Meckling, 1976). According to this theory reward mix is a significant control mechanism used by principals to ensure that agents act in the owners' best interests. Most of the reward research using agency theory as its theoretical base has been done on the compensation of top executives in organisations, usually the Chief Executive Officer, with lower level understanding of reward mix issues less well studied (Bloom & Milkovich, 1998; Trevor, 2008). Studies extending beyond executive reward have been conducted and will be examined below.

Agency theory provides insight into how goal incongruence, differing risk preferences and information asymmetry can be managed. At the centre of managing these issues is reward mix defined as the proportion of fixed and variable reward making up total compensation. Wiseman et al outlined the importance of "creat[ing] a common fate" through reward mix (2000: 312). Higher proportions of variable pay are intended to achieve this common fate by tying employees' interests to those of the organisation (Gomez-Mejia & Balkin, 1992; Delvey, 1999). How organisations attempt to achieve the common fate depends on the type of contracting arrangement they put in place and the reward mix arrangements that flow from this. Outcome based contracts link agent's reward to an outcome desired by the owner of the organisation, for example shareholder return. This is desirable for the owner as it aligns reward between owner and employee. However, the use of outcome contracts may be less appealing to employees as outcome measures are not fully in their control (Eisenhardt, 1989). For example, an organisation's share price will move not only due to the performance of the organisation, but also due to wider market moves independent of the organisation's performance (Hull, 2009). The transferring of risk, through outcome based contracts also has a cost, as the agent will require a risk premium through a higher level of total reward, to compensate for the increased risk that they are bearing (Eisenhardt, 1989). The level of risk premium will reflect the increased uncertainty of result, which comes from outcome based contracts (Eisenhardt, 1989). Agency theory predicts that high levels of business uncertainty lead to higher proportions of fixed pay, as the risk premium required to compensate employees for uncertainty about future compensation flows and lowered employment security becomes prohibitively expensive (Bloom & Milkovich, 1998). However, research has not shown this, with organisations in fast-paced uncertain markets adopting more flexible approaches to compensation to manage cash flow and attract the required skills (Stroh et al., 1996; Balkin & Gomez-Mejia, 1987; 1990).

Alternatively, behaviour based contracts can be used, which link employees' reward to specific behaviours or actions delivered by the employee regardless of their ultimate effect on the return accruing to the principal. This may be more appealing to employees as it is within their control, but may have less appeal to the principal given the monitoring costs associated with the subjective measurement and the fact that behaviours are not guaranteed to deliver the principals' goal (Eisenhardt, 1989). The decision about which form of contract to adopt is a key one for organisations, given the implications that it appears to have for how reward is distributed between fixed and variable reward elements.

Reviews by Eisenhardt (1989), Zajac and Westerphal (1995), Prendergast (1999) and Miller and Whitford (2007) indicate that agency theory research generally supports the prediction that reward mix can assist in controlling employees. However, agency research can be criticised on a number of fronts. Studies have typically focused on sectors and roles where measurement of performance is straightforward e.g. piece rates, sales and overall profitability when using CEOs as the target role (Prendergast, 1999). This may limit the usefulness of the approach in understanding roles where behavioural contracts are more common, due to outcome measurement difficulties. A cautious interpretation of the results would also take into account whether the activities performed in their own right carry any intrinsic motivation, which, according to Deci (1985), would be diminished by explicit monetary payment (Prendergast, 1999). Tosi et al. (1997) criticised the firm level econometric approach to testing agency theory, which required proxy variables to be developed based on the availability of data. They contend that the usefulness of these studies is limited by concerns over construct validity and reverse causality. Prendergast also notes the problem with "identification difficulties" (1999: 11), that although the theory often provides a good explanation, the outcomes observed could equally be explained by other theories.

Miller and Whitford asked the question that, in light of this support for the use of incentives to align outcomes, "why are incentives not used more often than they are?" noting that "even in those cases where the agent's performance can be directly linked to compensation, corporations often still choose to use contingency-free compensation schemes" (2007: 214). They concluded that this is driven by self interested principals accepting lower efficiency "out of a concern for the principal's own profit." (2007: 215). They outline that there are theoretical cases where the incentive levels required to induce effort are more costly, due to the risk premium required being significantly higher than the resulting increase in profitability. A degree of inefficiency is profit maximising. Consequently, "most organisations, and in particular public agencies, rely very little on pure incentive contracts and instead use coercive mechanisms of monitoring and sanctioning" (2007: 213).

The agency model has been criticised for its focus on reward mix as the pivotal mechanism for control and ignoring other elements of the agency relationship (Eisenhardt, 1989; Fernandez-Alles et al., 2006). The contract specification cannot capture all relevant dimensions, such as uncertainty, information shortages and the dynamic and political nature of the relationship (Tosi et al., 1997). A further criticism questions the agency theory assumption of a conflict of interest between principal and agent and consequently, whether there is a need for reward mix to act as a control mechanism (Deckop et al., 1999). For example, Ouchi (1980) contended that goal incongruence varied across the workforce. Where alignment was strong Deckop et al believed there was little need for incentive pay as the "clan-form" (1999: 421) would ensure behaviour consistent with organisational goals.

A final criticism comes from the fact that agency theory has generally been applied solely to cash compensation (Barringer & Milkovich, 1998). It could be extended to include other elements of reward with benefits considered as a fixed element. However, this approach has its drawbacks given the deferred nature of certain benefits and the rising value (i.e. variability) of this benefit as retirement approaches. Sheppard et al (1996) also showed the incentive effects that flexible work has, where workers are prepared to work hard enough not to lose this valued part of the mix through dismissal. This variable has not been incorporated, to the best of my knowledge, in any agency based research.

Agency and contingency theory have emerged as the main theoretical explanation of reward mix. However they both have focused on the fixed to variable reward relationship, not a wider mix definition incorporating benefits and relational returns. For this we need to look to other theories for insight. It has also been suggested that these theoretical approaches overemphasise the efficiency and rational drivers of decision making in reward mix choice and underestimate the institutional and political power related pressures that may be relevant to organisations (Barringer & Milkovich, 1998; Bartol & Locke, 2000). For example, Eisenhardt concluded that agency theory "is an empirically valid perspective, particularly when coupled with complementary perspectives" (1989: 57), and Barringer and Milkovich stated that "agency theory presents a partial view of the world that … ignores a good bit of complexity of organizations" (1998: 71). Further examination of these "complementary perspectives" is important to understand the role they may play in reward mix decisions to deepen our insight of how they interact and influence decision making.

Institutional Theory

Institutional theory[3] proposes that institutional forces create coercive, mimetic and normative pressures on organisations to be similar in how they operate (DiMaggio & Powell, 1991). The extent to which these constraints operate influences how much freedom of choice organisations may have over reward mix (Carpenter and Wade, 2002).

Coercive isomorphism "results from both formal and informal pressures exerted on organizations by other organizations upon which they are dependent" (DiMaggio & Powell, 1991: 67). These pressures can take a number of forms. First, legal, through laws and regulations. U.K. employment legislation has increased significantly since 1970 with, for example, minimum wage, working hours and holiday entitlements, share ownership and pension legislative requirements having been introduced. As components of reward mix, constraints on how they are managed are likely to influence the overall mix. For example, pension legislation has sought to influence organisations' behaviour towards this element of the reward mix, with direct coercion in the form of personal accounts to be introduced from 2012 (Crown, 2008). These politically driven influences on reward mix may mean

---

[3] This review is based on neo-institutional theory which took initial theorising on the influence external factors have on organisations and extended this through describing the processes by which external factors influence organisations (Hatch and Cunliffe, 2006).

specific benefits are provided, even though they are expensive (Festing et al., 2007). Perkins and White felt that the legal context was so significant that "while employers may wish as far as possible to create reward strategies for their own particular circumstances, the starting point will always be what the law allows or requires" (2008: 67). Second, as the tax system regarding pay and benefits has changed, tax efficiency, especially around the balance between benefits and cash wage payments, has become increasingly significant (Perkins & White, 2008). This led Long and Scott to conclude that "taxation is a major determinant of the compensation mix" (1982: 218). Finally, coercive pressures may arise from trade unions. Unions appear to have a particular interest in certain elements of the reward mix, such as holiday entitlement, pensions and sick pay (Forth & Millward, 2000). Budd and Mumford (2004) also showed how union representation was positively related to the extent to which family friendly policies were part of the reward mix.

Mimetic behaviour is when organisations adopt policies that others have adopted, in order to gain the security that conformity is perceived to bring (DiMaggio & Powell, 1991). Organisations look to avoid uncertainty as diverging from standard practice is seen to increase risk (Norman et al., 2007). Mimetic pressures appear to be commonplace in the reward field originating from a number of sources (Trevor, 2008). First, organisational knowledge may be held by particular individuals and through turnover, this knowledge may be spread across other organisations. Specific reward specialist recruitment agencies are established (such as TotalRewardCareers and Portfolio CBR) potentially indicating a specialist market in reward managers and a flow of their expertise across organisations. Diffusion of standard reward mix practice may also occur through the activities of consulting firms and trade associations (DiMaggio & Powell, 1991). The use of consultants has been shown to have a legitimising effect (Barkema & Gomez-Mejia 1998, Main et al. 2008). The reward consulting profession is well established in the U.K. A Chartered Institute for Personnel Development survey (CIPD, 2008) found that 32% of organisations had used a consultancy service to provide benchmarking data. Benchmarking has been identified as a key factor assisting the spread of isomorphism (Eisenhardt, 1988; Crystal, 1991). Specific reward professional bodies are also in place as mechanisms by which firms can establish the practices of others and can replicate them. In the U.K., the largest is the CIPD which has a specific reward forum for reward professionals, which provides access to data so that firms can replicate the position of other 'similar' organisations. Practitioners have also taken it upon themselves to develop semi formal gatherings of those from similar sectors, through the establishment of groups such as the Financial Services Reward Networking Group, with the intention of sharing benchmarking data. Support is also evident from research on executive reward. Bender concluded that "companies used performance-related pay because their peers did, and because that legitimised them in the eyes of the establishment" (2004: 521). Ogden and Watson (2004; 2007; 2008) found that Remuneration Committees felt under significant political pressure, which led to policies shaped by comparisons to other companies, rather than analysis of performance consequences of reward decisions. This conclusion was supported by Main et al. (2008), who noted the significance remuneration committees place on the market in determining which measure of performance was used in long-term incentive schemes.

Finally, normative pressures stemming from "the collective struggle of members of an occupation to define the conditions and methods of their work ... and legitimisation for their occupational autonomy" (DiMaggio & Powell, 1991: 70). For example, the 'New Pay'[4] prescription that pay should be linked to performance (Lawler, 1995; Schuster & Zingheim, 1996), which has been widely promoted by the consultancies and professional bodies, despite concern that they may not be appropriate prescriptions for all types of organisation (White, 1996). Eisenhardt (1988) found that the key driver in determining reward mix was acceptance of the practice within the sector, rather than alignment with strategic goals.

Table 2 summarises studies that have used institutional theory to specifically examine employee reward mix determination. The support for institutional influences on reward mix determination is strong. Eisenhardt (1988) concluded that contextual conditions at the time of the organisation being established were particularly significant on mix choice and, once chosen, the reward mix had longevity. Van der Stede identified the presence of "intracorporate isomorphism" (2003: 268), reflecting the strong influence of parent companies on business unit reward mix decisions. Whilst relatively little is known about cross national reward practices (Werner & Ward, 2004), Segalla et al's (2006) examination of cross-national sales compensation practices concluded that culture influences reward mix decisions through the effect it has on managers. This led them to question the applicability of institutional theory's theoretical prescriptions for effective reward mix decisions in all scenarios, particularly where national boundaries are concerned. Fernadez-Alles et al (2006) found that reward mix policy incorporates popular reward trends and practices stating that "variable compensation is sometimes designed to reward not those particular practices and procedures that rationally should enhance the performance of the company but those that enhance its social standing and reputation in its institutional context" (2006: 963).

The research on reward mix determination appears to show that institutional pressures are influential. However, the theory does not fully explain differences in practices between organisations. Critics argue that institutional theory fails to fully incorporate individual organisational strategic and leadership goals (Hambrick, 2007; Oliver, 1991). Given that reward mix can be changed without increasing costs (Lazear, 1998), then organisations may face less difficulty in differentiation themselves in this area. "[P]ay mix is where the action is in differentiating organisations" (Gerhart & Milkovich, 1992:669). In addition, despite the iso-morphic pressures that appear to exist, examples show changes in reward mix policies are occurring, such as the introduction of different types of performance related pay, closing of defined benefit pension schemes and the introduction of work-life balance initiatives (Armstrong & Brown, 2005). So, as with agency research, it would appear that the institutional theory explanation of mix determination is also incomplete.

---

[4] 'New Pay' became a label to what Lawler described as designing reward systems such that they attract and retain the individuals whose behaviour is consistent with that required for success and aligning costs of reward to the organisation's ability to pay at different points in its life cycle (Lawler, 1995).

Table 2: Studies that have used institutional theory to examine reward mix decisions

Study	Objective	Reward mix	Theory	Setting	Findings
Eisenhardt 1988	Evaluation of when organisations use salary compensation as opposed to compensation based on performance	Salary: Commission	Agency / Institutional	Retail sales	The store age is negatively related to the use of salaries and positively related to the use of commissions. Commissions are more common in shoe sales than in other types of retailing
Conlon and Parks 1990	How behaviour monitoring, and the presence of tradition of non contingent pay, interact to affect compensation arrangements	Fixed : variable	Agency / Institutional	Experiment on MBA / Graduates	Pay traditions can inhibit the economically rational thinking predicted by agency theory
Taras 1997	Assessment of the impact of managerial objectives on wage policies	Significance of wage	Institutional	Canadian petroleum industry	Managerial Objectives – in particular, a tendency toward imitative behaviour and a strategy of union avoidance – influences wage mix
Milne 2001	Investigation of the pattern of adoption of an HMO option as a component of a multiple choice health insurance plan	Adoption of HMO medical plans	Institutional / Resource dependency theory	US	Several factors both internal and external affect the responses of management
Van der Stende 2003	Examining the influence of variations in national culture on incentive mix	Percentage of compensation that is performance dependent	Institutional / Hofstede's cultural dimensions / Contingency	Belgian multi national enterprises	Corporate effects are dominant over national cultural effects with respect to incentive pay systems. Incentive systems tend to be uniformly implemented within firms
Segalla et al 2006	Investigation of why managers choose one sales compensation form than another	Fixed : variable	Expectancy, agency, Institutional, Hofstede's cultural dimensions	Branch banking in six European countries	Consideration of national culture was significant when designing sales force compensation
Fernadez-Alles et al 2006	Analysis of whether compensation design is an economically rational incentive to increase performance or whether it responds to other factors such as the search for legitimacy	Extent of variable compensation	Agency / Institutional	Middle managers in Spanish banking	Compensation design takes into account the company's adoption of popular management practices that increase its legitimacy but not necessarily its performance. Reward mix design often has social objectives, such as the search for legitimacy, as institutional theory suggests

Resource Dependency Theory

Resource dependency theory proposes that individuals and organisations have a desire to reduce their dependency on others, in order to increase the power they have over their own future (Pfeffer & Salancik, 2003). The extent to which an organisation is dependent on employees depends on whether employees are deemed as critical and the availability of substitutes for these employees. Employees are critical if their removal from the organisation would cause material disruption to the organisation (Pfeffer & Salancik, 2003). Dependence on an individual, or group of individuals, is likely to influence reward mix for this group (Tremblay et al., 2003; Pfeffer & Davis-Blake, 1987). Bartol and Martin (1988) raise seven factors that influence the level of dependence an organisation has on employees, and consequently the power they have over their reward mix. First, is the task uncertainty around the activities carried out by the employee where, due to the complexity of the task, the manager is unable to direct the activity. This is often the case for specialist research jobs (Balkin & Bannister, 1993). Second, is the extent to which performance can be monitored. Third, is performance visibility, defined as whether failures and successes are visible to both management and significant external parties. Management are also more dependent when employees have skills that are difficult to replicate. Replicability is also related to the fifth of Bartol and Martin's factors – replaceability. Where skills are difficult to replace, then organisations will be more dependent on those performing those skills. Next, the more important the task performed is to the organisation's success, then the more likely the organisation is to be dependent on the individuals performing the task. Finally, individuals with connections to powerful others, such as internal senior level sponsors, potentially provide increased power for those individuals.

A number of papers have examined the effect resource dependency may have on reward decision making and to a more limited extent reward mix decisions. Morgan and Miller (1992) showed how the proportion of women in an organisation influenced the extent that family friendly policies constituted part of the mix. However, the work can be criticised as the results did not meet tests of statistical significance and there was no indication as to whether the proportion of women controlled what were deemed to be critical resources, and therefore had power to dictate terms more aggressively. Resource dependency theory has been applied to the determination of CEO reward mix (Elvira, 2001). Studies in this area include Finkelstein and Hambrick's (1995) examination of the effect of ownership structure on CEO reward and Crystal's work on CEO and compensation consultant's role in executive pay determination (Crystal, 1991). Elvira (2001) noted that most incentives are paid at managerial and professional levels, due to attraction and retention considerations driven from higher levels of resource dependence for these types of roles. These studies suggest reward mix is influenced through the power dependency gives employees to negotiate mix in line with personal preferences, not organisational alignment. Fiss (2006) however challenged this resource dependent perspective. In his study of the social influence of the CEO on company boards, he argued that the strength of this social relationship was a significant driver of the top management team's compensation, not, as resource dependency predicts, scarcity of key human resource skills.

However, at lower levels Nienhuser (2008) found that organisations look to the market to recruit others with the required skills and thus reduce their dependency on them. Where this is not possible the dependency makes these staff more powerful. Consequently, organisations look to tie them into the organisation, through more attractive benefits and other forms of financial 'tie-in'. This supports the earlier conclusions of Balkin and Bannister (1993) that organisations will look to reduce uncertainty of operation by using means to reduce their dependency, or at least create mutual dependency through reward structures between the organisation and the critical individuals.

Union representation may also create a form of dependency and consequently influence reward mix for the workforce (Budd, 2004). Freeman and Medoff (1981) showed how unionised environments typically have a positive effect on benefit provision, due to the monopoly power they have in sectors where unions are strong, thereby increasing their bargaining power. Also, they provide a collective voice to employees. This may mean that benefits are increased as democratic preferences of employees are heard (Freeman & Medoff, 1981). Kaufman (2002) showed how the collective voice provided by unions was likely to lead to lower proportions of variable pay in the overall mix. Other research has supported these conclusions, showing in particular, that the proportion of benefits in the overall mix has fallen when union density has declined (Budd, 2004; Bloom & Freeman, 1992).

Balkin and Bannister (1993) examined how reward mix may be influenced by the relative power of certain employee groups holding critical positions by the specialist nature of their roles, the autonomy they have in how they operate and the overall effect they have on organisational performance. They conclude that the determining factor for the mix for specialist groups is the preferences they have to participate personally in higher returns relative to their risk tolerance. They concluded that the more powerful the individual or group is, the more the organisation will do to meet their preferences in reward mix. Managers may also be willing to overlook other reward issues, such as internal and external equity with other groups of staff. Consistent with resource dependence theory, this suggests that management will have greater control over reward mix for non critical groups of employees on whom they are less dependent.

Gomez-Mejia and Balkin also examined what they termed "strategic employee groups" (1992: 101). They also concluded that the reward mix of these critical groups should be tailored to better align to their preferences. In addition, they also noted a knock on effect on the reward mix of other 'non strategic groups'. They speculated, in contrast to Balkin and Bannister's (1993) conclusions, that this was down to organisations not wanting to totally separate reward mix for these critical groups of employees from other employee groups for internal equity reasons. Gustman et al. (1994) lent support to this view, finding that pension plans, whilst having a cross organisational structure, are sometimes built with particular employee groups in mind.

Abbott and De Cieri (2008), found that different environmental conditions were seen to influence the respective power of employees and consequently the extent of work-life benefits. They concluded that specific work-life balance provision is organisationally context specific and the influence of employee power is relevant. This, although not the focus of the study, provides some support for a resource dependency perspective on benefit provision. However, we need to exercise care in drawing too strong a conclusion from this work, given it focuses only on two companies, and with respect to reward mix, the fact that it is not examining the relative balance of the work-life benefit component relative to other elements of the mix.

From the above discussion, we can see that we only have a limited understanding of the influence resource dependence may have on reward mix, and the impact its provisions may have on organisational decision makers, when we may expect the approach to have some predictive capabilities. The literature examined, although identifying the link between resource dependency and reward mix decisions, is relatively limited. In addition, Neinhuser (2008) concludes that, although there is much confirming empirical evidence for resource dependency theory, it is not always strong and does not always explain a high proportion of variance in the situations reviewed. This led him to conclude that it may need combining with other theories to improve our understanding of the situation being examined.

Combining Theoretical Insights

Whilst agency contingency has emerged as the dominant perspective through which reward mix determination has been examined, the other theoretical viewpoints have been shown to potentially have further explanatory power. The approaches examined are summarised in table 3.

Agency, contingency and resource dependency theories assume that the interests of the organisation will prevail. Barringer and Milkovich termed this a "rational response", noting that underpinning the rationality was the assumption "that organizations actively manage environmental constraints, adopting structures that ensure the flow of resources, or minimize agency or transaction costs" (1998: 312). This can be contrasted with an institutional perspective, which they stated "assumes that organizations do not exercise active choice; rather they more passively conform to their environments" (1998: 312). Enhanced legitimacy was a separate objective from considerations of efficiency.

Table 4 summarises a number of research papers that have explicitly adopted combinations of the theoretical approaches of agency, institutional and resource dependency in examining reward strategy for employees. The range of studies employing both agency and institutional theory have generally concluded that the addition of institutional factors have enhanced results, given the partial understanding that agency research has brought (Eisenhardt, 1988; Trevor, 2008; Fernandez-Alles et al., 2006; Barringer & Milkovich, 1998; Conlon & Parks, 1990). Eisenhardt concluded that "the institutional emphasis on tradition complements the efficiency emphasis of agency theory, and the result is a better understanding of compensation" (1988: 72). Barringer & Milkovich (1998) felt resource dependency agency and transaction cost theories were predominately efficiency theories and were complemented by institutional theory which emphasises external pressures. Ear-

Table 3: Summary of agency, resource dependence and institutional theory

	Agency	Resource Dependence	Institutional
Purpose of reward mix decisions	Minimise shirking when monitoring is difficult / costly	Acquisition of business critical resources	Conformity with other organisations and market practice to gain legitimacy
Main Assumptions	Rational decisions People are self interested, risk averse Goal conflict exists between owners and employees Information asymmetry	Rational decision Control of critical resources leads to power	Organisations seek legitimacy Organisations conform to norms Process of satisfycing behaviour
Organisational reaction	Rational active management	Rational active management	Passive conformity or rational legitimacy seeking
Implications for reward mix	Relative weight of incentives versus fixed reward will be managed to optimise the alignment of agent and principals interests	Reward mix will be influenced by the relative strength of employee groups determined by their criticality to organisation success	Reward mix will be influenced by coercive, mimetic and normative pressures and the extent to which operating within these norms confers legitimacy

lier Eisenhardt (1989) noted how institutional and resource dependency are stronger when efficiency is not a pressing concern, giving large public bureaucracies as examples. Conlon and Parks (1990), in an experiment with MBA and undergraduate students, found that the institutionalisation of practises may come down to the influence of particularly powerful bodies. Resource dependency suggests these members would be those controlling critical resources. Their study led them to conclude that pay traditions, which may not be economically efficient, play a significant role in influencing reward mix. Whilst the results appear robust in the laboratory setting, their operationalisation of pay traditions in the fictional industry, i.e. telling the actors that a certain tradition did/did not exist, is questionable given the complexity with which institutional factors are formed and manifested in organisational life (DiMaggio & Powell, 1991).

Table 4: Combinations of agency, institutional and resource dependency theories

Study	Perspectives	Purpose
Eisenhardt 1988	Agency, institutional	Evaluation of when organisations use salary compensation and when they use compensation based on performance
Barringer and Milkovich 1998	Agency, institutional, resource dependence, transaction cost	Theoretical examination of the adoption and design of flexible benefit systems
Conlon and Parks 1999	Agency, institutional	How behaviour monitoring, and the presence of tradition of non contingent pay, interact to affect compensation arrangements
Milne 2001	Institutional, resource dependence	Investigation of the pattern of adoption of an HMO Option as a component of a multiple choice health insurance plan
Elvira 2001	Agency, resource dependency, power	Examination of the relationship between bonuses and promotions and whether these incentives are traded off
Tremblay et al 2003	Agency, resource dependence, transaction cost	Investigation of the influence of the theoretical perspectives on the proportion of salary in sales compensation
Segalla et al 2006	Expectancy, agency, institutional, Hofstede's cultural dimensions	Investigation of why managers choose one sales compensation form than another
Yanadori & Marler 2006	Agency, resource dependence	Examining whether innovation strategy effects compensation decisions in the high technology sector
Fernandez-Alles et al 2006	Agency, institutional	Analysis of whether compensation is designed as an economically rational incentive to increase organisational performance or whether it responds to other factors such as the search for legitimacy
Festing et al 2007	Resource dependence, institutional, cultural dimensions	Analysis of power relations in multi national enterprises and their influence on compensation strategies
Trevor 2008	Agency, institutional	Exploration of the contemporary realities of compensation strategy what, how and significantly why organisations are structuring reward as they are

Festing et al (2007) found that whilst institutional theory has given particular insight into reward decisions, it does not fully explain the pressures reward managers' face. They added that for this an understanding of relative power is also needed, as discussed in resource dependency theory. This followed Segalla et al.'s thoughts that reward mix decisions are influenced by "idiosyncratic factors related to their [reward managers] personal and cultural characteristics" (2006: 420). A number of studies have also shown that the explanatory power of agency, when combined with resource dependency, is stronger than when agency is applied on its own (Tremblay et al., 2003; Carpenter & Wade, 2002; Elvira, 2001; Yanadori & Marler, 2006). For example, Yanadori and Marler (2006) showed that the increased compensation risk that comes with longer term incentives, which they show are payable to strategic groups of employees, may be counterbalanced by the increased job security, due to their criticality, that these groups enjoy. The combination of resource dependence with institutional theory has also been shown to enhance insight into reward mix decisions, albeit with fewer studies taking these two perspectives (Festing et al., 2007; Festing & Sahakiants, 2010; Milne, 2001). Both resource dependence and institutional theory share the drivers of their actions as internal and external forces, with legitimacy as an important factor. The reactions to these pressures are deemed either strategic (resource dependence), or passive (institutional) based on the extent to which legitimacy can be pursued (resource dependency), or the extent to which it is just imposed (institutional).

In Barringer and Milkovich's model (1998) three perspectives, plus transaction costs theory, were used to derive pertinent determinants of reward mix. This integration of theoretical perspectives was a major contribution provided by this work. Again, they concluded that in this situation the explanatory power of flexible benefit system adoption would be improved by this multi-theoretical perspective.

Research Paradigms and Methodological Approaches

In examining the reward mix literature, the review investigated the basis on which knowledge had been formed. Review of the literature shows that positivist and critical rationalist approaches have directed the area of pay and compensation research, with quantitative methods dominating both experimental and field based work. For example, Werner and Ward's (2004) review of the compensation literature from 1996 to 2002 showed that of the 396 studies identified 1.8% were meta-analysis and 4.5% theoretical, with the rest being quantitative analysis of data either empirical or experimental. This is unsurprising given that pay is monetised.

Whilst the statistical analysis may have 'proved' relationships between the variables being examined, the authors could then only speculate on potential reasons for these relationships (Yanadori & Marler, 2006). Taras concluded that "it is perhaps troubling that while scholars clearly are able to develop strong rational models of wage determination based on inferences derived from large data sets of wage outcomes, they are caught short when exposed to the often intuitive or baffling decisions of actual compensation managers" (1997:

181). Consequently, she proposed that "it is appropriate now to simply ask compensation managers about their decisions, if for nothing else than to posit some plausible explanations for further testing" (1997: 181). Heneman and Judge, albeit in the context of research on employee pay satisfaction, noted that "we must enter the field, rather than merely survey it, if we are to fully understand and appreciate its context and changes" (2000: p369). Bloom and Milkovich add to this that "ours is a field of inquiry irrevocably intertwined with the decisions of practical people" (1996: p40). However, in the decade since that was written, the work remains one step removed through archival and survey research, rather than really field based to engage and interpret the social element implied by this intertwining.

Work on remuneration committees in the U.K. has taken a different approach to "look inside the black box" (Main et al., 2008: 226), of the decision making process through qualitative interviews (for example, Bender, 2004; Ogden & Watson, 2008; Main et al., 2008; Perkins & Hendry, 2005; Bender & Moir, 2006). Given this developing approach, it is perhaps surprising that so little qualitative work has been done below executive level. There have been exceptions (Festing et al., 2007; Trevor, 2008; Fernandez-Alles et al., 2006; Abbott & De Cieri, 2008; Taras, 1997; Darmon, 1982). Eisenhardt predominately used survey data in forming her seminal conclusions on agency and institutional influences on compensation approach in the retail industry, but did "enrich insights" (Eisenhardt, 1988) through qualitative questions which she asked of store managers. A similar approach was taken by Elvira (2001). Whilst predominately statistically driven, the research did follow up the results with interviews with human resource executives and a number of employees. This was considered justifiable to help counter the criticism that, economic based theories do not take into account the social structures which will influence behaviour (Elvira, 2001). Taras (1997) took a more inductive approach, using a combination of qualitative and quantitative methods and, with respect to the interviews she carried out, noting that she "found that managers were startlingly open about themes that rarely appear in existing wage-determination literature" (1997: 184). A further exception is Fernandez-Alles et al (2006) who used a case study approach to examine reward mix. The approach was justified as it was felt a case study approach was particularly suited to exploratory research in an area that lacked clarity or was subject to a number of different explanations. Trevor (2008) argues, in his review of compensation management practice, that a qualitative approach is the most effective way of not just getting at what firms are doing, but also why they are doing it.

To conclude, much of what we know about reward mix determination is known through positivist and critical rationalist research paradigms and quantitative methods. An emerging body of work is developing, taking a more constructionist approach to reward determination as a potential means to establish not only, what is driving reward decisions, but significantly why. This has developed in light of findings that institutional pressures exist and influence reward decisions. The implications of this and the wider findings of the review are now discussed through the development of a conceptual framework to guide future work and from this suggestions for the directions this work should take.

Conceptual Framework

Each of the theoretical perspectives reviewed has offered a slightly different explanation as to what factors influence reward mix policy choices in organisations. In this context, the main concepts that have been discussed in this review are:
– Reward mix, made up of cash compensation, benefits and relational returns;
– Principals;
– Employees;
– Monitoring;
– Control;
– Firm strategy;
– Firm characteristics;
– Coercive, mimetic and normative isomorphism;
– Critical resources; and
– Power.

These concepts and the relationships that are believed to exist between them should be helpful in providing direction to future research and are shown in the conceptual framework in figure 1.

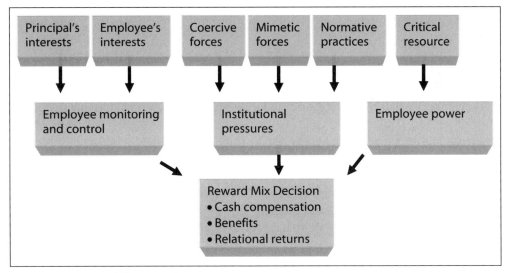

Figure 1: Conceptual framework

Gaps in the Literature for Further Examination

This literature review has attempted to review what is already known about reward mix policy decision making for employees and assessed how we come to know this, with a view to determining what gaps remain in our knowledge. Each of the theoretical perspectives examined has offered a slightly different explanation as to what factors influence reward mix policy choices in organisations.

If agency theory is to be believed, then we might expect reward executives to discuss how monitoring of employees and efficiency considerations around this monitoring and the span of controls of managers has determined the mix of at least fixed and variable pay. However it has little to say about the benefits or relational elements of the reward mix. Contingency theory examines organisational strategy characteristics looking for alignment between business strategy and reward mix determination. Resource dependency meanwhile focuses on the relative power between the actors involved in the employment exchange. Organisational success will be controlled by those, either individuals, groups of individuals or influential organisations, who control access to critical resources needed for that success. Consequently reward mix, including the benefit component, will be developed with the acquisition and retention of those critical resources in mind. Institutional theory questions these more economic and resource efficiency based approaches, identifying a societal dimension to the reward mix policy decision as organisations seek to gain wider ranging legitimacy. Reward mix decisions are therefore largely driven by fixed constraints, both legal and tax regulations, alongside pressure to conform to the practice of other successful organisations or prescribed best practice formulas, driven by professional bodies, networks and consultancy advice.

Given what we know, what must be asked next? The review has highlighted four significant areas where further research is required. First, although a range of studies have examined reward mix determination, they have been dominated by research at the executive level and in particular the Chief Executive level. This is unsurprising given the significant decision making authority that individual has and also the availability of data on executive reward, given the requirement for it to be published for many organisations. However, it may also be misguided given the significance of employee compensation relative to organisational cost. Focussing solely on the CEO attributes all the success of the organisation on that one compensation decision and the effect it has on one individual. Further research of reward mix determination (along with other areas of reward practices) at employee level would therefore appear to be needed, to allow us to understand whether there are significant differences between executive and employee reward mix determination and why this might be the case.

Second, the review highlighted that reward mix has been conceptualised in numerous ways in the academic literature. For example, a narrow definition of reward mix has been conceptualised through the use of the ratio of base salary to short term bonus payments, as this was perceived as the most common form of incentive pay (Gerhart &Milkovich, 1990; Eisenhardt, 1988; Boyd & Salamin, 2001; Werner & Tosi, 1995; Bloom & Milkovich, 1998; Gerhart & Trevor, 1996). Alternatively, others have widened this simple ratio to examine the proportion of base pay to cash compensation i.e. including both short and long term incentives (Tremblay et al., 2003; Roth & O'Donnell, 1996; Tremblay & Chenevert, 2005; Burke & Hsieh, 2006). This, of course, misses a proportion of reward mix with respect to the benefits that employees receive and the relational returns that also accrue from employment around the job and the work environment. Research should now look to widen its definition of reward mix and align more with the emerging practice of 'total reward' which organisations are pursuing.

Next, the literature review established a long list of factors that have been shown to be statistically related to reward mix. Within this 'list' agency and contingency theories are the dominant theoretical explanation for the reward mix decision. However, there is some more limited evidence that reward decisions are taken that are not always in line with the expectations of these theoretical approaches but, in addition, social interactions appear to have an influence (institutional and resource dependency theory). Empirical examination of these interactions and how they influence reward mix determination would be beneficial.

Finally, much of what we know about reward mix determination is known through a positivist research approach. Whilst clearly relevant for a field of this nature, it has meant that little time has been spent with the reward policy decision makers themselves to understand what issues they consider when determining reward mix and why these factors are used compared with others that the statistical research may be indicating as important. However an emerging body of work has developed taking a more constructionist approach to reward determination, as a potential means to establish not only what is driving reward decisions, but significantly why albeit at an Executive level (for example, Bender, 2004; Ogden and Watson, 2008; Main et al., 2008; Perkins and Hendry, 2005; Bender and Moir, 2006). This should be extended to further interaction with compensation decision makers to understand reward mix determination for the wider employee population. Building theory from a different research paradigm will add insight to the area through revised theory generation and potentially contribute to simplifying the field.

References

Abbott, J. & De Cieri, H. (2008). Influences on the provision of work-life benefits: Management and employee perspectives. Journal of Management and Organization, 14 (3), 303-322.

Abraham, S., Friedman, B. &Thomas, R. (2008). The relationship among union membership, facets of satisfaction and intent to leave: Further evidence on the voice face of unions. Employee Responsibilities and Rights Journal, 20 (1), 1-11.

Addison, J. T. & Blackburn, M. L. (1999). Minimum wages and poverty. Industrial & Labor Relations Review, 52 (3), 393-409.

Andersen, E. (1985). Contracting the selling position: The salesperson as an outside agent of employee. Marketing Science, 4, 234-254.

Ang, S., Slaughter, S. & Ng, K. Y. (2002). Human capital and institutional determinants of information technology compensation: Modeling multilevel and cross-level interactions. Management Science, 48 (11), 1427-1445.

Armstrong, M. & Murlis, H. (2007). Reward management: A handbook of remuneration strategy and practice, 5th ed. London: Kogan Page Limited.

Armstrong, M. & Brown, D. (2005). Reward strategies and trends in the United Kingdom: The land of diverse and pragmatic dreams. Compensation and Benefits Review, 37 (4), 41-53.

Artz, B. (2008). The role of firm size and performance pay in determining employee job satisfaction brief: Firm size, performance pay, and job satisfaction. Labour, 22 (2), 315-343.

Baeten, X. (2008). Executive remuneration: Towards a structured multi-theory approach. 5th Research Workshop on Corporate Governance, 26th-28th November 2008, EIASM, Brussels, EIASM.

Balkin, D. B. & Bannister, B. D. (1993). Explaining pay forms for strategic employee groups in organizations: A resource dependence perspective. Journal of Occupational and Organizational Psychology, 66 (2), 139-151.

Balkin, D. B. & Gomez-Mejia, L. R. (1990). Matching compensation and organizational strategies. Strategic Management Journal, 11 (2), 153-169.

Balkin, D. B. & Gomez-Mejia, L. R. (1987). Toward a contingency theory of compensation strategy. Strategic Management Journal, 8 (2), 169-182.

Barney, J. B. (1986). Organizational culture: Can it be a source of sustained competitive advantage? Academy of Management Review, 11 (3), 656-665.

Barringer, M. W. & Milkovich, G. T. (1998). A theoretical exploration of the adoption and design of flexible benefit plans: A case of human resource innovation. The Academy of Management Review, 23 (2), 305-324.

Barringer, M. W. & Milkovich, G. T. (1996). Employee health insurance decisions in a flexible benefits environment. Human Resource Management, 35 (3), 293-315.

Bartol, K. M. & Locke, E. A. (2000). Incentives and motivation. In Rynes, S. L. & Gerhart, B. (Eds.), Compensation in Organizations: Current Research and Practice (pp. 104-147). San Francisco: Jossey-Bass.

Bartol, K. M. & Martin, D. C. (1988). Influences on managerial pay allocations: A dependency perspective. Personnel Psychology, 41 (2), 361-378.

Batt, R. (2001). Explaining wage inequality in telecommunications services: Customer segmentation, human resource practices, and union decline. Industrial & Labor Relations Review, 54 (2A), 425-449.

Bender, R. (2004). Why do companies use performance-related pay for their executive directors? Corporate Governance: An International Review, 12 (4), 521-533.

Bender, R. & Moir, L. (2006). Does 'Best Practice' in setting executive pay in the UK encourage 'good' behaviour? Journal of Business Ethics, 67 (1), 75-91.

Blasi, J., Conte, M. & Kruse, D. (1996). Employee stock ownership and corporate performance among public companies. Industrial & Labor Relations Review, 50 (1), 60-79.

Bloom, M. C. & Milkovich, G. T. (1996). Issues in management compensation research. In Rousseau, D. M. & Cooper, D. M. (Eds.), Trends in Organizational Behavior (pp. 23-47). New York: Wiley.

Bloom, D. E. & Freeman, R. B. (1992). The fall in private pension coverage in the United States. The American Economic Review, 82 (2), 539-545.

Bloom, M. & Milkovich, G. T. (1998). Relationships among risk, incentive pay, and organizational performance. Academy of Management Journal, 41 (3), 283-297.

Boyd, B. K. & Salamin, A. (2001). Strategic reward systems: A contingency model of pay system design. Strategic Management Journal, 22 (8), 777-792.

Brown, C. & Campbell, B. (2001). Technical change, wages, and employment in semiconductor manufacturing. Industrial & Labor Relations Review, 54 (2A), 450-465.

Brown, C. & Campbell, B. A. (2002). The impact of technological change on work and wages. Industrial Relations, 41 (1), 1-33.

Budd, J. W. (2004). Non-wage forms of compensation. Journal of Labor Research, 25 (4), 597-622.

Budd, J. W. & Mumford, K. (2004). Trade Unions and family-friendly policies in Britain. Industrial and Labor Relations Review, 57 (2), 204-222.

Burke, L. A. & Hsieh, C. (2006). Optimizing fixed and variable compensation costs for employee productivity. International Journal of Productivity and Performance Management, 55 (1/2), 155-162.

Carpenter, M. A. & Wade, J. B. (2002). Microlevel opportunity structures as determinants of non-CEO executive pay. Academy of Management Journal, 45 (6), 1085-1103.

Chen, H. & Hsieh, Y. (2005). Incentive reward with organizational life cycle from competitive advantage viewpoint. Human Systems Management, 24 (2), 155-163.

Chiang, F. (2005). A critical examination of Hofstede's thesis and its application to international reward management. International Journal of Human Resource Management, 16 (9), 1545-1563.

Chiang, F. F. T. &Birtch, T. (2007). The transferability of management practices: Examining cross-national differences in reward preferences. Human Relations, 60 (9), 1293-1330.

Chiang, F. F. T. & Birtch, T. A. (2006). An Empirical examination of reward preferences within and across national settings. Management International Review, 46 (5), 573-596.

Christofides, L. N. & Laporte, A. (2002). Menu costs, nominal wage revisions, and intracontract wage behavior. Industrial Relations, 41 (2), 287-303.

CIPD (2008). Reward Management Survey Report 2008. London: CIPD.

Collins, J. C. & Porras, J. L. (1994). Built to last: Successful habits of visionary companies. New York: Harper Business.

Colvin, A. J. S., Batt, R. & Katz, H. C. (2001). How high performance human resource practices and workforce unionization affect managerial pay. Personnel Psychology, 54 (4), 903-934.

Conlon, E. J. & Parks, J. M. (1990). Effects of monitoring and tradition on compensation arrangements: An experiment with principal-agent dyads. Academy of Management Journal, 33 (3), 603-622.

Crown (2008). Pensions Act 2008. London, United Kingdom.

Crystal, G. S. (1991). In Search of Excess: The Overcompensation of American Executives. New York: Norton.

Darmon, R. Y. (1982). Compensation plans that link management and salesman's objectives. Industrial Marketing Management, 11 (2), 151-163.

Datta, S. K., Nugent, J. B. & Tishler, A. (2004). Contractual mix between cash and kind wages of casual workers in an agrarian economy. Review of Development Economics, 8 (4), 521-540.

Deci, E. L. & Ryan, R. M. (1985). Intrinsic motivation and self-determination in human behaviour. New York: Plenum.

Deckop, J. R., Mangel, R. & Cirka, C. C. (1999). Research Notes. Getting more than you pay for: Organizational citizenship behavior and pay-for-performance plans. Academy of Management Journal, 42 (4), 420-428.

Delvey, D. (1999). Practical lessons for designing an economic value incentive plan. Compensation and Benefits Review, 31 (2), 61-70.

Demougin, D. & Fluet, C. (2001). Monitoring versus incentives. European Economic Review, 45 (9), 1741-1764.

DiMaggio, D. P. & Powell, W. W. (Eds.) (1991). The New Institutionalism in Organizational Analysis. Chicago: University of Chicago Press.

Donaldson, L. (2001). The Contingency Theory of Organizations. California: Sage Publications, Inc.

Dreher, G. F., Ash, R. A. & Bretz, R. D. (1988). Benefit coverage and employee cost: Critical factors in explaining compensation satisfaction. Personnel Psychology, 41 (2), 237-254.

Eisenhardt, K. M. (1988). Agency – and institutional - theory explanations: The case of retail sales compensation. Academy of Management Review, 31, 1153-1166.

Eisenhardt, K. M. (1989). Agency Theory: An assessment and review. Academy of Management Review, 14 (1), 57-74.

Elvira, M. M. (2001). Pay me now or pay me later: Analyzing the relationship between bonus and promotion incentives. Work and Occupations, 28 (3), 346-370.

Fernandez-Alles, M., Cuevas-Rodríguez, G. & Valle-Cabrera, R. (2006). How symbolic remuneration contributes to the legitimacy of the company: An institutional explanation. Human Relations, 59 (7), 961-992.

Festing, M. & Sahakiants, I. (2010). Compensation practices in Central and Eastern European member states – An analytical framework based on institutional perspectives, path dependencies and efficiency considerations. Thunderbird International Business Review, 52 (3), 203-216.

Festing, M., Eidems, J. & Royer, S. (2007). Strategic issues and local constraints in transnational compensation strategies: An analysis of cultural, institutional and political influences. European Management Journal, 25 (2), 118-131.

Fiss, P. C. (2006). Social influence effects and managerial compensation evidence from Germany. Strategic Management Journal, 27 (11), 1013-1031.

Forth, J. & Millward, N. (2000). The determinants of pay levels and fringe benefit provision in Britain, Discussion paper 171. London: National Institute of Economic and Social Research.

Freeman, R. B. & Medoff, J. L. (1981). The impact of the percentage organized on Union and Nonunion wages. The Review of Economics and Statistics, 63 (4), 561-572.

Friesen, J. (1996). The response of wages to protective labor legislation: Evidence from Canada. Industrial & Labor Relations Review, 49 (2), 243-255.

Gerhart, B. & Milkovich, G. T. (1992). Employee compensation: Research and practice. In Dunnette, M. D. & Hough, L. M. (Eds.), Handbook of Industrial and Organizational Psychology (2nd ed, pp. 481-569). Palo Alto, California: Consulting Psychologists Press.

Gerhart, B. & Rynes, S. L. (2003). Compensation: Theory, Evidence, and Strategic Implications. California: Sage Publications Inc.

Gerhart, B. & Milkovich, G. T. (1990). Organizational differences in managerial compensation and financial performance. Academy of Management Journal, 33 (4), 663-691.

Gerhart, B. & Trevor, C. O. (1996). Employment variability under different managerial compensation systems. Academy of Management Journal, 39 (6), 1692-1712.

Gomez-Mejia, L. R. & Balkin, D. B. (1992). Compensation, Organizational Strategy, and Firm Performance. Cincinnati, Ohio: Southwestern Publishing.

Gomez-Mejia, L. R. (1992). Structure and process of diversification, compensation strategy, and firm performance. Strategic Management Journal, 13 (5), 381-397.

Gomez-Mejia, L. R. & Balkin, D. B. (1992). Determinants of faculty pay: An Agency Theory perspective. Academy of Management Journal, 35 (5), 921-955.

Gomez-Mejia, L. R. & Balkin, D. B. (1989). Effectiveness of individual and aggregate compensation strategies. Industrial Relations, 28 (3), 431-445.

Gomez-Mejia, L. R. & Welbourne, T. M. (1988). Compensation strategy: An overview and future steps. Human Resource Planning, 11 (3), 173-189.

Gustman, A. L., Mitchell, O. S. & Steinmeier, T. L. (1994). The role of pensions in the labor market: A survey of the literature. Industrial and Labor Relations Review, 47 (3), 417-438.

Hambrick, D. C. (2007). Upper echelons theory: An update. Academy of Management Review, 32 (2), 334-343.

Hambrick, D. C. & Finkelstein, S. (1995). The effects of ownership structure on conditions at the top: The case of CEO pay raises. Strategic Management Journal, 16 (3), 175-193.

Hambrick, D. C. & Mason, P. A. (1984). Upper Echelons: The organization as a reflection of its top managers. Academy of Management Review, 9 (2), 193-206.

Hatch, M. J. & Cunliffe, A. L. (2006). Organization Theory: Modern, Symbolic, and Postmodern Perspectives. Oxford: Oxford University Press.

Heneman III., H. G. & Judge, T. A. (2000). Compensation attitudes. In Rynes, S. L. & Gerhart, B. (Eds.), Compensation in Organizations: Current Research and Practice (pp. 61-103). San Francisco: Jossey-Bass.

Heneman, R. L., Ledford, G. E. J. & Gresham, M. T. (2000), The changing nature of work and its effect on compensation design and delivery. In Rynes, S. L. & Gerhart, B. (Eds.), Compensation in Organizations: Current Research and Practice (pp. 195-240). San Francisco: Jossey-Bass.

Hofstede, G. H. (2001). Culture's consequences: comparing values, behaviors, institutions, and organizations across nations, 2nd ed. California: Thousand Oaks.

Hull, J. C. (2009). Options, Futures, and Other Derivatives, 7th ed. India: Prentice Hall India Pvt. Ltd.

Ippolito, R. A. (1987). Why federal workers don't quit. The Journal of Human Resources, 22 (2), 281-299.

Ittner, C. D., Larcker, D. F. & Pizzini, M. (2007). Performance-based compensation in member-owned firms: An examination of medical group practices. Journal of Accounting and Economics, 44 (3), 300-327.

Jensen, M. C. & Meckling, W. H. (1976). Theory of the firm: Managerial behavior, agency costs, and ownership structure. Journal of Financial Economics, 3, 305-360.

John, G. & Weitz, B. (1989). Salesforce compensation: An empirical investigation of factors related to use of salary versus incentive compensation. Journal of Marketing Research, 26 (1), 1-14.

Johnson, G., Scholes, K. & Whittington, R. (2008). Exploring Corporate Strategy, 8th ed. Harlow: Financial Times Prentice Hall.

Kaestner, R. & Simon, K. I. (2002). Labor market consequences of state health insurance regulation. Industrial & Labor Relations Review, 56 (1), 136-156.

Kaufman, B. E. (2002). Models of union wage determination: What have we learned since Dunlop and Ross? Industrial Relations, 41 (1), 110-158.

Kerr, J. L. (1985). Diversification strategies and managerial rewards: An empirical study. Academy of Management Journal, 28 (1), 155-179.

Krashinsky, H. (2002). Evidence on adverse selection and establishment in the labor market. Industrial & Labor Relations Review, 56 (1), 84-96.

Kuhn, K. M. & Yockey, M. D. (2003). Variable pay as a risky choice: Determinants of the relative attractiveness of incentive plans. Organizational Behavior and Human Decision Processes, 90 (2), 323-341.

Lawler, E., L. (1971). Pay and Organizational Effectiveness: A Psychological View. New York: McGraw-Hill.

Lawler, E. E., III (1995). The new pay: A strategic approach. Compensation and Benefits Review, 27 (4), 14-22.

Lazear, E. P. (1998). Personnel Economics for Managers. New Jersey: John Wiley & Sons Inc.

Long, J. E. & Scott, F. A. (1982). The income tax and nonwage compensation. The Review of Economics and Statistics, 64 (2), 211-219.

Main, B. G. M., Jackson, C., Pymm, J. & Wright, V. (2008). The remuneration committee and strategic human resource management. Corporate Governance: An International Review, 16 (3), 225-238.

Milkovich, G. T. (1988). A strategic perspective on compensation management. Research in Personnel and Human Resources Management, 6, 263-288.

Milkovich, G. T. & Newman, C. (2008). Compensation, 9th ed. Boston: McGraw-Hill/Irwin.

Miller, G. J. & Whitford, A. B. (2007). The principal's moral hazard: Constraints on the use of incentives in hierarchy. Journal of Public Administration Research and Theory, 17 (2), 213-233.

Miller, J. S., Hom, P. W. & Gomez-Mejia, L. R. (2001). The high cost of low wages: Does Maquiladora compensation reduce turnover? Journal of International Business Studies, 32 (3), 585-595.

Milne, S. H. (2001). Employer adoption of an HMO option for employees: An integrated institutional and resource dependence perspective (unpublished Ph.D. thesis). Georgia, USA: Georgia Institute of Technology.

Montemayor, E. F. (1996). Congruence between pay policy and competitive strategy in high-performance firms. Journal of Management, 22 (6), 889-908.

Morgan, H. & Milliken, F. J. (1992). Keys to action: Understanding differences in organizations' responsiveness to work and family issues. Human Resource Management, 31 (3), 227-248.

Nienhüser, W. (2008). Resource dependence theory – How well does it explain behavior of organizations? Management Revue, 19 (1/2), 9-32.

Norman, P. M., Artz, K. W. & Martinez, R. J. (2007). Does it pay to be different? Competitive non-conformity under different regulatory regimes. Journal of Business Research, 60 (11), 1135-1143.

Ogden, S. & Watson, R. (2008). Executive pay and the search for legitimacy: An investigation into how UK Remuneration Committees use corporate performance comparisons in long-term incentive pay decisions. Human Relations, 61 (5), 711-739.

Ogden, S. & Watson, R. (2007). The influence of comparative pay, customer service measures and accounting profits upon CEO pay in the UK privatised water industry. Accounting and Business Research, 37 (3), 199-215.

Ogden, S. & Watson, R. (2004). Remuneration committees and CEO pay in the UK privatized water industry. Socio-Economic Review, 2 (1), 33-63.

Oliver, C. (1991). Strategic responses to institutional processes. Academy of Management Review, 16, 145-179.

Olson, C. A. & Schwab, A. (2000). The performance effects of human resource practices: The case of inter-club networks in professional baseball, 1919-1940. Industrial Relations, 39 (4), 553-577.

Ouchi, W. G. (1980). Markets, bureaucracies, and clans. Administrative Science Quarterly, 25 (1), 129-141.

Pappas, J. M. & Flaherty, K. E. (2006). The moderating role of individual-difference variables in compensation research. Journal of Managerial Psychology, 21 (1), 19-35.

Perkins, S. J. & White, G. (2008). Employee Reward Alternatives, Consequences and Contexts. London: Chartered Institute of Personnel and Development.

Perkins, S. J. & Hendry, C. (2005). Ordering top pay: Interpreting the signals. Journal of Management Studies, 42 (7), 1443-1468.

Pfeffer, J. & Salancik, G. R. (2003). The External Control of Organizations: A Resource Dependence Perspective, New Edition ed. California: Stanford University Press.

Pfeffer, J. (1993). Barriers to the advance of organizational science: Paradigm. The Academy of Management Review, 18 (4), 599-620.

Pfeffer, J. & Davis-Blake, A. (1987). Understanding organizational wage structures: A resource dependence approach. Academy of Management Journal, 30 (3), 437-455.

Prendergast, C. (1999). The provision of incentives in firms. Journal of Economic Literature, 37 (1), 7-63.

Rajagopalan, N. (1996). Strategic orientations, incentive plan adoptions, and firm performance: Evidence from electric utility firms. Strategic Management Journal, 18, 761-785.

Raphael, S. (2000). Estimating the union earnings effect using a sample of displaced workers. Industrial and Labor Relations Review, 53 (3), 503-521.

Roth, K. & O'Donnell, S. (1996). Foreign subsidiary compensation strategy: An agency theory perspective. Academy of Management Journal, 39, 678-703.

Russell, R. & Callanan, V. (2001). Firm-level influences on forms of employment and pay in Russia. Industrial Relations, 40 (4), 627-634.

Schuster, J. R. & Zingheim, P. K. (1996). The New Pay: Linking Employee and Organizational Performance. California: Jossey-Bass.

Segalla, M., Rouzies, D., Besson, M. & Weitz, B. A. (2006). A cross-national investigation of incentive sales compensation. International Journal of Research in Marketing, 23 (4), 419-433.

Shepard, E. M.,III, Clifton, T. J. & Kruse, D. (1996). Flexible work hours and productivity: Some evidence from the pharmaceutical industry. Industrial Relations, 35 (1), 123-139.

Stroh, L. K., Brett, J. M., Baumann, J. P. & Reilly, A. H. (1996). Agency theory and variable pay compensation strategies. Academy of Management Journal, 39 (3), 751-767.

Taras, D. G. (1997). Managerial intentions and wage determination in the Canadian petroleum industry. Industrial Relations, 36 (2), 178-205.

Tosi, H. L., Katz, J. P. & Gomez-Mejia, L. R. (1997). Disaggregating the agency contract: The effects of monitoring, incentive alignment, and term in office on agent decision making. Academy of Management Journal, 40 (3), 584-602.

Tremblay, M. & Chenevert, D. (2005). The effectiveness of compensation strategies in international technology intensive firms. International Journal of Technology Management, 31 (3/4), 222-239.

Tremblay, M., Cote, J. & Balkin, D. B. (2003). Explaining sales pay strategy using agency, transaction cost and resource dependence theories. The Journal of Management Studies, 40 (7), 1651-1682.

Trevor, J. (2008). Can compensation be strategic? A review of compensation management practice in leading multinational firms. Judge Business School Working paper series; Cambridge.

Umanath, N. S., Ray, M. R. & Campbell, T. L. (1996). The effect of uncertainty and information asymmetry on the structure of compensation contracts: A test of competing models. Management Science, 42 (6), 868-874.

Van der Stede, W. A. (2003). The effect of national culture on management control and incentive system design in multi-business firms: Evidence of intracorporate isomorphism. European Accounting Review, 12 (2), 263-285.

Van Fleet, D. D., McWilliams, A. & Siegel, D. S. (2000). A theoretical and empirical analysis of journal rankings: The case of formal lists. Journal of Management, 26 (5), 839-861.

Werner, S. (2002). Recent developments in international management research: A review of 20 top management journals. Journal of Management, 28 (3), 277-305.

Werner, S. & Tosi, H. L. (1995). Other people's money: The effect of ownership on compensation strategy and managerial pay. Academy of Management Journal, 38 (6), 1672-1691.

Werner, S. & Ward, S. G. (2004). Recent compensation research: An eclectic review. Human Resource Management Review, 14 (2), 201-228.

White, G. (1996). The new pay – losing sight of reality? Management Research News, 19 (4/5), 56-58.

Wiseman, R. M., Gomez-Mejia, L. R. & Fugate, M. (2000). Rethinking compensation risk. In Rynes, S. L. & Gerhart, B. (Eds.), Compensation in Organizations: Current Research and Practice (pp. 311-348). San Francisco: Jossey-Bass.

World at Work (2007). The WorldatWork Handbook of Compensation, Benefits & Total Rewards: A Comprehensive Guide for HR Professionals. New Jersey: John Wiley & Sons, Inc..

Yanadori, Y., Sturman, M. C., Milkovich, G. T. & Marler, J. H. (2002). Organizational Pay Mix: The Implications of Various Theoretical Perspectives for the Conceptualization and Measurement of Individual Pay Components. CAHRS Working Paper, vol. 2. Ithaca, NY: Cornell University.

Yanadori, Y. & Marler, J. H. (2006). Compensation strategy: does business strategy influence compensation in high-technology firms? Strategic Management Journal, 27 (6), 559-570.

Zajac, E. J. & Westphal, J. D. (1995). Accounting for the explanations of CEO compensation: Substance and symbolism. Administrative Science Quarterly, 40 (2), 283-308.

Expatriate Compensation: A Theoretical Approach

Christelle Tornikoski

The complexity of managerial compensation is undeniable. The multiple theoretical perspectives used to examine this strategic issue has, however, segmented its global understanding and blurred the relationships between its numerous facets, determinants and outcomes. Compensation complexity is even greater in the context of expatriation. The aim of this paper is to highlight the global picture when designing an expatriate package. For that purpose the traditional organisational control perspective, deemed to be adopted by Human Resource specialists, is examined. Expatriates' motivations for accepting an international assignment are then considered before turning to their social exchange relationship with their supervisor. This brings to the fore possible divergences in terms of focus and package design as well as tensions within the organisation itself; and leads to the definition of the expatriate compensation package as a "bundle" of total rewards, namely, a collection of interrelated valued rewards differentiated according to the dimensions of particularism and concreteness (Foa & Foa, 1975). This bundle can be considered the outcome of an "idiosyncratic deal" between the three parties. The impact of the international environment on the constituents of the package is in turn examined before offering some propositions to guide research and practice.

1. Introduction

Compensation is of strategic business importance since it is used by organisations to attract, motivate and retain valuable employees. In the context of expatriation this importance is increased because foreign assignments are seen as a normal part of a business career rather than as an exception in a career in international companies (e.g., Schell & Solomon, 1997). Moreover, the use of expatriation is expected to increase in the future (Bonache, Brewster, Suutari & De Saá, 2010). Still, compensation is the aspect of expatriation, which has received least attention (Bonache & Fernandez, 1997; Suutari & Tornikoski, 2000, 2001; Bonache, 2006) and no study has focused entirely on the content of expatriate compensation packages.

Expatriate compensation is often considered extremely costly and time consuming for the organisations involved (Bonache & Pla-Barber 2005). These two perceived two inherent handicaps when it comes to the management of contemporary employment relationships

(Rousseau, 2001). Indeed this perception pressures companies to either decrease their investment in international experience and knowledge[1]; or to look for alternate international employee populations (such as self-initiated expatriates)[2] and alternate forms of assignments[3]; or to decrease the coverage and amount of their expatriate compensation packages (Perkins & Daste, 2007). There is a danger that these pressures may lead to an alteration in expatriates' perceptions not only of their compensation package, but also of their whole employment relationship prompting expatriates to change their attitude toward their employer or simply change their employer. So there is the need to understand possible ways of designing expatriate compensation package while limiting the risk of the end of the employment relationship.

The purpose of this article is to examine expatriate compensation through different theoretical lenses to see if it might help understanding the perspectives of the different parties involved in the expatriate employment relationship. These are considered to be first, Human Resource (HR) specialists, who stand guarantor for the organisational interests in expatriation through the use of expatriate compensation package design; then the expatriate supervisor who has the responsibility of managing, motivating and committing the expatriate to the organisation through their relationship while standing for the organisation; and finally the expatriates who nowadays tend to manage their own career (e.g., Segers, Inceoglu, Vloeberghs, Bartram & Henderickx 2008; Sullivan & Baruch, 2009). The article also examines the international environment in which the employment relationship is embedded. The objective in doing so is first to globally understand the role of each perspective in the design and content of the expatriate package. Second, it is to show that expatriate compensation packages need to fit both organisational and individual objectives to ensure the success of the international assignment (Cerdin & Le Pargneux, 2009). Third, the objective is to lead to propositions, which might guide future research and practices on expatriate compensation issue. The structure of the paper follows the same logic and starts with a general presentation of compensation and the parties having an impact on it in expatriation.

2. Compensation and Concerned Parties in Expatriation

Compensation is one of the means used by organisations to control expatriates' behaviours and attitudes (Eisenhardt, 1989) with the ultimate objective of reaching their strategic goals such as performance. Compensation is also considered as one of the most salient signals and earliest practices interpreted by employees regarding the nature and status of their employment relationship (Rousseau & Ho, 2000). Furthermore, it is at the core of any employment relationship and one of the most basic reasons why people engage them-

[1] e.g, Bonache and Pla-Barber, 2005; Pate and Scullion, 2010, Schell and Solomon, 1997
[2] e.g, Meyskens, Von Glivow, Wether & Clarke, 2009; Thite, Srinivasan, Harvey & Valk, 2009
[3] e.g, Collings, D.G. Scullion, H. & Morley, M.J., 2007

selves in working for an organisation (Bloom & Milkovich, 1996) and to accept an international assignment (Miller & Chen, 1978; Pate & Scullion, 2010).

Compensation has for long been considered as a total compensation package, however Bloom and Milkovich (1996: 27) state that *"defining compensation as a bundle of valued returns offered in exchange for a cluster of employee contributions"* provides a broader view of compensation. Depending on who considers or which theoretical perspective is adopted to examine compensation, this bundle might not mean the same or encompass the same "returns". For this reason, when considering the employment relationship previous research (e.g., Macneil, 1980; Yan, Zhu & Hall, 2002; Perkins & Daste, 2007; Pate & Scullion, 2010) have been concerned about who actually stands for the organisation when communicating and setting realistic expectations for the employee. Indeed research has shown that HR specialists frequently face troubles in their dealings with discontented expatriates (Paik, Segaud, & Malinowski, 2002).

Examining the employer-employee relationship from an agency theory perspective in the context of international assignments, Yan, Zhu and Hall (2002: 338) indicate that the focus should be on *"the organizational entity lowest within the hierarchy that is directly involved in selecting, dispatching, and managing the assignee, including conducting performance reviews and repatriating the employee when the assignment is completed. This entity, however, should not be a particular individual who holds no institutionally binding power."* This is in line with the argument of Macneil (1980) according to which players in the corporate hierarchy on behalf of the organisation usually perform the principal's functions.

However, when considering the employment relationship from the bilateral view of the psychological contract (Rousseau, 1989), Pate and Scullion (2010) stress that a clear definition of whom the employer stands for in the organisation is not an easy issue to deal with. Indeed, multiple agents may represent the organisation's perspective, such as line, senior and HR managers at the headquarters and at the subsidiary. The recent article of Perkins and Daste (2007) shed some light on this issue. They distinguish between expatriate policy specialists who are *"personnel and development specialists responsible for design and quality assurance monitoring of expatriation policy (Ibid: 551)"* and expatriate supervisors who are *"the senior managers to whom expatriate report up-the-line (Ibid: 551)"*. The authors show the potential tensions between these two categories of organisational representatives. It is considered in this paper that the former category is accountable for designing, communicating and applying corporate expatriation policy to expatriate thus adopting "organisational control" lenses. The latter manages individual expatriates whom they need to keep motivated and committed to the organisation to ensure the success of the international assignment. Henceforth, expatriate supervisors might wear "motivational and exchange" lenses. This difference in perceiving what the organisation-expatriate relationship means and what the related returns are, creates tensions between the different parties involved. Still, a fit between these different perspectives and the criteria used both by expatriates and the organisation to assess their respective success, is argued to be critical to the success of the international assignment and the repatriation (Cerdin & Le Pargneux, 2009).

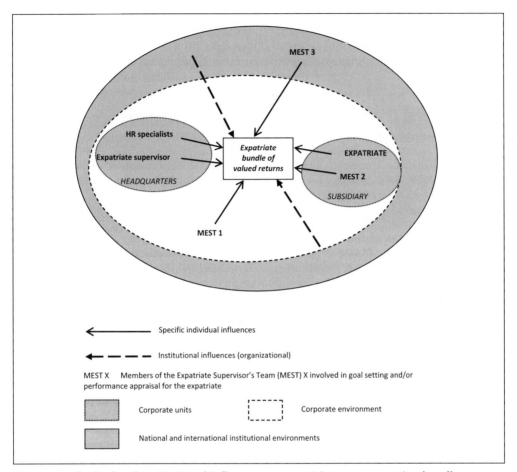

Figure 1: Individual and institutional influences on expatriate compensation bundle

In this article, the distinction by Perkins and Daste (2007) between **HR specialists** and **expatriate supervisors** is adopted to anthropomorphise the organisation. In addition, other potential supervisors will be referred to as the **supervisor's team**. Indeed, the findings by Black, Gregersen and Mendenhall (1992), Gregersen, Hite and Black (1996), and Suutari and Tahvanainen (2002) indicate that expatriates might also have other potential international relationships with other supervisors or professionals who are also involved in his/her goal setting and outcome appraisal. Furthermore, it is argued here that expatriate compensation package is not only embedded into this employment relationship (Bloom & Milkovich, 1996) but also into the international environment surrounding the international assignment. Therefore, Figure 1 summarises the specific individual and institutional influences on the expatriate package environments considered in this paper. The institutional context is going to be examined later on in this paper.

In the following section the traditional approach used by research to examine expatriate compensation is presented. Secondly, the tenets of agency theory are combined with a resource-based view perspective to explain how organisations might consider expatriates and thus design their compensation package. Thirdly, a brief description of the content of the traditional total compensation package of expatriates is presented.

3. Traditional Theoretical Approach to Expatriate Compensation

The focus of the scarce previous compensation studies in the context of expatriation has been on how to control subsidiaries (e.g., Roth & O'Donnell, 1996; Bonache & Fernández, 1997) through the adequate compensation of CEOs or top managers (Sanders & Carpenter 1998, Björkman & Furu, 2000; Carpenter, Sanders & Gregersen, 2001), namely variable pay, for instance. This research has been guided by the prescriptions of organisational control theories which view financial compensation as a pivotal control, and incentive mechanisms as flexible means to be used by organisations to achieve business objectives such as organisational performance. Thus, they have mainly used agency theory as a theoretical underpinning (see for instance, Roth & O'Donnell, 1996, Björkman & Furu, 2000). The understanding of such theoretical perspectives is important to grasp how an expatriate compensation package might have been designed and what components it might consist of. Consequently, this section describes how a traditional approach to expatriate compensation, such as an agency theory perspective and completed by a resource-based approach, enables understanding factors that might explain the difference of expatriate compensation packages in terms of proportions of fixed pay vs. variable pay.

3.1 Compensation from an Agency Theory Perspective

Agency theory originated from Adam Smith's (1937) observation that corporate directors used "other people's money" to pursue their own interests. It then evolved to examine the employment relationship at the individual level (e.g., Jensen & Meckling, 1976; Fama & Jensen, 1983; Eisenhardt, 1989). It thus describes that a "principal" (considered to be HR specialists, here) hires an "agent" (namely, expatriates) for his/her specialised knowledge, skills and, his expected capabilities to fulfil the organisational objectives and goals. This employment relationship is symbolised, based on and directed by a contract. This contract or agreement describes rights of each party, rules according to which expatriates' base salary will be determined, and performance evaluated and then paid. Central to the agency relationship is the conflict between the parties' self-interest that guides their behaviour and the low availability of information from the agent to the principal (also referred to as "information asymmetries"). The higher "information asymmetries" are the more the significance of this problematic situation, called "moral hazard" (Eisenhardt, 1988) increases. This situation increases further the more autonomy and independence the expatriate enjoys and the greater the specialised knowledge required to performe the task (Gomez-Mejia & Balkin, 1992; Holmstrom, 1979). HR specialists fear that the rational, self-interest motivated and risk-adverse expatriate will shirk or not provide the work efforts he engaged himself for (Stroh, Brett, Bauman & Reilly, 1996). They then look then for ways to deal with this agency problem.

According to agency theory HR specialists have basically two options (Demski & Feltham, 1978; Eisenhardt, 1988). They can either invest in information gathering to ensure that the expatriate acts according to the corporate interests and objectives (Eisenhardt, 1988, 1989; Jensen, 1983; Ouchi, 1977), or design a reward system to motivate the agent and monitor his/her actions according to objectives/goals to be performed to the satisfaction of HR specialists (Gomez-Mejia & Balkin, 1992; Jensen, 1983). When seeking to align the expatriate's behaviour, HR specialists design and develop compensation systems including fixed pay (behaviour-based pay) and variable pay (outcome-based pay). Tosi and Gomez-Mejia (1989) showed that "when an agent has high autonomy, independence and highly specialised knowledge, monitoring becomes very difficult and expensive, so principals depend on incentives to reward agents for appropriate outcomes" (Gomez-Mejia & Balkin, 1992: 923).

Thus, from the perspective of organisational control theories such as agency theory, money or tangible financial compensation is a pivotal control of employees' behaviours and incentive mechanism that HR specialists can use flexibly to achieve business objectives such as organisational performance (Gomez-Mejia & Balkin, 1992).

3.2 Determinants of Expatriate Total Compensation

In the following paragraphs the tenets of agency theory are mainly examined from a resource-based view (RBV) perspective. This theory indeed aims at identifying whether the firms' resources (see human capital theory, Becker, 1964) are valuable, rare, non-substitutable and inimitable to determine the sustainable corporate competitiveness on the global market. Individually. these four characteristics are necessary but not a sufficient of a sustainable corporate competitiveness.

Sole their combination provides such a sustainable competitive advantage (Barney, 1991). The aim here is to understand how organisations and HRM specialists may consider international assignments and expatriates from that RBV perspective to determine the financial content of expatriate compensation packages. Table 1 (see next page) summarises the key developments.

3.2.1 Degree of Expected Challenge Related to the International Assignment Task

Task programmability has been identified as an important determinant of variable pay systems (Eisenhardt, 1989; Gomez-Mejia & Balkin, 1992; Stroh et al., 1996; Ouchi, 1977). It is defined as the degree to which the appropriate behaviour by expatriates can

Table 1: Agency theory tenets and corresponding concepts in the context of expatriation

Considered agency theory tenets	Corresponding concepts into the expatriation context	Operationalisation
Task programmability	Degree of expected challenge related to the international assignment task	– Degree of autonomy – Degree of independence – Degree of specialised knowledge – Degree of intensity of expatriate's interaction with locals
Outcome measurability	Degree of information gathering	– Size of expatriate supervisor's team – Frequency of communication between expatriates and their supervisor

be clearly specified and defined in advance to achieve the organisation's desired outcome (Eisenhardt, 1988; Ouchi, 1977). According to agency theory, the principal chooses between behaviour-based contracts (fixed pay) and outcome-based contracts (variable pay) by examining the ease of monitoring the expatriate's job performance (behaviours). The more programmable the assignment task of expatriates, the easier for the principal to specify the behaviours that expatriates need to perform.

In their study on the determinants of faculty members' pay, Gomez-Mejia and Balkin (1992) showed that in situations where an agent has an inherently non-programmable job, the principal chooses to monitor performance by assessing outcomes, in that specific case the number of publications. Tosi and Gomez-Mejia (1989) also showed earlier that an agent with highly specialised knowledge, high autonomy and high independence is difficult and expensive for the principal to monitor. Therefore, the principal favours variable pay to reward agents for their appropriate outcomes.

By definition expatriates are strategic resources (Hsieh, Lavoie & Samek, 1999). They differ from their national counterparts, as they are scarce employees due the rarity or uniqueness of their specified knowledge, skills and capabilities. They are also *valuable* employees in creating and sustaining firm competitive advantage. Moreover they have been considered as *inimitable* since they are transferors of the strategic tacit knowledge of the company. Finally they are holders of qualities that make them *irreplaceable* such as being highly socialised and trustworthy. This resource-based definition of expatriates helps to introduce the discussion related to the difficulty for principals to define the programmability of the international assignment task, or in other words defining the extent of challenges inherent in the assignment tasks expatriates are expected to cope with.

Expatriates are likely to have been socialised into the organisational culture and management practices. As such they are sent abroad for either specific staffing needs, or organisation development purposes such as control and coordination, knowledge transfer and instilling corporate culture (Riusala & Suutari, 2004), or alternatively management development purposes (e.g., Edström & Galbraith, 1977; Welch, 1998; Stahl & Cerdin, 2004). Those assignment tasks often imply high levels of trust from the supervisor in the expatriate, which often results, as Riusala and Suutari (2004) illustrate, in expatriates' high degree of autonomy.

When considering the agency relationship, expatriates' **degree of autonomy**, within the strategic frames given by their supervisor for achieving the international assignment goals, is defined here as the degree to which their decision making process and authority (discretion), regarding how to pursue the goals they have been assigned, are expected to be free and independent from the intervention by their principal, or by any other member of the principal's team (see definition of "task autonomy" by Hackman, 1980). This construct is perceived as the horizontal limit of expatriates' decision-making freedom within strategic frames set by the supervisor, whereas the notion of degree of independence is perceived as its vertical limit. Following the logic of the previous definition, expatriates' **degree of independence** (or of financial discretion), within the strategic frames given by their supervisor for achieving the international assignment goals, is the financial level up to which their decision, regarding the means they will use to pursue their assigned goals, are not expected to require the intervention by the principal, or by any other member of the supervisor's team (see Tosi & Gomez-Mejia, 1989).

Moreover, expatriates' inimitability makes them extremely valuable for their organisation from a strategic point of view, whilst their scarcity increases this strategic value. These qualities are conceptualised here as the expected **degree of specialised knowledge** required from expatriates by the assignment task. This construct is defined as the perceived and expected difficulty for the supervisor and HR specialists of replacing the expatriate by equally competent employees for the same assignment task.

The international assignment involves a wide variety of situational contexts, which reinforces the inimitability of the expatriates based on very specific backgrounds and knowledge acquirement histories (Barney, 1991). However, beside this RBV perspective, these contexts, which differ from domestic assignment (Murphy & Cleveland, 1991), may also shake the supervisor's confidence and predictions regarding the ability of their "trusted" and autonomous expatriates to behave adequately and perform efficiently and successfully in contact with locals and international counterparts. Consequently, the notion of "agency moral hazard" previously linked to information asymmetries still seems to be valid in the case of expatriates, even though Roth and O'Donnell (1996) and then Björkman and Furu, (2000) argue the contrary in the case of an agency relationship between executives at corporate headquarters and expatriate managers at the head of subsidiaries. The uncertainty related to the difficulty of predicting expatriates' adequate and efficient behaviours while on assignment abroad can be also related to the **degree of intensity of expatriates' interaction with locals** (Chen, Choi & Chi, 2002; Bonache, Sanchez & Zárraga-Oberty, 2010). This construct describes the expected international characteristics of the international assignment tasks to which expatriates will have to adapt and correctly respond in order to efficiently and successfully perform their assigned task.

The four defined degrees of high autonomy, high independence, specialised knowledge and intensity of interaction with locals seem to be inherent characteristics of expatriates' international assignment task. They are considered all together as **the degree of expected challenge related to the international assignment task for the expatriate**. The higher this expected challenge, the less programmable the expatriates' task is expected to be. As a consequence, and following the agency theory logic, it is suggested here that the higher the expected degree of challenge, the more difficult it will be for the principal to programme the outcomes of expatriates, therefore a contract more based on outcome-related pay might be favoured by the principal.

3.2.2 Degree of Information Gathering

Agency principals look for means to monitor expatriates' behaviour and appraise their outcomes while limiting their costs. The first option available to the principal is a mechanism to motivate and encourage expatriates to act according to the organisation's interest and display the type of behaviour required in the subsidiary's compensation and incentive system (e.g., Bonache & Fernández, 1997). This system can be defined as "a pivotal control and incentive mechanism that can be flexibly used by management to achieve business objectives" (e.g., Gomez-Meija & Balkin, 1992:18). This concept leads to the agency constructs of outcome measurability (e.g., Anderson, 1985, Eisenhardt, 1988, 1989); also identified as an important determinant of variable pay systems (e.g., Eisenhardt, 1989; Gomez-Mejia & Balkin, 1992; Stroh et al., 1996). It refers to the extent to which performance/contribution outcomes of expatriates can be measured reliably and in a valid way.

In the case of an international assignment many factors like government policies, economic climate, competitors' actions, the weather, expatriates' family adaptation to the host country and other factors may intervene to cause variations in expatriates' outcomes in an international environment (Eisenhardt, 1989). In case the degree and complexity of external pressures on expatriates are high, the specification of their expected behaviour and the definition of the expected outcomes are arduous, then the possible geographical distance between the supervisor and the expatriate and other factors render the expatriates' outcomes difficult to measure. According to agency theory, in such a situation, the HR specialists will favour another option to reduce the agency moral hazard and will prefer to compensate expatriates with fixed pay. Therefore they will information to ensure that the agent acts according to the principal's interests and objectives based on local conditions and comparability.

Furthermore, in her study Tahvanainen (1998) shows that typically more than one person evaluate expatriates' performance. Suutari and Tahvanainen (2002) also indicate that performance goal setters and appraisal raters might not always be the same persons, even though a main supervisor is usually named. As previously indicated, other supervisors or professionals are involved in the expatriate's goal setting and outcome appraisal and are referred in this paper as the expatriate supervisor's team. Each member of the team represents an additional possibility or perspective in gathering information on the expatriates' behaviours as well as the external contextual features of the international environment in which the agent evolves. This team can provide important and multiple insights to appreciate the various facets of the host context and an expatriate's work (Gregersen et al., 1996) and thus help reduce information asymmetries. In addition, the frequency of communication between the supervisor and the expatriate is another means for the supervisor to appreciate and monitor the assignee's behaviour. Therefore, the size of the principal's team as well as the frequency of communication between the expatriate and the supervisor, in other words the **degree of information gathering** regarding the expatriate's behaviour, is expected to have a negative impact on an expatriates' proportion of variable pay.

3.3 Traditional Expatriate Total Compensation Components

The academic literature review on managerial compensation (see Werner & Ward, 2004) shows that most research on compensation either on national or international grounds mainly focuses on financial components of compensation, also referred to as total compensation package in the case of expatriate compensation.

In the case of the expatriate package, financial components include elements such as fixed pay and bonuses, benefits and allowances (Stone, 1986). The fixed pay corresponds to the compensation where the amount and payment is guaranteed. Its basis is influenced by the compensation approach adopted by the organisation, i.e., either home country-, or host country-, or hybrid-, or global-approach (e.g., Suutari & Tornikoski, 2001; Bonache, 2006). Bonuses are significant elements of the total compensation package (Bailey, 1995) and include compensation whose amount varies or the distribution is uncertain such as performance-related pay, for instance (Igalens & Roussel, 1999). When comparing national compensation packages with international ones, the main differences also lay in the composition of the remaining components of the total compensation package, namely the allowances and benefits (Guzzo et al., 1994).

The previous literature points out the important role that allowances play in expatriate financial compensation (e.g. Bonache, 2005; Guzzo et al., 1994; Suutari & Tornikoski, 2001). Such allowances refer to payments that are typically used to bridge the gap between reasonable expenditure in the home and the host country (Torrington, 1994) as well as to cover the costs of moving overseas and motivate the individual to make such a career move. When making the parallel between Herzberg's theory (1968) they appear to be what the author called "the KITA" (or "kick in the pants") to make the employee accept the job or assignment. It includes typical allowances such as an overseas premium, a cost of living allowance, or housing allowance. Moreover benefits such as insurances provided by the organisation may cover not only the expatriate's assignment-, travel-, health-, life-, accident-insurances, but also the family members' who move with the expatriate (e.g. Bonache, 2006; Festing & Perkins, 2009). They are difficult to deal with for organisations but nevertheless offered for business or moral reasons and support.

However, in the context of expatriation an employee-employer relationship encompasses much wider terms (Guzzo et al., 1994) than just financial or "monetizable" components (Rousseau & Ho, 2001). The international employee compensation package is consequently much broader in terms of components. Financial rewards alone have been shown to be insufficient in binding the employee to the organisation (Barringer & Milkovich, 1995; Herzberg, 1968; Malhotra, Budhwar, & Prowse, 2009). Other rewards seem critical and decisive to the employee's decision to stay in a company (Stahl, Miller & Tung, 2002; Stahl & Cerdin, 2004), especially in an international context (Suutari, Mäkelä & Tornikoski, 2009). Therefore after looking at expatriate compensation though the organisational control lenses deemed to be worn by HR specialists, the following section presents the perspective of expatriates.

4. Expatriate Compensation Embedded into the Employment Relationship

4.1 Expatriates' Perspective

The results of the study by De Vos and Meganck (2007) highlight that there is a discrepancy between HR specialists and employees' views regarding financial rewards. The former develops retention policies related to financial rewards while employees attach most importance to inducements related to the social atmosphere, career development and job content. Dickmann, Doherty, Mills and Brewster (2008) as well as Pate and Scullion (2010) indicate that HR specialists seem to overestimate the weight of financial compensation over other motivators expressed by expatriates. Furthermore, Stahl et al. (2002) and Stahl and Cerdin (2004) show that financial considerations were ranked at the fifth or sixth position after non-financial motivators among French and German expatriates. The respective studies of Stahl, Chua, Caligiuri, Cerdin and Taniguchi (2009) and Suutari, Mäkelä and Tornikoski (2009) stress how expatriates and global careerists value the on-going developmental opportunities linked to their international jobs, the meaningfulness and importance of the jobs, as well as their high levels of autonomy.

All these motivators have previously been reported to be typical characteristics of international jobs (Boies & Rothstein 2002; Bossard & Peterson 2005). Expatriate managers also value the international aspect of their career environment (Segers et al., 2008) as reported in earlier research among global careerists (Suutari & Mäkelä, 2007) or expatriates (Cerdin & Le Pargneux, 2010). The financial aspects of compensation are seen as important too but are more often considered as prerequisite and implicit conditions of the job offer rather than a motivation. In fact, financial considerations occupy only the fourth position after job-related characteristics, location of the assignment and the type of organisation as pull factors for employees (Suutari et al., 2009). All in all, it appears that expatriates are greatly concerned about their career success all along their international assignment (Tung, 1988; Cerdin & Le Pargneux, 2009).

Therefore, organisational control theories, such as agency theory, seem to reach their limits when it comes to explaining contemporary employment relationship (Rousseau, 2001) of expatriates. Moreover, despite the efforts of HR specialists in designing very effective total compensation packages the marginal to non-significant relationship between financial rewards and employee outcomes (De Vos & Megank, 2007; Malhotra et al., 2007) tends to question this sole financial perspective. Thus it is asserted that researchers and HR specialists need to identify what expatriate value most to motivate, commit them to the organisation and consequently retain them during and after their international assignment. The fact that HR specialists frequently face issues dealing with discontented expatriates (Paik et al., 2002) seems partly originating from the fact that they provide them with inadequate packages.

The following paragraph examines the expatriate supervisor's perspective on expatriate compensation.

4.2 Expatriate Supervisor's Perspective

Typically the expatriate supervisor has developed a personal relationship with the assignee since he/she had a time period long enough before the international assignment to get to know the expatriate. Based on this personal relationship, the expatriate supervisor is aware of and knows what the expatriate values most and looks for in his/her work and their international assignment. He/she is able to perceive what is essential to keep the expatriate motivated and willing to achieve the goals of the organisation. In return, the relationship with the supervisor is perceived as a trusted one by the expatriate. As seen previously, the exchanged returns are mostly intangible and non-financial, such as recognition, development support for instance (Rousseau & Ho, 2000; Rousseau, Ho & Greenberg, 2006).

When comparing expatriate supervisors' perspective with the one of HR representative described previously, clear differences emerge. This observation adds insights to the existence of socio-political tensions between these two corporate representatives identified and described by Perkins and Daste (2007).

4.3 Theoretical Perspectives

4.3.1 Psychological Contract

The expatriate supervisor is the one who embodies the organisation in the expatriate's eyes and thus the party with whom expatriates consider having an exchange relationship (Blau, 1964), and the basis of their psychological contract[4] (Rousseau, 1989). Bloom and Milkovich (1996) state that:

---

[4] *"By definition, the psychological contract is subjective, reflecting an individual's beliefs regarding an exchange of agreement binding that individual and another party (Rousseau & Ho 2000: 276)".*

> *"Psychological contracts theory views the relationship between employer and employee as a collection of promises; a set of obligations to exchange contributions for returns. As this exchange becomes less like a simple sales transaction and more like an on-going relationship, the location of valued returns moves from an exclusive focus on cash wages to a variety of socio-emotional benefits (Macnecil, 1980, 1985; Rousseau and Parks, 1993). Psychological contracts theory asserts that what the organization offers [i.e. [a] bundle of valued returns] is crucial for understanding what the employee contributes in exchange. Psychological contracts are schemas (Cantor, 1990) which give meaning to the bundle and direct individual reactions to it* (Ibid: 27-28)".

In their quantitative studies Guzzo et al., (1994) and Tornikoski (2011) consider the relationship between expatriate compensation and psychological contract. They show the mediating role played by the latter between expatriate compensation package and expatriates' attitudes. The psychological contract based on the exchange relationship between the expatriate and his/her supervisors provides an interpretative means of their relationship. It enables understanding the signal sent by the content of the compensation package in terms of the conditions and the nature of their relationship. Henceforth, the communicating role of the expatriate supervisor with regard to the content of the compensation package is essential in keeping the expatriate's psychological contract intact throughout the employment relationship including international assignment and repatriation. The underpinning of the psychological contract theory can be found in social exchange theory (Blau, 1964). According to this theory, social exchange relationships are those in which voluntary actions are contingent on rewarding reactions. This theory will be used to describe the concept of the "bundle of returns" exchanged between the expatriate supervisor and the assignee during the international assignment in the following paragraph.

4.3.2 Expatriate Bundle of Valued Returns: A Total Reward Package

The previous developments show that the "bundle of valued returns" (Bloom & Milkovich, 1996) exchanged between the expatriate supervisor and the expatriate is much broader than just the financial components considered in the traditional total compensation package. It encompasses returns, which are closely linked to the relationship between the expatriate and his/her supervisor. The value of these returns is mainly understood by and known of these two parties.

In social exchange theory (Blau, 1964) the notion of returns or rewards is central. According to Blau a social exchange occurs any time a social behaviour is motivated by an expected return or response from another. The perceived value of these exchange returns, entails reciprocal obligations of this social exchange, and is what matters most in this social exchange. The nature of these returns is to be left to the discretion of the parties who provide them. So Blau (1964) embedded the notion of returns within the social exchange relationship. Following the work of Blau (1964), Foa and Foa (1975) also "attached" the context of the relationship to the exchanged rewards, but in addition provided two dimensions to classify these returns. The first dimension labelled particularism "indicates the extent to which the value of a given resource [i.e. return] is influenced by the particular persons involved in exchanging it and by their relationship" (Foa & Foa, 1975: 80). This dimension varies from particularistic when the return exchanged is very specific to the parties of the exchange relationship (for instance recognition) to universalistic when the return can be exchanged without specific relationship between the two parties (for instance money). The second dimension, concreteness, "ranges from concrete to symbolic and suggests the form or type of expression characteristic of the various resources [or returns]" (Foa & Foa 1975: 80-81).

Foa and Foa (1975) considered "particularism" to be similar to Blau's (1967) notion of extrinsic and intrinsic rewards previously mentioned. This distinction has been widely used in compensation psychology (see Werner & Ward, 2004 for a short description of their area of research). However, as noted by Guzzo as early as 1979 the definition of these concepts has evolved (see Deci, 1975) and is far from reaching a consensus when it comes to its components and their respective effects on each other (e.g., Werner & Ward, 2004). Furthermore, Sachau (2007) who addresses the misinterpretations of Herzberg's Motivation-Hygiene theory, stresses that what researchers nowadays refer to as extrinsic rewards can clearly be assimilated to the "hygiene factors", while intrinsic rewards can be understood as Herzberg's "motivator factors". In his motivational model, "the two factor model", Herzberg (1966) makes the distinction between hygiene factors, which prevent employees from dissatisfaction and motivator factors, which, as their names indicate it, motivate and satisfy employees. Hygiene factors include for instance the working environment, interpersonal relationship status and pay while rewards such as achievement, recognition, responsibility are included in motivator factors. The parallel with intrinsic/extrinsic and with particularism is important because Herzberg (1966) described how those categories of factors are qualitatively different. In particular he stressed how hygiene factors, which are primarily in the job context, are linked to the perception of escalating needs. This escalation of needs means that *once a person has experienced a new level of a given hygiene factor, the new level becomes the minimal acceptable level*" (Sachau, 2007: 386). At the same time, other authors such as Armstrong and Stephens (2005) make the distinction between transactional and relational rewards. They define the first ones as "tangible rewards arising from transactions between the employer and employees concerning pay and benefits" whereas the second ones as "*intangible rewards concerned with learning and development and the work experience*" (Ibid: 14).

For clarification purposes and based on social exchange theory (Blau, 1965) and the work of Foa and Foa (1975) it is argued here that particularistic returns encompass intrinsic rewards, motivator factors and non-financial rewards whereas non-particularistic ones, which are also referred to as universal, encompass extrinsic rewards, hygiene factors and financial rewards. In terms of "concreteness", rewards which are neither visible symbolically and physically, nor easily computable and comparable, or with those of other employees, are included in the intangible category. Those that are easily computable and comparable by employees are encompassed by the tangible category. Thus the content of the "bundle of valued returns" (Bloom & Milkovich, 1996)[5] exchanged between expatriates and their supervisors should be defined according to these two dimensions. Furthermore, it should be acknowledged that the notion of the "bundle of valued returns" finds echoes in the concept of total reward (O'Neal, 1998: 6; Manus & Graham, 2003) grounded in business practice (CIPD, 2011). Even though this concept is not new, very little academic research has been devoted to this topic (Giancola, 2009). Cohen's (2007) analysis of the Academy of Management Journal's in the preceding five years of publication uncovered approximately 300 articles in total with only eighteen articles concerning total rewards. She also had only found five articles related to that topic in Personnel Psychology. Even though the list of constituent elements of a total reward package does not seem to gather unanimity either from academics or professionals and evolves with time (Giancola, 2009), it "embraces everything that employees value in the employment relationship" (O'Neal, 1998). As for the bundle of valued rewards, the total reward approach implies that "each aspect of reward, namely base pay, contingent pay, employee benefits and non-financial rewards, which include intrinsic rewards from the work itself, are linked together and treated as an integrated and coherent whole". (Armstrong & Stephens, 2005: 13). So in the present article, the expatriate bundle of valued rewards and the expatriate total reward package are considered as synonyms and as interrelated to the employment relationship.

In order to shed more light on the complexity of designing expatriate total reward packages, it is important to adopt a recently developed theoretical approach, still in its infancy: the one of idiosyncratic deals (i-deals) (Rousseau, 2001). This approach updates social exchange theory to apply more fully to the ever changing and more complex world of the relationship between organisations and their employees. This approach differentiates itself from the traditional theoretical stream by emphasising the bargaining power of valuable employees in the negotiation of the terms and the content of their contract with their organisation. As such this approach perfectly fits the case of expatriates.

4.3.3 Expatriate Total Reward Package: Outcome of an I-Deal

Cerdin and Le Pargneux (2009) examined how the fit between career and international assignment is likely to affect the success of the international assignment from pre-expatriation until repatriation both from the organisational and individual perspectives. They argue that for success both the individual criteria of success and those of the organisation have to mesh. Individual criteria include career success (measured by career satisfaction, promotion, pay increase), job success assessed through job satisfaction, and development success through the acquisition of international knowledge, skills and abilities (KSA) and the building of networks and relationships. When it comes to the organisational criteria

---

[5] Defined as *"a collection of interrelated returns an organization offers"* to employees, including *"a set of reparations, benefits, and items of value"* (Bloom & Milkovich, 1996:27)

of success of the international assignment, they include corporate performance assessment denoting the achievement of key organisational objectives, accomplishment of organisational tasks, but also the transfer of expertise, network and relationship building and, retention of expatriates.

The previous criteria of success are closely related to the returns that each party tends to include in or attach to the expatriate bundle of total rewards during the expatriate package negotiation. The notion of fit in turn appears clearly linked to the concept of idiosyncratic deal (i-deal). This notion was first developed by Rousseau (2001) and then with her colleagues (Hornung, Rousseau & Glaser, 2008; Rousseau, et al., 2006). Indeed they state that, in the case of valuable employees, the special terms and conditions of the employment relationship preferred by the worker can be negotiated between the two parties while at the same time helping the employer attract, motivate, and/or retain this highly valued contributor. Thus this kind of deal benefits both parties. These individualised employment arrangements differ then, to some extent, from what other workers in the company may get, but remain at the discretion of the parties and have to be transparent and justifiable to prevent perceptions of injustice. Furthermore, the individualisation of the contract can vary from a few elements in a larger standardised employment package to a total idiosyncratic employment bundle arrangement (Rousseau et al., 2006). Therefore when examining what might influence the composition of expatriate total reward package, the degree of standardisation of those packages and their negotiability are critical aspects.

Rousseau and her colleagues stress how the timing of i-deal in the employment relationship is important to understand the bargaining power of each party on the content of compensation package. I-deals can be negotiated prior to employment, during the recruitment, of a high market valued employee. These i-deals are called ex-ante i-deals. This kind of contract can easily concern self-initiated expatriates for instance (e.g., Inkson, Arthur, Pringle & Barry, 1997; Peel & Inkson, 2004). I-deals can also take place once on the job, after months or years of employment relationship. These i-deals are called ex-post i-deals. This is the particular case of most expatriates who have been working for many years within the organisation before being assigned abroad.

Depending on this timing, each party will have a very different degree of power in bargaining over terms or conditions. For instance, if we consider the case of a valuable employee chosen to be assigned abroad, the assignment abroad might jeopardise the career of his/her spouse and the education of his/her children. Due to the employment relationship prior to the assignment, the employee is in a better position to negotiate a possible dual career allowance and education allowance than if he or she was just being recruited. The negotiation behind this idiosyncratic deal may be considered as a symmetric power exchange as both parties benefit from it.

This dimension of the i-deal relationship significantly differs from the traditional approach to compensation and challenges its paradigms. Indeed, the previous sections of this article have highlighted the extent to which a multinational company's HR specialist's perspective is mainly concerned with corporate interests and outcomes, and differs from the approaches of the expatriate and their supervisor based on their socio-exchange relationship. This latter relationship is driven by a reciprocal exchange of returns to reach individual's outcomes, even though the expatriate supervisor acts the organisation. In his seminal and critical article on Human Resource Management research Guest (1999: 5) advocates that *"any concern for the impact of HRM should be as much with outcomes of relevance to workers as to business"*. He also shows that understanding employees' reactions to HRM practices is necessary to better design HR practices and reach organisational outcomes. This implies that the design of the expatriate total reward package would have to encompass both organisational and individual concerns and returns perceived as necessary to reach success. This total reward package would have to be the outcome of a negotiation between the three parties concerned. This goes back to the notion of i-deal developed by Rousseau and her colleagues in which bargaining powers are based on trust. This notion of i-deal also goes along with the arguments of Cerdin and Le Pargneux (2009) regarding the necessity of a fit between organisational and expatriates' success criteria related to career and international assignment to ensure their mutual success.

However, only focusing on the employment relationship risks the exclusion of external factors. Indeed, this employment relationship, the subsidiary and the corporation are all embedded in an international environment which pressures them to follow normative, cognitive and regulatory institutions for their individual or organisational legitimacy (Kostova, 1999; Kostova & Zaheer, 1999; Scott, 1995). From an agency theory perspective, these external institutional pressures transfer a financial risk to agents, as their outcomes are only partially a function of their behaviours. Therefore, international institutional dimensions of the expatriates' assignment deserve specific attention. In the following section institutional theory is considered as a means to explain and identify the international institutional elements that might impact upon an expatriate total reward package.

5. Compensation: The Importance of Context

From an institutional perspective both human and organisational behaviours are under pressure to adapt and be consistent with their institutional environment. They are expected gradually to behave similarly to other individuals or resemble other organisations in the environment in which they are embedded (Bloom & Milkovich, 1996). In the context of international compensation management, the idea of a country-level effect on individual and organisational behaviour is central. As an alternative to Hofstede's (1984) work mainly focusing on cultural aspects of countries, and based on the work of Scott (1995) and other institutional theorists, Kostova (1997) presented the country institutional profile construct. This construct describes the external organisational environments at the country level and is particularly adapted for describing the environments in which multinational enterprises evolve (Kostova & Zaheer, 1999; Xu & Shenkar, 2002) and, by extension, in which expatriates and their supervisors work. This country institutional profile *"reflects the institutional environment in that country defined as the set of all relevant institutions that have been established over time, operate in that country, and get transmitted into or-*

ganizations through individuals (Kostova, 1997: 180)." Scott (1995) described the three "pillars" or main types of institutions that constitute an institutional environment: regulatory, cognitive and normative. The *regulatory* component reflects national laws and rules existing to ensure stability and order in societies. It rests on the setting, monitoring and enforcement of rules. This component *"is based on instrumental logic and uses legal sanctioning as the basis of legitimacy* (Xu & Shenkar, 2003: 610)." So subsidiaries and individuals working in those companies have to comply with this legal logic to be legitimate in the country where they are located. The *cognitive* component *"reflects the cognitive structures and social knowledge shared by the people in a given country* (Kostova, 1997: 180)." Therefore organisations and individuals have to conform to what is taken for granted in the society in order to achieve legitimacy. *"The normative component consists of social norms, values, beliefs, and assumptions about human nature and human behaviour that are socially shared and are carried by individuals* (Kostova, 1997: 180)." Individuals as well as organisations get legitimacy by achieving prescribed desirable goals using adequate social norms (e.g., Xu & Shenkar, 2002).

This country institutional profile is used here to examine the country-effect on the expatriates' total reward package composition. Three perspectives are used: the parent company's home country; the subsidiary's founding conditions, implying the dominance of either the home country institutional profile or the one of the host country; and the country where the main expatriates' agency principal is located. Finally, the institutional measure "institutional distance" based on the country institutional profile construct is also a link between agency and institutional theory.

5.1 A Country Institutional Profile Perspective

5.1.1 Home Country of the Parent Company

It is also important to consider the possible impact of the home country of the parent company on the "zone of negotiability and composition"[6] of the total reward package of expatriates. According to the construct of the country institutional profile, firms located in the same country are likely to have similar kinds of policies and practices as they are expected to establish, and maintain similar external legitimacy in their home institutional environment. It can be expected that the institutional pressures of the parent company will affect incentives and reward practices. Legitimacy requirements vary across countries (Kostova & Zaheer, 1999). This is illustrated by the findings of Rousseau (2001) and her colleagues that one of the most fundamental differences among 13 democratic nations was the "zone of negotiability." She described that every country and every organisation "sets a zone of negotiability through the constraints and guarantees it has, which establishes certain conditions of employment (e.g., wage rates, retirement benefits, termination

---

[6] Defined as the extent to which terms and conditions of contracts are negotiable (Rousseau, 2001)

practices) or customs (e.g., strict separation between work and nonwork time characteristics of many European countries) (Rousseau, 2001: 264)." The previous description explains differences in compensation and more specifically incentive and reward practices. Based on institutional theory, Björkman and Furu (2000) showed that top-managers in subsidiaries owned by US multinational companies received a higher proportion of variable pay than others. The nationality of the multinational company was also found to be a significant determinant of the compensation packages of Finnish expatriates in Suutari and Tornikoski's (2000) empirical study. On average foreign employers offered better compensation terms and more commonly cost-of-living, hardship and dual-career allowances than Finnish employers did. In addition, Ferner's (1997, 2001) review of the literature on the effects of the country of origin of multinational companies (MNCs) on their foreign practices indicated strong support for the nationality of a multinational company as a determinant of compensation practices abroad.

5.1.2 The Founding Conditions of the Subsidiary (or the Pressure of the Dominant Country Institutional Profile on the Subsidiary)

Moreover, it is suggested that the incentive and reward practices in the subsidiary might be affected by its founding conditions. Therefore, it is important to consider its possible impact on the zone of negotiability and consequently the composition of the expatriate total rewards package. In their examination of the organisational legitimacy of multinational enterprises Kostova and Zaheer (1999) described that each subunit of a multinational faces its own institutional environment in the host country where it is located. This external institutional pressure increases the complexity of the legitimisation of the subsidiary, as it also has to face internal institutional pressures within the organisation. Based on their work and the construct of institutional distance defined by Kostova (1997) (see definition in the second following paragraph), Xu and Shenkar (2003) proposed different entry strategies of a multinational company. They argued that the existence of normative, cognitive or regulative distances between the country of the parent company and the targeted host country of its subunit would cause the firm to choose a different entry mode (acquisition, greenfield investment, wholly owned subsidiary or joint venture). Furthermore, in their paper explaining HRM practices in international joint ventures, Björkman and Lu (2001) found some strong support for the impact of founding conditions of joint ventures on the similarity of HRM practices to those of the parent company. They based their theoretical arguments on the work by Stinchcombe (1965) and Scott (1987) referring to the influence of the initial resource mix that an organisation acquires at its founding context and the institutional pressures existing at the time of their creation. Later on Kostova (1999) argued that the successful transfer of strategic organisational practices from a parent company to a subsidiary is affected by three sets of factors at the country, organisation and individual levels.

5.1.3 Country where the Expatriate Supervisor is Located

The expatriate supervisor can be located in the home country, the host country or even a third country (Gregersen et al, 1996; Tahvanainen, 1998). To illustrate the implications that the location of the expatriate supervisor can have on expatriates' variable pay Perkins and Hendry (2001) quoted the comments of Clive Wright from the multinational enterprise BOC which was moving by then to a more transnational form of organisation:

> *"How does a "line of business" executive who's sitting in South Africa look at the pay of people who are reporting to him in North America, Australia, UK, and Japan? What do the comparabilities need to be on that? How do we determine where they sit in the market? What do you do about performance parameters (because the performance systems are different in each of those countries)? (Clive Wright, BOC) (2001:68)."*

Thus individual expatriates face institutional pressures and in particular, the expatriate supervisor who sets assignment goals with respect to performance and contribution as well as appraises expatriates' related achievements. Therefore, it would be logical to consider that the institutional profile of the country where the principal is located would have an impact on the way performance and contribution are perceived, measured, appraised and the extent to which terms and conditions of contracts are negotiable (Rousseau, 2001).

5.2 Institutional Distance: A Link between Agency and Institutional Theories

Building on the role of context, Kostova and Zaheer (1999) highlight the importance of *institutional distance* between the home country of the firm and the host country where the subsidiary is located. This institutional distance refers to the difference or similarity between the three institutional pillars (regulatory, cognitive and normative) of the two countries that affect the firms' legitimacy, the transfer of routines to the corporate sub-units and the transfer of strategic organisational practices. Following this logic, the institutional distance should be a key determinant of compensation policies and practices and therefore affect the expatriate's compensation mix. Combined with the perspective of agency theory, institutional distance describes the complexity of the environment in which the expatriate evolves. It also illustrates how commonly information asymmetries will be exacerbated by the difference in ways used by expatriates and HR specialists (as well as the corporate unit, division or subsidiary in which each of them are located) to articulate, disseminate and arbitrate cultural and social cues as well as strategic and organisational information (Kostova, 1999; Xu & Shenkar, 2002). Based on agency theory arguments and the notion of zone of negotiability described by Rousseau (2001), it can be expected that the greater the institutional distance, the more difficult it will be for HR specialists to obtain and accurately interpret information regarding expatriates' outcomes.

It will also more difficult to find common grounds of negotiation. Therefore, it is expected that information asymmetries will increase. Consequently, HR specialists will be more inclined to pay expatriates on outcome-based contracts. They will favour the use of variable pay as a motivator, as well as control of expatriates' performance and contribution to goals achieved.

An extension of this previous line of reasoning would be to consider the cultural distance between the host-country of the subsidiary and the country where the expatriate supervisor is located. The existence of this additional institutional distance would increase information asymmetries between expatriates and their supervisor. It would therefore reinforce the use of variable pay.

To conclude this section, it is important to return to the relationship between HR specialists, expatriate supervisors and the assignee. All are embedded in institutional environments and adapt themselves accordingly and progressively. HR specialists, who are the architects and communicators of expatriate compensation policies, play the role of translators of all these institutional pressures. The way they look at expatriate assignments and compensation is indisputably influenced by these regulations, norms and cognitive structures. Consequently, the expatriate compensation packages they design tend to integrate all institutional requirements. The expatriate supervisor and his/her team, wherever they are located, confront the same situation; they must adapt and modify their behaviour according to the institutional pressures they face. This is necessarily reflected into their social exchange relationship with the expatriates they manage and the returns they exchange with them. As far as expatriates are concerned, various institutional influences shape their values and motivations differently (e.g. Segers et al, 2008; Ward, 2008) throughout their international assignment. These influences might include their country of origin, their location abroad, the nationality and the organisational background of their co-workers to name a few. Consequently, it is argued that ultimately institutional influences are encompassed in i-deals of total rewards and that these i-deals need to be adapted all along the international employment relationship, namely before, during and after an international assignment.

6. Towards an Integration of Different Perspectives

Employees often perceive an international assignment as recognition of their value and good qualities. The distinctive and strategic purpose of their assignment also signals to them how important they are to their principal. Their organisation's decision to assign them abroad confers them some power to bargain what is, and will be, the most valuable to them once abroad. This symmetrical beneficial exchange means that the more the degree of expected challenge related to the task of the expatriate, the more the organisation, embodied by HR specialists, should be ready to negotiate particularistic terms and conditions of the expatriate contract to ensure the success of the international assignment.

Proposition 1: *In contemporary employment relationships, the more the degree of expected challenge related to the task of the expatriate, the more the organisation is ready to make an idiosyncratic deal to ensure the success of the international assignment.*

In addition, when considering traditional expatriation, based on internal recruitment, expatriate total reward packages are outcomes of ex-post i-deals. This means that they occur after years of social exchange between the expatriate and his/her supervisor. As a consequence the returns exchanged include forms of personal or emotional support, which are particularistic to this relationship and more difficult for others outside the relationship to identify and compare. Following the arguments of Rousseau et al. (2006) that ex-post i-deals are more likely to be based on intangible particularistic rewards, it implies that:

Proposition 2: *In contemporary employment relationships, the more valuable the expatriate to the organisation, the more the organisation proactively includes intangible particularistic rewards in their total reward package.*

Thanks to his/her knowledge of the expatriate, the supervisor should play a critical role in the i-deal negotiation as he/she is the main person able to identify and understand what particularistic rewards the expatriate values most. Consequently, the HR specialists' perspective to compensation and theirs should be combined to support:

Proposition 3: *In contemporary employment relationships, organisations whose HR specialists and expatriate supervisors work together on the design of adequate total reward packages for their expatriate, have a competitive advantage over competitors.*

The proactive collaboration of HR specialists and expatriate supervisors protects the organisation from the risk of a pervasive and escalating use of financial universalistic rewards. This also reduces the risk that their expatriates behave in a way that goes against the strategic corporate goals and consequently reduces the need to seek external information about the behaviour of the agent (decrease of information asymmetries). If this collaboration is an improvement on what the traditional organisational control approach to compensation dictates, it is not enough. Indeed expatriates need to have a chance to state if they are even interested in the international assignment (Cerdin & Le Pargneux, 2009). Moreover they need to have the possibility of negotiating their returns to ensure that they and the organisation really correlate with what they value and seek in the international assignment. Therefore it is argued that:

Proposition 4: *In contemporary employment relationships, the more an expatriate total reward package fits to the perspectives of HR specialists, the expatriate supervisor and the expatriate, the greater chance the international assignment has to be a success from both organisational and individual point of view.*

While being abroad expatriates are often geographically isolated from the people they worked with in the organisation. The virtual communication with their supervisors can also become difficult and sporadic. Depending on the degree of challenge inherent to the assignment, the support and the link to the organisation are, however, essential to expatriates since many aspects of their work and life depend on it (Guzzo et al. 1994; Pate & Scullion, 2010). However, very often, during the international assignment, the expatriate supervisor becomes unreachable due to promotion to other responsibilities or simply because (s)he has left the organisation. Consequently, the person who has followed the assignee for many years in the organisation, with whom intangible particularistic rewards that they value most have been negotiated for the international assignment, who embodies the organisation in the expatriate's eyes and with whom their psychological contract disappears. At the stage, it is clear that:

Proposition 5: In contemporary employment relationships, an organisation that ensures that their expatriates are managed and followed by the same team of HR specialists and supervisors all along the international assignment will commit their expatriates to the organisation in the long run and prevent breaking their psychological contract.

7. Conclusion

7.1 Summary of the Arguments of this Article

This paper addresses the complex and challenging issue of expatriate compensation. It shows the limits of the traditional organisational approach to compensation in explaining the contemporary employment relationships of a multinational company with their valuable expatriates, and in designing an adequate compensation package to retain them. The example of an agency theory perspective deemed to be the one used by HR specialists is considered. This theory assumes an asymmetrical relationship in which a principal attempts to control the self-interest motivated and risk-adverse behaviour of the agent. However, this perspective does not apply to the way many contemporary organisations operate in expatriation (e.g., Perkins & Daste, 2007) and deal with their valuable employees. De Vos and Meganck (2007) showed that HR specialists, who design expatriate compensation, relate to financial rewards while employees attach most importance to other inducements related to their work environment and career success. Consequently, expatriate compensation packages which are composed mainly of fixed and variable pay do not correspond to current realities of expatriates' expectations and results in their discontentment (Barley, 1995, Pate & Scullion, 2010). The compensation package asked by assigned employees nowadays is what is considered to be "a total reward bundle" (Bloom & Milkovich, 1996), meaning a collection of interrelated intangible/tangible and particularistic/universalistic elements (Foa & Foa, 1975) exchanged with the organisation in return of their contributions. This bundle should include the intangible particularistic rewards that they get from their social relationship with their supervisor and the returns they value most and look for in their international assignment. It is stated that the package should be the outcome of an idiosyncratic deal (Rousseau, 2001) between HR specialists, the expatriate supervisor and the expatriate.

7.2 Theoretical Contributions

Firstly, the main contribution of this paper is to provide a global theoretical background to the field of expatriate compensation. The dearth of theoretical grounded studies in that field has been stressed by many authors such as Bonache (2006), Rousseau and Ho (2000). Furthermore, Bloom and Milkovich (1996) have pointed to the fact that the multitude of theories available to researchers and practitioners to examine managerial compensation has led to a segmented perception of this complex issue. This limits the understanding of the link between the findings of very specific research. Secondly, this article provides an original choice of theories since both the more classical and more recent ones are taken into account. By translating these theories in the context of expatriate compensation this article provides an overall, even though non-exhaustive, review of factors that might have an impact on the design and composition of expatriate compensation package.

Thirdly, by anthropomorphising the organisation through the consideration of HR specialists and the expatriate supervisor and associating different theoretical perspectives to each of them, the present article provides a theoretical explanation of the socio-political tensions existing between the two, originally described by Perkins and Daste (2007). Fourthly, this article shows the limits of traditional organisational control approaches to compensation in contemporary organisation. Nowadays, a package of financial rewards is not sufficient to satisfy and commit expatriates to the organisation. Therefore, the consideration of other theories such as social exchange theory combined with concepts such as the "bundle of returns" (Bloom & Milkovich, 1996), "particularism" and "concreteness" of returns (Foa & Foa, 1975) both pointing at the notion of total rewards used in business life is necessary. The fifth theoretical contribution is to show that the high risk and uncertainty linked to the challenge of the task, the very complex international environment in which the employment relationship takes place, and the behaviour of the agent can be significantly reduced by the organisation by negotiating idiosyncratic deals with their valuable expatriates. The content of this i-deal needs to benefit and encompass what is the dearest, to both organisational and individual parties. In other words the expatriate compensation package needs to fit both parties' perceptions of what is needed to be successful.

A sixth contribution was to make the link between the Career-Assignment fit model developed by Cerdin and Le Pargneux (2009) and the notion of the total reward bundle. Indeed this bundle thus encompasses all returns considered as necessary to achieve success both according to the individual and organisational criteria. A last contribution is to provide propositions for future research. It should be noted here that even though this article focuses on assigned expatriates, the recent study by Tornikoski (2011; 2010) shows that self-initiated expatriates interpret the signals send by their compensation package and react in the same way as assigned expatriates.

7.3 Practical Managerial and Business Contributions

A first practical managerial contribution of this article is to translate the tenets of agency theory in the context of expatriation: task programmability is translated into the degree of expected challenge related to the international assignment and the outcome measurability into the degree of information gathering. This translation provides a possible operationalisation of these concepts in the context of expatriation.

A second practical managerial contribution is to point at the decisive role of expatriate supervisors in the design of expatriate compensation packages. This article stresses the need of collaboration between HR specialists and expatriate supervisors to successfully and proactively answer expatriates' expectations in terms of their compensation package. Since they are the ones who know expatriates best they are also the ones who understand what is needed to lead to a successful assignment. However, HR specialists as guarantors of the organisational interest need to indicate to which extent returns, especially the financial ones, are possible. Besides being crucial, the role of expatriate supervisors is also a difficult one, because they are between two "self-interested" parties: the organisation represented by HR specialists and the one of expatriates. Thus their role appears to be the one "mediating translator" so that both parties understand each other's objectives, success criteria and expectations. Furthermore, they are also employees with their own career perspectives and expectations. The role should be clearly supported by the organisation. This also sheds light on the high importance to the term "human" in the Human Resource Management expression (Inkson, 2008). A good and trustworthy relationship between "a individual principal" and his/her agent is essential to a successful employment relationship, especially in an expatriation context.

A third contribution is to show the corporate goals in contemporary organisations can no longer be achieved unilaterally. Contemporary organisations have to take their employees' criteria of success into account. Pate and Scullion (2010) confirmed this by showing that the expatriate psychological contract is nowadays transactional, showing that expatriates are *"most inclined towards more robust bargaining with an individualistic and calculating interpretation of the employment relationship* (Ibid: 66)." Henceforth, idiosyncratic deals offer means for organisations and their expatriates to align their expectations in terms of international assignment success. This alignment is achieved through the negotiation of the compensation between the expatriate, his/her supervisor and the HR specialists. Furthermore, since i-deals fit to the parties' values and benefit both the organisational and the expatriate, they provide legitimacy and a means to explain such an individualised bundle to other employees of the organisation. So where other employees perceive some injustice in such treatment, these particularistic rewards, which are aligned with the values of the organisation, can be justified, and thus decrease, this organisational threat.

A last comment would be to stress that idiosyncratic deals are very difficult to copy since intangible particularistic exchanges between expatriate supervisors and assignees lack fixed metrics. In addition they are often not visible and make the exchange difficult to standardise or to govern by rules (Rousseau et al., 2006). Thus i-deals provide a strategic and sustainable competitive advantage to the organisation on the market.

References

Anderson, E. (1985). The salesperson as outside agent or employee: A transaction cost analysis. Marketing Science, 4, 234-254.

Armstrong, M. & Stephens, T. (2005). Handbook of employee reward management and practice. London and Sterling, VA: Kogan Page.

Bailey, E.K. (1995). International Compensation. In O. Shenkar (Ed.), Global Perspectives of Human Resource Management. Englewood Cliffs: Prentice-Hall, Inc.

Barney JB. (1991). Firm resources and sustained competitive advantage. Journal of Management, 17 (1), 99-120.

Barringer, M. & Milkovich, G. (1995). Changing employment contracts: the relative effects of proposed changes in compensation, benefits and job security on employment outcomes. Cornell Centre for Advanced Human Resource Studies.

Baruch, Y. & Steel, D.J. & Quantrill, G.A. (2002). Management of expatriation and repatriation for novice global player. International Journal of Manpower, 23 (7), 659-673.

Björkman, I. & Furu, P. (2000). Determinants of variable pay for top managers of foreign subsidiaries in Finland. International Journal of Human Resource Management, 11, 698-713.

Björkman, I. & Lu, Y. (2001). Institutionalization and bargaining power explanations of HRM practices in international joint ventures – The case of Chinese-Western Joint Ventures. Organization Studies, 22 (3), 491-512.

Black, J. S. (1991). When Yankees come home: Returning expatriates feel foreign in their native land. Journal of International Business Studies, 22 (4), 671-695.

Black, J.S., Gregersen, H.B. & Mendenhall, M. (1992). Global assignments: Successfully expatriating and repatriating international managers. San Francisco: Jossey-Bass.

Blau, P. (1964). Exchange and Power in Social Life. New York: Wiley & Sons.

Blau, P. (1967). Exchange and Power in Social Life. New York: Wiley.

Bloom, M. C. & Milkovich, G. T. (1996). Issues in managerial compensation research. Journal of Organizational Behavior, 3, 23-47

Bonache, J. (2006). The compensation of expatriates: a review and future research agenda. In Stahl, G. & Björkman, I. (Eds.), Handbook of research in international human resource management. Edward Elgar Publishing, Lmt.

Bonache, J., Brewster, C., Suutari, V. & De Saá, P. (2010). Expatriation: Traditional criticisms and international careers: Introducing the special issue. Thunderbird International Business Review, 52 (4), 263-274.

Bonache, J. & Fernández, Z. (1997). Expatriate Compensation and Its Links to Subsidiary Strategic Role: a Theoretical Analysis. The International Journal of Human Resource Management, 4, 457-475.

Bonache, J. & Pla-Barber, J. (2005). When are international managers a cost effective solution? The rationale of transaction cost economics applied to staffing decisions in MNCs. Journal of Business Research, 58, 1320-1329.

Bonache, J., Sanchez, J. I. & Zárraga-Oberty, C. (2010). The interaction of expatriate pay differential and expatriate inputs on host country national's pay unfairness. The International Journal of Human Resource Management, 20 (10), 2135-2149.

Cantor. N. (1990). From thought to behaviour: "Having" and "doing" in the study of personality and cognition. American Psychologist, 45, 745-750.

Carpenter, M. A., Sanders, W. G. & Gregersen, H. B. (2001). Bundling human capital with organizational context: the impact of international assignment experience on multinational firm performance and CEO pay. Academy of Management Journal, 44 (3), 493-511.

Cerdin, J.-L. & Le Pargneux, M. (2009). Career and international assignment fit: Towards an integrative model of success. Human Resource Management, 48 (1),5-25.

Chen, C.C. & Choi, J. & Chi, S-C. (2002). Making justice sense of local-expatriate compensation disparity: Mitigation by local referents, ideological explanations, and interpersonal sensitivity in China-Foreign joint ventures. Academy of Management Journal, 45 (4), 807-817.

Chen, H-F. (2010). The relationships of organizational justice, social exchange, psychological contract, and expatriate adjustment: an example of Taiwanese business expatriates. The International Journal of Human Resource Management, 21 (7), 1090-1107.

CIPD (2011). Total Reward, revised in January 2011. http://www.cipd.co.uk/hr-resources/factsheets/strategic-reward-total-reward.aspx

Cohen, D. J. (2007). The very separate worlds of academic and practitioner publications in Human Resource Management: Reasons for the divide and concrete solutions for bridging the gap. Academy of Management Journal, 50 (5), 1013-1019.

Collings, D.G. Scullion, H. & Morley, M.J. (2007). Changing patterns of global staffing in the multinational enterprise: Challenges to the conventional expatriate assignment and emerging alternatives. Journal of World Business, 42 (2), 198-213.

De Vos, A. & Meganck, A. (2009). What HR managers do versus what employee value – Exploring both parties – views on retention management from a psychological contract perspective. Personnel Review, 38 (1), 45-60.

Deci, E. L. (1975). Intrinsic Motivation. Plenum, New York.

Demski, J. & Feltham, G. (1978). Economic incentives in budgetary control systems. Accounting Review, 53, 336-359

Dickmann, M., Doherty, N., Mills, T. & C. Brewster (2008). Why do they go? Individual and corporate perspectives on the factors influencing the decision to accept an international assignment. The International Journal of Human Resource Management, 19 (4), 731-751.

Edström, A. & Galbraith, J. (1977). Transfer of managers as a coordination and control strategy in multinational organizations. Administrative Science Quarterly, 22, 248-263.

Eisenhardt, K. M. (1988). Agency and institutional theory explanations: The case of retail sales compensations. Academy of Management Journal, 31, 488-511.

Eisenhardt, K. M. (1989). Agency theory: An assessment and review. Academy of Management Journal, 14, 57-74.

Fama, E. & Jensen, M. (1983). Separation of ownership and control. Journal of Law and Economics, 26, 301-325.

Ferner. A. (1997). Country of origin effects and human resource management in multinational companies. Human Resource Management Journal, 7 (1), 19-37.

Festing, M. & Perkins, S.J. (2009). Rewards for internationally mobile employees. In Dickmann, M., C. Brewster & P. Sparrow (Eds.), International Human Resource Management: A European Perspective. Oxon, Routledge.

Foa, U. G. & Foa, E. B. (1975). Societal structures of the mind. Springfield, IL: Charles C. Thomas.

Gerhart, B. & Milkovich, G. T. (1993). Employee compensation: Research and Theory. In Dunette, M. D. & Hough, L.M. (Eds.), Handbook of Industrial and Organizational Psychology (Second edition, volume 3, pp. 481-569). Palo Alto, Ca: Consulting Psychology Press.

Giancola, F. L. (2009). Is total rewards a passing fad. Compensation Benefits Review, 41, 29-35.

Gomez-Mejia, L. R. & Balkin, D.B. (1992). Determinants of faculty pay: An agency theory perspective. Academy of Management Journal, 35, 921-955.

Gregersen, H. B., Hite, J. M. & Black, J. S. (1996). Expatriate performance appraisal in U.S. Multinational Firms. Journal of International Business Studies, 27 (4), 711-738.

Guzzo. R.A. (1979). Types of Rewards, and work motivation. Academy of Management Review, 4 (1), 75-86.

Guzzo, R.A., Noonan, K. A. & Elron, E. (1994). Expatriate managers and the psychological contract. Journal of Applied Psychology, 79 (4), 617-626.

Hackman. R. J. (1980). Work Redesign and Motivation. Professional Psychology, 11 (3), 445-455.

Harvey, M. (1993). Empirical evidence of recurring international compensation problems. Journal of International Business Studies, 24 (4), 785-799.

Herzberg, F. I. (1968). One more time: How do you motivate employees? Harvard Business Review, 46 (1), 53-62.

Herzberg, F. I. (1966). Work and the nature of man. Cleveland: World Publishing.

Hsieh, T-Y., Lavoie, J. & Samek, R. A. P. (1999). Are you taking your expatriate talent seriously? The McKinsey Quarterly, 3.

Hofstede, G. (1984). Culture's consequences: International differences in work-related values. Thousand Oaks, CA: Sage Publications, Inc.

Holmstrom, B. (1979). Moral hazard and observability. Bell Journal of Economics, 10 (1), 74-91.

Hornung, S., Rousseau, D. M. & Glaser, J. (2008). Creating flexible work arrangements through idiosyncratic deals. Journal of Applied Psychology, 93 (3), 655-664.

Igalens, J. & Roussel, P. (1999). A study of the relationship between compensation package, work motivation and job satisfaction. Journal of Organizational Behavior, 20, 1003-10025.

Inkson, K. (2008). Are humans resources? Career Development International, 13 (3), 270-279.

Inkson, K, Arthur, M., Pringle, J. & Barry, S. (1997). Expatriate assignment versus overseas experience: Contrasting models of international Human Resource development. Journal of World Business, 32 (4), 351-368.

Jensen, M. C. (1983). Separation of ownership and control. Journal of Law and Economics, 26, 301-325.

Jensen, M. & Meckling, W. H. (1976). Theory of the firm: Managerial behavior, agency costs, and ownership structure. Journal of Financial Economics, 3, 305-360.

Kostova, T. (1999). Transnational transfer of strategic organizational practices: A conceptual perspective. Academy of Management Review, 24, 308-324.

Kostova, T. (1997). Country institutional profiles: Concept and measurement. Academy of Management Proceedings, pp. 180-184.

Kostova, T. & Zaheer, S. (1999). Organizational legitimacy under conditions of complexity: The case of the multinational enterprise. Academy of Management Review, 24, 64-81.

Macneil, L.R. (1980). The new social contracts: An inquiry into modern contractual relations. New Haven, CT: Yale University Press.

Malhotra, N., Budhwar, P. & Prowse, P. (2009). Linking rewards to commitment: an empirical investigation of four UK call centres: International Journal of Human Resource Management, 18 (12), 2095-2127.

Manus, T.M. & Graham, M.D. (2003). Creating a total rewards strategy: a toolkit for designing business-based plans. American Management Association: New York.

Meyskens, M., Von Glivow, M.A., Wether, W.B. & Clarke, L. (2009). The paradox of international talent: Alternative forms of international assignments. The International Journal of Human Resources Management, 20 (6), 1439-1450.

Miller, E.L. & Cheng, J. (1978). A closer look at the decision to accept an overseas position. Management International Review, 25-33.

Murphy, K. R. & Cleveland, J. N. (1991). Performance appraisal: An organizational perspective. Boston: Allyn & Bacon.

O'Neal, S. (1998). The Phenomenon of Total Rewards. ACA Journal, 7 (3), 6-18.

Ouchi, W. F. (1977). The relationship between organizational structure and organizational control. Administrative Science Quarterly, 22, 95-113.

Paik, Y., Segaud, B. & Malinowski, C. (2002). How to improve repatriation management. International Journal of Manpower, 23 (7), 635-648.

Pate, J. & Scullion, H. (2010). The changing nature of the traditional expatriate psychological contract. Employee Relations, 32 (1), 56-73.

Peel, S. & Inkson, K. (2004). Contracting and careers: choosing between self and orgnizational employment. Career Development International, 9 (6/7), 542-558.

Perkins, S. J. & Daste, R. (2007). Pluralistic tensions in expatriating managers. Journal of European Industrial Training, 31 (7), 550-569.

Perkins, S. J. & Hendry, C. (2001). Global Champions: Who's Paying Attention? Thunderbird International Business Review, 43 (1), 53-75.

Riusala, K. & Suutari, V. (2004). International knowledge transfer through expatriates: A qualitative analysis of international stickiness factors. Thunderbird International Business Review, 46 (6), 743-770.

Roth, K. & O'Donnell, S. (1996). Foreign subsidiary compensation strategy: An agency theory perspective. Academy of Management Journal, 39, 678-703.

Rousseau, D. M. (2001). Idiosyncratic deals: Flexibility versus fairness? Organizational Dynamics, 29, 260-271.

Rousseau, D. M. (1989). Psychological and implied contracts in organizations. Employee Rights and Responsibilities Journal, 37 (2), 121-139.

Rousseau, D. M. & Ho, V. T. (2000). Psychological contract issues in compensation. In Rynes, S. L. & Gerhart, B. (Eds.), Compensation in organizations: current research and practice. Jossey-Bass: San Francisco (CA).

Rousseau, D. M., Ho, V. T. & Greenberg, J. (2006). I-deals: Idiosyncratic terms in employment relationships. Academy of Management Review, 31, 977-994.

Rousseau, D. M. & Parks, J.M. (1993). The contracts of individuals and organizations. In Cummings, L.L. & Staw, B. M. (Eds.), Research in Organizational Behavior (Volume 15, pp. 1-47). Greenwitch, Ct: JAI Press.

Sachau, D. (2007). Resurrecting the motivation-hygiene theory: Herzberg and the positive psychology movement. Human Resource Development Review, 6 (4), 377-393.

Sanders, W. G. & Carpenter, M. A. (1998). Internationalization and firm governance: The roles of CEO compensation, top team composition, and board structure. Academy of Management, 14 (2), 158-178.

Schell, M.E. & Solomon, C.M. (1997). Capitalizing on the global worksforce: A Strategic Guide to Expatriate Management. New York: McGraw-Hill.

Scott, R. (1995). Institutions and Organizations. Thousand Oaks, CA: Sage Publications.

Scott, R. (1987). The adolescence of institutional theory. Administrative Science Quarterly, 32 (4), 493-511.

Segers, J., Inceoglu, I., Vloeberghs, D., Bartram, D & Henderickx, E. (2008). Protean and boundaryless careers: A study on potential motivators. Journal of Vocational Behavior, 73, 212-230.

Smith, A. (1937). The wealth of nations. New York: Modern Library.

Stahl, G.K. & Cerdin, J. L. (2004). Global careers in French and German multinational corporations. Journal of Management Development, 23 (9), 885-902.

Stahl, G. K., Chua C.H., Caligiuri, P., Cerdin, J.-L. & Taniguchi, M. (2009). Intentions in learning-driven and demand-driven international assignments: The role of repatriation concerns, satisfaction with company support, and perceived career advancement opportunities. Human Resource Management, 48 (1), 89-109.

Stahl, G. K., Miller, E. L. & Tung, R. (2002). Toward the boundaryless career: a closer look at the expatriate career concept and the perceived implications of an international assignment. Journal of World Business, 37 (3), 216-227.

Stinchcombe, A. L. (1965). Social structure and Organizations. In March, J.G. (Ed.), Handbook of Organizations. Chicago: Rand McNally.

Stone, R.J. (1986). Compensation: Pay and Perks For Overseas Executives. Personnel Journal, 64, 67-69.

Stroh, L. K., Brett, J.M., Bauman, J. P, & Reilly, A.H. (1996). Agency theory and variable compensation strategies. Academy of Management Journal, 39, 751-767.

Sullivan, S.E. & Baruch, Y. (2009). Advances in career theory and research: A critical review and agenda for future exploration. Journal of Management, 35, 1542-1571.

Suutari, V. & Mäkelä, K. (2007). The Career Capital of Managers with Global Careers. Journal of Managerial Psychology, 22 (7), 628-648.

Suutari, V., Mäkelä, L. & Tornikoski, C. (2009). How to attract and retain global careerists: A total compensation perspective on career decisions of global careerists. Conference proceedings of the 10th Vaasa Conference on International Business. Vaasa, Finland.

Suutari, V. & Tahvanainen, M. (2002). The antecedents of performance management among Finnish expatriates. International Journal of Human Resource Management, 13 (1), 55-75.

Suutari, V. & Tornikoski, C. (2000). Determinants of Expatriate Compensation: Findings among Expatriate Members of SEFE. Finnish Journal of Business Economics, 49 (4), 517-539.

Suutari, V. & Tornikoski, C. (2001). The Challenge of Expatriate Compensation: The Sources of Satisfaction and Dissatisfaction among Expatriates. International Journal of Human Resource Management, 12 (3), 1-16.

Tahvanainen, M. (1998). Expatriate performance management. The case of Nokia. Telecommunications. Acta Universitatis Oeconomicae Helsingiensis A-134. Helsinki, HeSE prist.

Thite, M., Srinivasan, V., Harvey, M. & Valk, R. (2009). Expatriates of host-country origin: "Coming home to test the waters". The International Journal of Human Resource Management, 20 (2), 269-285.

Toh, S. M. & Denisi, A. S. (2003). Host country national reactions to expatriate pay policies: A model and implications. Academy of Management Review, 28 (4), 606-621.

Tornikoski, C. (2011). Fostering expatriate affective commitment: a total reward perspective. Cross-Cultural Management-An International Journal, 18 (2). Issue entitled, Expatriate Management: New Issues and New Insights.

Tornikoski, C. (2010). Expatriate's compensation information processing and affective commitment: A psychological contract and total reward perspective. EIBA Conference Proceedings 2010. Competitive paper. Porto, Portugal.

Torrington, D. (1994). International Human Resource Management – Think Globally, Act Locally. UK: Prentice Hall International.

Tosi, H. L. & Gomez-Mejia, L.R. (1989). The decoupling of CEO pay and performance: An agency theory perspective. Administrative Science Quarterly, 34, 169-189.

Tung, R. L. 1988. Career issues in international assignments. The Academy of Management Executive, 2 (3), 241-244.

Warr, P. (2008). Work values: some demographic and cultural correlates. Journal of Occupational and Organizational Psychology, 81 (4), 751-775.

Welch, D. (1998). The psychological contract and expatriation: A disturbing issue for IHRM? Paper presented at 6th Conference on International Human Resource Management, University of Paderborn.

Werner, S. & Ward S. G. (2004). Recent compensation research: An eclectic review. Human Resource Management Review, 14, 201-227.

Whitener, E.M., Brodt, S.E., Korsgaard, M.A. & Werner, J.M. (1998). Managers as Initiators of Trust: An Exchange Relationship Framework for Understanding Managerial Trustworthy Behavior. Academy of Management Review, 23 (3), 513-30.

Xu, D. & Shenkar, O. (2002). Institutional distance and the multinational enterprise. Academy of Management Journal, 27 (4), 608-618.

Yan, A., Zhu, G. & Hall, D. (2002). International assignments for career building: A model of Agency relationships and psychological contracts. Academy of Management Review, 27 (3), 373-391.

Talent vs Performance-Based Managerial Pay

Marco Celentani, Rosa Loveira

In this paper we consider a market for managerial services in which managers are assumed to have superior information on their own talent or ability to make an appropriate observable decision on a given investment project and in which firms compete for managers offering menus of contracts. We study equilibrium contracts and investment decisions when exogenous noisy information becomes costlessly available after the manager has accepted an employment contract. We consider two different cases: 1) The information on the manager is contractible; 2) The information on the manager is non-contractible. We use this latter case to characterize equilibrium contracts, which are made dependent on internal and non-contractible managerial evaluations, and we find that information on talent is ignored in equilibrium.

1. Introduction

The concept of War for Talent has been popularized by a book of the same name by three McKinsey consultants (Michaels, Handfield-Jones & Axelrod, 2001). These authors claimed that a common factor among successful companies is that they found and rewarded talent and defended the idea that success in the modern economy requires the *"talent mind-set"*: the *"deep-seated belief that having better talent at all levels is how you outperform your competitors"*.

The War for Talent – both the book and the principle – has been criticized on several grounds. As Gladwell (2002) points out, those companies that took the talent mind-set closest to heart, as Enron did, ended up doing performance evaluations that were not based on performance. Taken literally the war for talent suggests that employees reputed to be talented should be rewarded on the basis of their perceived talent even when how a company would measure its employee's talent was not clear.

In this article we try to give some theoretical argument that supports the idea that „The War for Talent" seems not to be such a brilliant idea, i.e., that it would not make sense to pay „talent" independent of the performance. We focus on whether a particular source of information on manager's talent should be used in the design of incentives schemes in an environment where firms compete to hire a manager with private information on his ability. We find that the contract the manager accepts in equilibrium is independent of the realization of a competency signal: information on the manager's type is ignored in equilibrium and compensation depends exclusively on return realizations. This signal is related to the talent of the corporate management but it is independent of his performance, i.e., it is a subjective assessment.[1] This result is shown to arise because competition between firms implies that no compensation scheme is accepted in equilibrium that (i) depends on the realization of the non-contractible signal and (ii) such that firms have incentives to acknowledge the true realization of the signal.

The informativeness principle argues that all informative measures of performance should be included in an employment contract (Holmstrom, 1979, 1982). In this work we show that what classical principal theory postulates: "there is never any loss, and there are, in general, benefits in using all available information in the design of incentives schemes" has not to be necessarily true. We can think in the Enron scandal. According to Gladwell (2002): "the management of Enron did exactly what the consultants at McKinsey said that companies ought to do in order to succeed in the modern economy. It hired and rewarded the very best and the very brightest and is now in bankruptcy. The reasons for its collapse are complex, needless to say. But what if Enron failed not in spite of its talent mind-set but because of it?". In this line, this paper shows that perhaps compensating managers according to their talents and independently of their performance is not a good idea when asymmetric information exists and firms compete to hire managers offering menus of contracts.

The paper is organized as follows. Chapter 2 presents the related literature. In chapter 3 we explain the methodology adopted. Chapter 4 presents the model and introduces the equilibrium concept used. In chapter 5 we propose as a benchmark a situation in which no post-contractual exogenous information is available. Chapter 6 analyses the equilibrium when post-contractual exogenous information on the manager's type becomes available. Chapter 7 concludes.

2. Related Literature

Our work starts from the observation that reneging on the part of the firm is an obvious problem when pay is based on non-contractible information. Reneging occurs when contracted performance is not rewarded in order to save on wages. When performance is verifiable reneging is not a problem, because contracts can be made explicit and legally enforceable (Prendergast & Topel, 1993). The existing literature on performance pay and employer cheating has been mainly concerned with providing conditions under which an efficient use of non-contractible information is made in the equilibrium of a repeated

---

[1] According to Baker, Gibbons and Murphy (1994): "Many firms mitigate the effects of distortionary objective performance measures by augmenting objective measures with subjective assessments of performance. Investment bankers, for example, could be measured by several objective performance measures, such as the fees generated. Nonetheless, compensation at most investment banks relies heavily on subjective assessments of other factors".

moral hazard relation (Bull (1987), MacLeod & Malcomson (1989), Prendergast & Topel (1993), Gibbons (1998), Prendergast (1999), and Levin (2003)). Most of these studies assume that incentives to renege are often non-existent because of reputational concerns. In our work there exists a short-term employment relationship and firms are not assumed to be honest. However, the interest in suppressing the information on agent's type goes beyond the obvious financial incentive of firms to renege on payments when performance is non-verifiable. Here, information is ignored as a consequence of competition.

Other works states that organizations may have an interest in suppressing information on agent's performance because ignoring information on relative performance may enhance incentives and output. In this line, Crémer (1995) studied a situation in which a principal gets a costless signal correlated with the agent's type after the latter has carried out production. Despite of the fact that the information is useful ex-post to screen the agent's type, Crémer showed that the principal finds it optimal to commit ex-ante to disregard this information, because this increases the incentives for the agent to exert high effort. This result is independent on whether the information is contractible or not.

Our work differs from Crémer's in that we consider a situation in which post-contractual information could be used to screen managers' type ex-ante, at the contracting stage, and because we find that the result differs according to the information being contractible or not: if it is non-contractible competition implies that it is ignored in equilibrium.

3. Methodology

Most of the theoretical papers on managerial compensation have designed compensation based on performance measures in order to provide the manager with appropriate incentives to take actions in benefit of the firm he works for. This is the traditional way to ameliorate the moral hazard problem that arises once the manager is hired and his actions are not observable by shareholders. In this work we consider an adverse selection model in which managers have private information about their talent, so, when firms offer compensation contracts to hire a manager, this latter knows better than the firm how talented he is. We assume that a higher talented manager has a higher ability to distinguish a profitable investment project from an unprofitable one. Once the manager is hired, a principal-agent problem between ownership (shareholders) and corporate management arises because shareholders lack information to determine what led to the manager to choose an investment project or another, i.e., shareholders observe the action taken by the manager (which means that there is no a moral hazard problem, as is traditional in a principal-agent model) but they do not know if this action maximizes firm's value. As in Caruana & Celentani (2003), we subscribe to the view that *"when operating uncertainty is not minimal, managerial compensation is designed much more as an instrument to induce managers to make decisions in the interest of shareholders than as an attempt to provide lazy managers with incentives to work hard"*. So, the problem for shareholders combines adverse selection ex-ante and principal-agent problem with hidden information ex-post. We assume that once the manager is hired shareholders (or the Board of Directors or the Compensation Committee) obtain a competency signal related to the ability or talent of the corporate management and independent of his performance and we ask whether this information should be used when designing an optimal contract. We can think of shareholders activists that have a say in the design of compensation plans. In order to avoid a "no" vote on executive compensation packages (because it would affect negatively to their reputation), public companies: (i) would increase communication with shareholders to convince them how good or talented they are and consequently, shareholders obtain new or additional information on their corporate management's talent; and (ii) would feed this additional information that arises in the process of play back to the compensation plan.

In this environment, an optimal contract is the least-cost contract that helps to sort heterogeneous talented managers and to provide them with incentives to make appropriate decisions once hired.

We depart from the view of analysing the trade-off between risk and distortions that characterizes much of the performance measures. We focus on whether a particular source of information on manager's talent should be used in the design of incentives schemes in an environment where firms compete to hire a manager with private information on his ability. We consider two different situations. One in which the noisy signal on manager's talent is publicly observable (the case of contractible information) and one in which the signal is privately observed by the firm, which then announces the signal it observed (the case of non-contractible information). When the information on manager's talent is contractible, the contract that the manager accepts in equilibrium gives him higher pay when the realization of the signal increases his relative likelihood of being highly talented, i.e., the manager is paid more when there is more compelling evidence that he is good. When the information on manager's talent is not contractible, his pay may be made dependent on the realization of the signal privately observed only if the firm has incentives to truthfully disclose its information. For this case we find that the contract that the manager accepts in equilibrium is independent of the realization of the signal and therefore the information on the manager's type is ignored in equilibrium: compensation depends exclusively on return realizations.

4. The Model

All firms are risk neutral and each has an investment project available whose revenue is z > 0 with probability p, and 0 with probability $1 - p$. We normalize the cost of the investment project to 1 and assume that the investment project is ex-ante profitable, $pz - 1 > 0$.[2]

Each manager has an innate ability to forecast the realization of a given investment project. To simplify computations we assume that only two types of managers exist, good and bad, $\tau \in \{G, B\}$. A good manager is always able to forecast the realization of the investment

---

[2] Qualitatively similar results are obtained in the case in which $pz - 1 < 0$

project, whereas a bad manager is never able to do so. Each manager knows his own type but it is common knowledge that firms believe that he is good with probability μ and bad with probability $1 - μ$. To economize on notation we assume that, before making the decision to invest or not a manager receives a signal $ρ \in \{V,L,H\}$. The bad manager will get V, the void signal, with probability 1 and the good manager will get signals L or H, the low and the high signal, with probabilities $1 - p$ and p. The probability of the project having the high return conditional on the received signal will be

$$\Pr(z \mid \rho) = \begin{cases} p & \text{if } \rho = V \\ 0 & \text{if } \rho = L \\ 1 & \text{if } \rho = H \end{cases}.$$

In other words, while signals H and L ensure, respectively, the success or the failure of the investment project, the void signal, V, provides no additional information and the conditional probability of success is, therefore, equal to the prior, p.[3]
A manager has to decide whether to invest (I) or not (N) in the project available to the firm. We denote the observable final outcome of the investment project by $P \in \{F,S,N\}$, where N indicates that no investment took place and F and S indicate that the investment was carried out and it was, respectively, a failure or a success. An investment action profile for a manager is a vector $i = (i_V, i_L, i_H) \in \{I,N\}^3$, where i_V, i_L, and i_H denote the decision to invest (I) or not (N) when the signal received by the manager is respectively V, L, or H. Managers are risk neutral, which means that they maximize their expected salary.
After the manager receives signal $ρ \in \{V,L,H\}$ but before he invests, the firm and the manager receive a signal on manager's type, $α \in \{\underline{α}, \bar{α}\}$ with

$$\Pr(\bar{α} \mid \tau) = \begin{cases} \gamma & \text{if } \tau = G \\ 1 - \gamma & \text{if } \tau = B \end{cases}$$

and $\gamma \in \left[\frac{1}{2}, 1\right]$.
We consider two different cases, each corresponding to a different assumption on additional information accruing to players. Under case 1 the signal is public and therefore contractible and under case 2 the firm receives a private and therefore non-contractible signal on manager's type.
After managers learn their type, firms offer contracts to managers. A contract specifies that if the manager accepts it he will receive a non negative payment from the firm for each

---

[3] Managers with high ability are often described in the literature as being able to generate high-expected return investment projects, i.e., as being able to come up with good ideas. In contrast to this, we refer to managerial ability to forecast the realization of a given project: all investments projects are drawn from the same distribution, regardless of the manager's ability, but different managers may have different abilities to forecast their realization.

subsequent public history of the game, i.e., for each $(P,\alpha)\in\{N,F,S\}\times\{\underline{\alpha},\overline{\alpha}\}$ in case 1 and for each $(P,\hat{\alpha})\in\{N,F,S\}\times\{\underline{\alpha},\overline{\alpha}\}$ in case 2.

To simplify notation we will denote a contract by

$$w = \left(\underline{w},\overline{w}\right) = \left(\underline{w}_N,\underline{w}_F,\underline{w}_S,\overline{w}_N,\overline{w}_F,\overline{w}_S\right)\in\mathfrak{R}_+^6,$$

where $\underline{w}_P$ (respectively, $\overline{w}_P$) denotes the non-negative payment to the manager when the outcome of the investment process is $P\in\{N,F,S\}$ and when $\alpha=\underline{\alpha}$ in case 1 and $\hat{\alpha}=\underline{\alpha}$ in case 2 (respectively, when $\alpha=\overline{\alpha}$ in case 1 and $\hat{\alpha}=\overline{\alpha}$ in case 2).

We finally make the assumption that a firm can function without a manager, but that in this case it will get signal V with probability 1. Given investment projects are assumed to be ex-ante profitable, investing is the optimal decision for a firm with no manager (and therefore, without a signal on the profitability of the investment project). This implies that a firm with no manager gets and expected profit of $pz - 1$.[4]

We consider the case in which two firms compete for every single manager. In particular, we assume that every manager is offered a countable set of contracts $w\in\mathfrak{R}_+^6$ by each firm and chooses one contract (if any) out of them. All our results generalize to the case in which the measure of the set of managers is lower than the measure of the set of firms and firms are allowed to make offers to all managers.[5]

In the following we summarize the extensive form of the game.

N *Nature* chooses the type of the manager, G with probability μ and B with probability $1 - \mu$, and (independently) the realization of the investment project, S with probability p and F with probability $1 - p$.

τ The *manager* observes his own type.

F Without observing nature's choices, each of the two *firms* competing for a given manager offers him a countable set of contracts each of them of the form

$$\left(\underline{w},\overline{w}\right) = \left(\underline{w}_N,\underline{w}_F,\underline{w}_S,\overline{w}_N,\overline{w}_F,\overline{w}_S\right)\in\mathfrak{R}_+^6$$

M The *manager* either accepts an offer or rejects them all.

R If the manager rejects all offers, play ends, the manager gets a 0 payoff and the firm invests and gets an expected payoff equal to $pz - 1$.

A If the manager *accepts* an offer, he is hired.

ρ The manager receives a private signal, $\rho\in\{V,L,H\}$.

α The firm receives signal $\underline{\alpha}$ or $\overline{\alpha}$. In case 1 this implies that the manager will be paid according to $\underline{w}$ or $\overline{w}$. In case 2, the firm announces $\underline{\alpha}$ or $\overline{\alpha}$ and depending on this

---

[4] The qualitative nature of the results of the paper would not change if we made the assumption that the reservation level for the firm is 0 rather than $pz - 1$, i.e., if we assumed that a manager is an essential input in the production process.

[5] In this case firms are allowed to offer different countable sets of contracts to managers with different beginning of period probabilities of being good.

announcement the manager will be paid according to $\underline{w}$ or $\overline{w}$. (Notice: The announcement does not have to be necessarily equal to α).

i The manager decides whether to invest or not in the given project, $i \in \{I, N\}$.

P The manager's play and the realization of the investment project in case the manager decides to invest are observed, $P \in \{N, F, S\}$.

S The firm pays the manager a salary. In case 1, the salary payment is $\underline{w}_P$ or $\overline{w}_P$ when the signal received was $\underline{\alpha}$ or $\overline{\alpha}$, respectively. In case 2, the salary payment is $\underline{w}_P$ or $\overline{w}_P$ when the signal announced by the firm was $\underline{\alpha}$ or $\overline{\alpha}$, respectively.

Strategies and equilibrium concept:

In each of the two cases, the two firms competing for a manager believed to be good with probability $\mu \in [0,1]$ offer countable sets of short run contracts, $(\underline{w}, \overline{w}) \in \Re_+^6$, conditioning on the public history of the game.

The manager either accepts a contract or none out of the sets of contracts offered to him by the two firms. If the manager accepts, he receives a private signal on the profitability of the project owned by the firm that employs him, $\rho \in \{V, L, H\}$.

Then the firm receives a signal $\alpha \in \{\underline{\alpha}, \overline{\alpha}\}$, which can be a public or a private signal. In the first case, the manager will be paid according to $\underline{w}$ or $\overline{w}$, but in the second one the manager will be paid according to $\underline{w}$ or $\overline{w}$ depending on firm's announcement about the signal received. Because of its private character this announcement does not have to be necessarily equal to α.

Consider a manager who is believed to be good with probability μ and who has accepted contract w. His investment strategy can be denoted as

$$i(w) = \left(\underline{i}(w), \overline{i}(w)\right) = \left(\underline{i}_V(w), \underline{i}_L(w), \underline{i}_H(w), \overline{i}_V(w), \overline{i}_L(w), \overline{i}_H(w)\right) \in \{I, N\}^6$$

Where $\underline{i}_\sigma$ (respectively, $\overline{i}_\sigma$) denotes the manager's investment decision conditional on private signal $\rho \in \{V, L, H\}$ and on $\alpha = \underline{\alpha}$ in case 1 and $\hat{\alpha} = \underline{\alpha}$ in case 2 (respectively, on $\alpha = \overline{\alpha}$ in case 1, $\hat{\alpha} = \overline{\alpha}$ in case 2).

The equilibrium concept we use is subgame perfect Nash equilibrium. To ensure the existence of such an equilibrium we will assume the following standard tie-breaking rules: (i) whenever indifferent between the two investment actions (I and N), the manager will play the one with the higher expected profit; (ii) whenever indifferent between accepting a contract or rejecting all, the manager will accept a contract.

5. The Benchmark Case (Case 0, No Exogenous Information)

Proposition 1 (Caruana & Celentani, 2003)

In all equilibria:

The unique contract which is accepted by both types of managers is w with:

$$w_N = \frac{\mu(1-p)}{1+\mu(1-p)}$$

$$w_F = 0$$

$$w_S = \frac{\mu(1-p)}{p\left[1+\mu(1-p)\right]}$$

The investment action profile played by the manager on the equilibrium path is efficient.

Proposition 1 analyses the impact of asymmetric information about managers ability on equilibrium contracts and shows that they are

1. *Pooling:* A manager that is believed to be good with probability μ at the beginning of play will accept offer $w(\mu)$ regardless of whether he is in fact good or bad.
2. *Efficient:* On the equilibrium path the manager plays the efficient investment action profile.

To see why equilibria are efficient, note that competition for managers' tends to lead to surplus maximization (efficiency).

To see that equilibria are pooling it is necessary to show that offers that are more attractive to a good manager are not profitable deviations for the firms. The following argument will show that this is the case because, once the incentive compatibility constraints are kept into account, the indifference curves of the two types of managers do not intersect, and offers that are preferred by a good manager are also preferred by a bad manager.

Without loss of generality assume first that $w_F = 0$[6] and consider pairs $(w_N, w_S) \in \mathfrak{R}_+^2$. Figure 1 depicts the indifference curves for the good and the bad manager in that space keeping into account their incentive compatibility constraints. Given that the incentives are simply determined by explicit compensation, it is easy to see that so long as $w_s \geq w_N$ (i.e., below the 45 degree line) the typical indifference curve for the good manager is the negatively sloped line represented as U^G as a good manager's expected utility is $pw_s + (1-p)w_N$. Note that if $w_s < w_N$ the manager would always refrain from investing and his utility would be w_N. The typical indifference curve for the bad manager instead is like the kinked line represented as U^B: above line (i.e., whenever $pw_s < w_N$) a bad manager chooses not to invest and gets w_N, whereas below line (*IC*) (i.e., whenever $pw_s \geq w_N$) he chooses to invest and gets pw_s.

Since it is easy to check that in equilibrium managers fully extract their expected value (and firms only make $pz - 1$ in expected terms), in Figure 1 we represent the condition ensuring this as the broken double line (*FE*). Given this, it is easy to verify that any contract on (*FE*) but different from the intersection of lines (*IC*) and the rightmost part of (*FE*) is such that a profitable deviation for a firm exists (attracting only good managers),

---

[6] By this we mean that: (i) in equilibrium $w_F = 0$ has to hold and (ii) if no profitable deviation with $w_F = 0$ from a proposed equilibrium exists, then no profitable deviation exists at all.

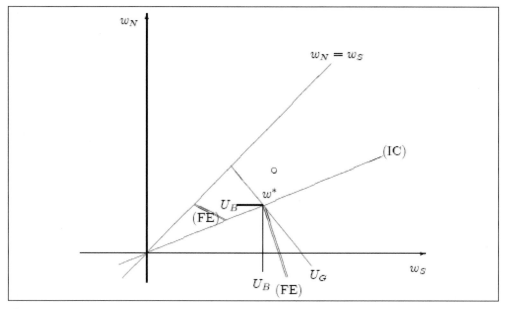

Figure 1

whereas no such deviation exists for the contract at that intersection. Since it is easy to verify that this last contract is the one mentioned in Proposition 1[7], the result follows.

6. Information About the Manager

The exogenous information is privately observed by the firm and the manager and is contractible.

Proposition 2
In all equilibria:
1. The unique contract which is accepted with positive probability by both types of managers is $(\bar{w},\underline{w})$ such that:

$$\underline{w}_N = 0$$
$$\underline{w}_F = 0$$
$$\underline{w}_S = 0$$
$$\bar{w}_N = \frac{\mu(1-p)}{\mu\gamma(2-p)+(1-\mu)(1-\gamma)}$$
$$\bar{w}_F = 0$$
$$\bar{w}_S = \frac{\mu(1-p)}{p\left[\mu\gamma(2-p)+(1-\mu)(1-\gamma)\right]}$$

---

[7] Notice that the contract in Proposition 1 is such that $pw_s = w_N$ and gives the firm expected profit $pz - 1$

2. The investment action profile played by the manager on the equilibrium path is efficient.

Proof. Appendix

Proposition 2 analyses the impact of exogenous noisy contractible information about manager's talent on equilibrium contracts and shows that they are
1. *Efficient* in the sense that the manager plays the efficient investment action profile.
2. *Separating* in the sense that the set of contracts offered to the managers differ according to the signal received by the firms. It means that firms make compensation contingent on the additional information about managers' ability to better identify individual talents. Note that the equilibrium is pooling in the sense that both types accept the same contract.

Equilibria are efficient because competition for managers tends to lead to surplus maximization.

To see that equilibria are separating in the sense explained before we study the compatibility constraints and the indifference curves for both types in different planes according to the public signal received by the firm. As before we can assume without losts of generality that $\underline{w}_F = \overline{w}_F = 0$ [8] and consider pairs $\left(w_S, \overline{w}_N\right) \in \Re_+^2$.

In Figures 2(a) and 2(b) we depict in a way similar to Proposition 1 the indifference curves and the full extraction conditions keeping into account the incentive compatibility constraints when the signal is good and bad respectively. Given that the incentives are determined by explicit compensation, it is easy to see that so long as $\overline{w}_S \ge \overline{w}_N$ the typical indifference curve for the good manager in Figure 2(a) is the negatively sloped line represented as $\overline{U}^G$ as a good manager's expected utility is $p\overline{w}_S + (1-p)\overline{w}_N$. If $\overline{w}_S < \overline{w}_N$ the manager would always refrain from investing and his utility would be $\overline{w}_N$. The indifference curve for the bad manager is the kinked line represented by $\overline{U}^B$: above line $\left(\overline{IC}\right)$ (i.e., whenever $p\overline{w}_S < \overline{w}_N$) a bad manager chooses not to invest and gets $\overline{w}_N$, whereas below line $\left(\overline{IC}\right)$ (i.e., whenever $p\overline{w}_S \ge \overline{w}_N$) he chooses to invest and gets $p\overline{w}_S$. In equilibrium managers fully extract their expected value (and firms only make $pz - 1$ in expected terms). We represent the condition ensuring this in Figure 2(a) as the broken line $\left(\overline{FE}\right)$. Given this, it is easy to verify that any contract on $\left(\overline{FE}\right)$ but different from the intersection of lines $\left(\overline{IC}\right)$ and the right most part of $\left(\overline{FE}\right)$ is such that a profitable deviation for a firm exists provided that only the good manager accept it, whereas no such deviation exists for the contract at that intersection. In equilibrium we have that $p\overline{w}_S = \overline{w}_N$.

The same analysis follows in the case that the signal received by the firm is bad. We represent in Figure 2(b) the indifference curves for both types keeping into account their incentive compatibility constraint $\left(\underline{U}_G, \underline{U}_B\right)$ and the condition that ensures in equilibrium managers fully extract their expected value (*FE*). It is easy to check that in equilibrium it has to be that $p\underline{w}_S = \underline{w}_N$.

---

[8] By this we mean that: (i) in equilibrium $\underline{w}_F = \overline{w}_F = 0$ has to hold and (ii) if no profitable deviation with $\underline{w}_F = \overline{w}_F = 0$ from a proposed equilibrium exists, then no profitable deviation exists at all.

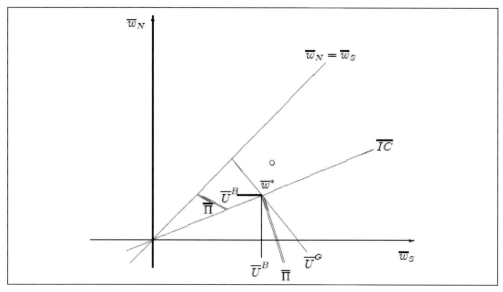

Figure 2a

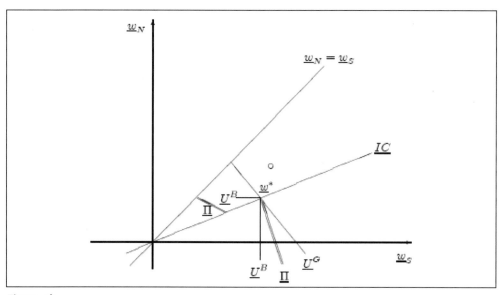

Figure 2b

With this result we can study the equilibrium in the plane $(\underline{w}_N, \overline{w}_N) \in \mathfrak{R}_+^2$. We have that the good manager has an expected utility:

$$U^G = \gamma \left[p\overline{w}_S + (1-p)\overline{w}_N \right] + (1-\gamma)\left[p\underline{w}_S + (1-p)\underline{w}_N \right] = \gamma(2-p)\overline{w}_N + (1-\gamma)(2-p)\underline{w}_N,$$

and the bad one:

$$U^B = \gamma p\underline{w}_S + (1-\gamma)p\overline{w}_S = \gamma\underline{w}_N + (1-\gamma)\overline{w}_N.$$

It is easy to check that because

$$MRS^G_{\underline{w}_N, \overline{w}_N} = -\frac{\partial U^G / \partial \underline{w}_N}{\partial U^G / \partial \overline{w}_N} = -\frac{1-\gamma}{\gamma} > MRS^B_{\underline{w}_N, \overline{w}_N} = -\frac{\partial U^B / \partial \underline{w}_N}{\partial U^B / \partial \overline{w}_N} = -\frac{\gamma}{1-\gamma},$$

there exists a profitable deviation for a firm offering a contract, which is strictly preferred by the good manager as long as $\underline{w}_N > 0$.

Now it is easy to verify that the contract that results is the one mentioned in Proposition 2.

The exogenous information is privately observed but it is non-contractible.

Proposition 3
In all equilibria:
1. The unique contract which is accepted with positive probability by both types of managers is $(\overline{w}, \underline{w})$ such that:

$$\underline{w}_N = \overline{w}_N = \frac{\mu(1-p)}{1+\mu(1-p)}$$

$$\underline{w}_F = \overline{w}_F = 0$$

$$\underline{w}_S = \overline{w}_S = \frac{\mu(1-p)}{p\left[1+\mu(1-p)\right]}$$

2. The investment action profile played by the manager on the equilibrium path is efficient.

Proof. Appendix.

Proposition 3 analyses the impact of exogenous noisy non-contractible information about manager's talent on equilibrium contracts and shows that they are
1. *Efficient* in the sense that the manager plays the efficient investment action profile.
2. *Pooling* in the sense that the set of contracts offered to the managers do not depend on the signal received by the firms. Therefore the information keeps being private.

Equilibria are efficient because competition for managers tends to lead to surplus maximization.

As before, to see that equilibria are pooling we study the incentive compatibility constraints and the indifference curves of the two types of managers in different planes according to the signal received. Note that here we have two additional incentive compatibility constraints of no deviation for the firms according to the signal received such that for the firm it is not profitable to offer a contract based on the signal it has not received. It is easy to see that whenever $p\underline{w}_s > \underline{w}_N$ it is possible to find another offer on $(\underline{FE})$ such that it is only preferred by the good manager and firms have no incentives to deviate. If we choose an offer with $p\bar{w}s > \bar{w}_N$ it is possible to reduce $\underline{w}_N$ and to increase $\bar{w}_N$ such that firms have no incentives to offer a contract based on a different signal and the new offer is profitable provided that only the good manager accept it. Because a necessary condition to firms not deviate is that $\bar{w}_N \le \underline{w}_N$ we have that when $\bar{w}_N = \underline{w}_N$ and $p\bar{w}s = \bar{w}_N$ there exists no profitable deviation and an equilibrium is obtained.

Hence, in equilibrium it has to be that $p\underline{w}_s = \underline{w}_N = \bar{w}_N = p\bar{w}s$, which is the contract mentioned in Proposition 2.

7. Conclusion

In this paper we study the impact on equilibrium contracts and investment decisions of exogenous noisy information on managers' talent that becomes costlessly available after the latter has accepted an employment contract. We realize this analysis in a context where firms compete to hire managers with superior information on their own ability to make an appropriate decision on a given investment project.

We show that when additional exogenous information on manager's talent is contractible it is used in equilibrium. However, if this information is non-contractible it is not used. This result is shown to arise not because of the obvious financial incentive of firms to renege on payments when information is non-verifiable, but because of competition among firms for the "talented" managers and the existence of asymmetric information on managers' abilities to forecast the realization of investment projects.

In contrast to the Holmstrom's informativeness principle (1979), we find that it is possible that equilibrium contracts do not make payments contingent on the available information. Note that the informativeness principle is a result based on a standard principal-agent model without asymmetric information and where principals are assumed to be honest.

References

Baker, G., Gibbons R. & Murphy K. (1994). Subjective performance measures in optimal incentive contracts. Quarterly Journal of Economics, 439, 1125-1156.

Bull, C. (1987). The existence of self-enforcing implicit contracts. Quaterly Journal of Economics, 102, 147-159.

Caruana, G. & Celentani, M. (2003). Career concerns and contingent compensation. Mimeo. Universidad Carlos III de Madrid.

Cremer, J. (1995). Arm's length relationship. Quarterly Journal of Economics, CX, 275-295.

Gibbons, R. (1998). Incentives in organizations. Journal of Economic Perspectives, Vol. 12, Nº 4.

Gladwell, M. (2002). The talent myth: are smart people overrated? The New Yorker, July 22.

Holmström, B. (1979). Moral hazard and observability. Bell Journal of Economics, 10, 231-259.

Holmström, B. (1982). Managerial incentive problems: a dynamic perspective. In Essays in Economics and Management in Honor of Lars Wahlbeck, Helsinki, Swedish School of Economics, 31, Helsingors, 177-208.

Levin, J. (2003). Relational Incentive Contracts. American Economic Review, 93, 835-857.

Macleod, W. B. & Malcomson, J. M. (1989). Implicit contracts, incentive compatibility, and involuntary unemployment. Econometrica, 57 (2), 447-480.

Michaels, E., Handfield-Jones, H. & Axelrod, B. (2001). The War for Talent. Harvard Business School Press, Boston, MA.

Prendergast, C. (1999). The provision of incentives in firms. Journal of Economic Literature, (1), 7-63.

Prendergast, C. & Topel, R. (1993). Discretion and bias in performance evaluation. European Economic Review, 37, 355-365.

Appendix

Proof of Proposition 2:

We will prove a sequence of claims. All of them, except the last one, are as in Caruana and Celentani (2003).

1. No separating equilibrium exists in which managers accept different offers. Each offer accepted by the good manager will be strictly preferred by the bad one and a contradiction with a separating equilibrium arises. Given this, in the following we focus on pooling equilibria.

2. The pooling equilibrium has to be such that firm's expected profits are $(pz - 1)$:

$$\Pr\left(\alpha = \overline{\alpha}\right)\left(E\left[\pi \mid \overline{\alpha}\right] - E\left[w \mid \overline{\alpha}\right]\right) + \Pr\left(\alpha = \underline{\alpha}\right)\left(E\left[\pi \mid \underline{\alpha}\right] - E\left[w \mid \underline{\alpha}\right]\right) = (pz - 1)$$

   This result is immediate from a standard Bertrand pricing argument.

3. The pooling equilibrium has to be such that the Pareto optimal investment strategy is played.

   Given that incentives are determined by explicit compensation, there exists weak monotonicity in firm absolute performance and the assumption that a manager who is indifferent between different investment decisions chooses the one which has a higher expected profit is sufficient to guarantee that both types of managers always make the efficient investment decision.

4. The offer accepted by both types of managers is such that $\overline{w}_F = \underline{w}_F = 0$.

   Suppose that the offer accepted in equilibrium by both types of managers, $w = \left(\overline{w}_N, \overline{w}_F, \overline{w}_S, \underline{w}_N, \underline{w}_F, \underline{w}_S\right)$ is such that $\overline{w}_F, \underline{w}_F > 0$. Consider another offer $\hat{w} = \left(\overline{w}_N, 0, \overline{w}_S + \varepsilon, \underline{w}_N, 0, \underline{w}_S + \alpha\right)$ It's not difficult to see that there exists a pair of values ε, $\alpha > 0$ such that is strictly preferred only by the good manager and such that gives an expected payoff to the firm strictly larger than $pz - 1$.

5. No equilibrium can exist in which both managers accept an offer different from

$$\left(\overline{w}_N,\overline{w}_F,\overline{w}_S,\underline{w}_N,\underline{w}_F,\underline{w}_S\right)=\left(\overline{w}_N,0,\frac{\overline{w}_N}{p},\underline{w}_N,0,\frac{\overline{w}_N}{p}\right)$$

and such that

$$\mu(1-p)=\left[\mu\gamma(2-p)+(1-\mu)(1-\gamma)\right]\overline{w}_N+\left[\mu(1-\gamma)(2-p)+(1-\mu)\gamma\right]\underline{w}_N.$$

By the incentive compatibility constraint for the good manager playing the efficient investment strategy in the good state we have that $p\overline{w}_S \geq \overline{w}_N$. Suppose that the offer accepted in equilibrium by both types of managers is such that $p\overline{w}_S > \overline{w}_N$ and let $w=\left(\overline{w}_N,\overline{w}_F,\overline{w}_S,\underline{w}_N,\underline{w}_F,\underline{w}_S\right)$ denote such an offer. Consider another offer $\hat{w}=\left(\overline{w}_N+\alpha,0,\overline{w}_S-\varepsilon,\underline{w}_N,0,\underline{w}_S\right)$ It is easy to check that there exists a pair of values $\varepsilon,\alpha>0$ such that $\hat{w}$ is strictly preferred only by the good manager and that gives an expected payoff to the firm strictly larger than $pz-1$. Therefore the offer accepted in equilibrium is such that $p\overline{w}_S = \overline{w}_N$.

With the same argument it is easy to show that the offer accepted in equilibrium is such that $p\underline{w}_S = \underline{w}_N$.

6. There exists an equilibrium in which both types of manager accept offer

$$\left(\overline{w}_N,\overline{w}_F,\overline{w}_S,\underline{w}_N,\underline{w}_F,\underline{w}_S\right)=\left(\frac{\mu(1-p)}{\left[\mu\gamma(2-p)+(1-\mu)(1-\gamma)\right]},0,\frac{\mu(1-p)}{p\left[\mu\gamma(2-p)+(1-\mu)(1-\gamma)\right]},0,0,0\right)$$

Suppose that the offer accepted in equilibrium by both types of managers,

$$w=\left(\overline{w}_N,\overline{w}_F,\overline{w}_S,\underline{w}_N,\underline{w}_F,\underline{w}_S\right)$$

is such that $\underline{w}_N>0$. Consider another offer

$$w'=\left(\overline{w}_N+\varepsilon,0,\frac{\overline{w}_N+\varepsilon}{p},0,0,0\right)$$

Under w and w' the expected salary payments to the good and the bad manager are,

$$E\left[w\mid G\right]=\Pr\left(\alpha\mid G\right)\left[p\frac{\overline{w}_N}{p}+(1-p)\overline{w}_N\right]+\Pr\left(\underline{\alpha}\mid G\right)\left[p\frac{\underline{w}_N}{p}+(1-p)\underline{w}_N\right]=$$

$$=\gamma(2-p)\overline{w}_N+(1-\gamma)(2-p)\underline{w}_N$$

respectively $E\left[w\mid B\right]=\Pr\left(\alpha\mid B\right)p\frac{\overline{w}_N}{p}+\Pr\left(\underline{\alpha}\mid B\right)p\frac{\underline{w}_N}{p}=(1-\gamma)\overline{w}_N+\gamma\underline{w}_N$

$$E\left[w'\mid G\right]=\gamma(2-p)\left(\overline{w}_N+\varepsilon\right)>\gamma(2-p)\overline{w}_N+(1-\gamma)(2-p)\underline{w}_N\Leftrightarrow\varepsilon>\frac{(1-\gamma)}{\gamma}\underline{w}_N$$

$$E\left[w'\mid B\right]=(1-\gamma)\left(\overline{w}_N+\varepsilon\right)<(1-\gamma)\overline{w}_N+\gamma\underline{w}_N\Leftrightarrow\varepsilon<\frac{\gamma}{(1-\gamma)}\underline{w}_N$$

Given this it is easy to see that

$$E[w'|G] > E[w|G] \Leftrightarrow \varepsilon > \frac{(1-\gamma)}{\gamma} \underline{w}_N$$

$$E[w'|B] < E[w|B] \Leftrightarrow \varepsilon < \frac{\gamma}{(1-\gamma)} \underline{w}_N,$$

and for all $\varepsilon \in \left(\frac{(1-\gamma)}{\gamma} \underline{w}_N, \frac{\gamma}{(1-\gamma)} \underline{w}_N \right)$ only the good manager prefers w' to w. Given that the expected payoff to the firm if only a good manager accepts w' is strictly larger than $pz - 1$ a profitable deviation exists and a contradiction is obtained.

Proof of Proposition 3:

The information is not verifiable and we must impose the following incentive compatibility conditions to the firms.

For the firm who receives the good signal it has to be that

$$\bar{\mu}(1-p)\overline{w}_N + p\overline{w}_S \leq \bar{\mu}(1-p)\underline{w}_N + p\underline{w}_S \Leftrightarrow \bar{\mu}(1-p)\left(\overline{w}_N - \underline{w}_N\right) + p\left(\overline{w}_S - \underline{w}_S\right) \leq 0 \quad (1)$$

and in the same way for the firm who obtains the bad signal

$$\underline{\mu}(1-p)\underline{w}_N + p\underline{w}_S \leq \underline{\mu}(1-p)\overline{w}_N + p\overline{w}_S \Leftrightarrow \underline{\mu}(1-p)\left(\overline{w}_N - \underline{w}_N\right) + p\left(\overline{w}_S - \underline{w}_S\right) \geq 0 \quad (2)$$

Notice the following:

1. $\overline{w}_N > \underline{w}_N$ implies $\overline{w}_S < \underline{w}_S$ and both conditions are verified if and only if $\bar{\mu} \leq \underline{\mu}$, which is never true for $\gamma > \frac{1}{2}$. Firms have always incentives to deviation.

2. $\overline{w}_N \leq \underline{w}_N$ implies $\overline{w}_S \geq \underline{w}_S$ and both conditions are verified $\forall \gamma$.

The incentive conditions for the managers verify that $\overline{w}_N \leq p\overline{w}_S$ and $\underline{w}_N \leq p\underline{w}_S$.

We have the following relationship between salaries:

$$\overline{w}_N \leq \underline{w}_N \leq p\underline{w}_S \leq p\overline{w}_S \quad (3)$$

A necessary condition for the existence of a separating equilibrium is $\overline{w}_N < p\overline{w}_S$. However we have that $\underline{w}_N$ has to be equal to $p\underline{w}_S$. If $\underline{w}_N < p\underline{w}_S$ there would be a deviation strictly preferred only by the good manager and such that the firms don't find a better offer.

What is the maximum $\overline{w}_N$ we can fix when firms have incentives to deviation?

From (1)

$$\overline{w}_N \leq \frac{[1 + \bar{\mu}(1-p)]\underline{w}_N - p\overline{w}_S}{\bar{\mu}(1-p)}$$

From (2) it has to be

$$\overline{w}_N \geq \frac{[1 + \underline{\mu}(1-p)]\underline{w}_N - p\overline{w}_S}{\underline{\mu}(1-p)}$$

We have that both conditions are verified if and only if $\underline{w}_N \leq p\overline{w}_S$, which is true from (3).
Let's fix

$$\overline{w}_N = \frac{[1+\overline{\mu}(1-p)]\underline{w}_N - p\overline{w}_S}{\overline{\mu}(1-p)} \tag{4}$$

Then,

$$\frac{[1+\overline{\mu}(1-p)]\underline{w}_N - p\overline{w}_S}{\overline{\mu}(1-p)} \leq p\overline{w}_S$$

if and only if

$$\overline{w}_S \geq \frac{\underline{w}_N}{p} \tag{5}$$

Therefore we have the contract

$$\left(\overline{w}_N, \overline{w}_F, \overline{w}_S, \underline{w}_N, \underline{w}_F, \underline{w}_S\right) = \left(\frac{[1+\overline{\mu}(1-p)]\underline{w}_N - p\overline{w}_S}{\overline{\mu}(1-p)}, 0, \overline{w}_S, \underline{w}_N, 0, \frac{\underline{w}_N}{p}\right)$$

such that

$$\begin{aligned}\mu(1-p) &= \Pr(\overline{\alpha})[\overline{\mu}(1-p)\overline{w}_N + p\overline{w}_S] + \Pr(\underline{\alpha})[\underline{\mu}(1-p)\underline{w}_N + p\underline{w}_S] \\ &= \mu[\gamma[(1-p)\overline{w}_N + p\overline{w}_S] + (1-\gamma)(2-p)\underline{w}_N] + (1-\mu)[(1-\gamma)p\overline{w}_S + \gamma\underline{w}_N]\end{aligned}$$

Expected salaries for the good and the bad manager are, respectively,

$$\begin{aligned}E[w \mid G] &= \gamma[(1-p)\overline{w}_N + p\overline{w}_S] + (1-\gamma)[(1-p)\underline{w}_N + p\underline{w}_S] = \\ &= \gamma\left[\frac{[1+\overline{\mu}(1-p)]\underline{w}_N}{\overline{\mu}} - \frac{(1-\overline{\mu})}{\overline{\mu}}p\overline{w}_S\right] + (1-\gamma)(2-p)\underline{w}_N\end{aligned}$$

$$E[w \mid B] = (1-\gamma)p\overline{w}_S + \gamma p\underline{w}_S = (1-\gamma)p\overline{w}_S + \gamma\underline{w}_N$$

Given that

$$\frac{\partial E[w \mid G]}{\partial \overline{w}_S} = -\gamma\frac{(1-\overline{\mu})}{\overline{\mu}}p < 0$$

$$\frac{\partial E[w \mid B]}{\partial \overline{w}_S} = (1-\gamma)p > 0,$$

firms have incentives to make offers with the smallest $\overline{w}_S$ which will be strictly preferred only by the good manager. The minimum feasible $\overline{w}_S$ is given by (5), $\overline{w}_S = \frac{\underline{w}_N}{p}$ .Substituting into (4) we obtain $\overline{w}_N = \underline{w}_N$. From (3) we have that $\overline{w}_N = p\overline{w}_S$ and a separating equilibrium will not exist:

Introducing Performance-based Reward Systems within Collectivistic National Cultures

Biljana Bogićević Milikić

In this paper I attempt to address the issue of the interdependence between culture and reward system, which has received considerable attention in management theory and practice. To date research suggests that Individualism vs. Collectivism is an important cultural value concerning its influence on the reward system design in a way that Individualism favours the performance-based reward system, whereas Collectivism emphasizes job security, group rewards and internal equity achieved through seniority based pay based on hierarchical status. In this study, I used a case study method in one Serbian company in order to contribute to the existing knowledge by answering particularly the following research question: Is it possible to introduce the performance-based reward system within the collectivistic cultural context, and, if it is possible, how? Following the research findings I propose that Collectivism strongly influences the employees` equity perceptions, but is not necessarily unable to coexist with the performance-based reward system.

1. Introduction

Companies use reward systems to show employees who, why and how will be rewarded or punished (i.e. which behaviours in organization are desirable or undesirable). At the same time, employees are exposed to an additional group of signals about an expected and desirable behaviour set in the organizational culture. Values provide individuals with a reference frame how to make judgments and how to choose among alternative options or courses of action (Schwartz & Bilsky, 1987). These two groups of signals (reward system and culture) may be, but not necessarily, compatible.

The interdependence between culture and reward system has received considerable attention in management theory and practice. Substantial effort has been devoted to investigation of the transferability of management practices around the world. Many authors argued that HR systems are the business practices most likely to be affected by the cultural context within which they are applied (Laurent, 1986; Li & Karakowsky, 2001; Schneider, 1992). The influence of culture on HRM practices and policies is particularly convincingly claimed by the proponents of the cultural divergence perspective (Holden, 2001), who suggest that cultural differences cause differences in organisational behaviour (Schuler, Jackson, Jackofsky, & Slocum, 2001) including work motivation, performance appraisal and rewarding (Rollinson & Broadfield, 2002). Some authors argue that some HRM practices are more culture-bound than others, although their research has produced contradictory results (Easterby-Smith, Malina, & Yuan, 1995; Sparrow & Wu, 1998).

Many studies have argued that, in general, culture makes an influence on the characteristics of the reward system, whereas Individualism vs. Collectivism proves to be an important cultural value influencing the design of a reward system (Gomez.Mejia & Welbourne, 1991; Hofstede, 1980, 1983; Kim, Park, & Suzuki, 1990; Ramamoorthy & Carroll, 1998; Triandis, 1995). Several studies have suggested that in collectivistic cultures contingent rewards are less likely related to employee performance (Aycan, Kanungo, & Sinha, 1999; Podsakoff, Dorfman, Howell, & Todor, 1986).

However, earlier empirical work seldom explores the influence of culture on the different dimensions of reward preference (Chiang & Birtch, 2007, p. 1295). In addition, little empirical work specifically explores the transferability of the reward practices preferred in individualistic cultures to and from collectivistic cultures, which is one of the main challenges for the transition economies in the South East Europe, which are high on Collectivism. Some studies even argue that the HRM concept that is advocated in the United States is neither espoused nor practiced elsewhere in Europe (Brewster, 1993, 2006; Hofstede, 1980), or in the transition economies (Alas & Svetlik, 2004; Bogićević Milikić, Janićijević, & Petković, 2008; Koubek & Brewster, 1995; Koubek & Vatchkova, 2004; Tung & Havlovic, 1996; Zupan & Kaše, 2005).

In order to provide for deeper understanding of the relationship between the reward system and the cultural values, specifically in terms of transferability of performance-based reward system to highly collectivistic cultural contexts, we used a case study method in one Serbian company. We believe that the research findings may contribute to the existing knowledge by answering particularly the following research question: Is it possible to introduce the performance-based reward system within the collectivistic cultural context, and, if it is possible, how? The findings may be of particular importance for the transition economies, which are seeking to implement management systems and tools recognized in developed Western economies, whereas the culture seems to be the main barrier to radical organisational changes (Newman & Nollen, 1998).

In this article we have addressed this issue in five sections. The first section, reviewing the relevant literature, defines the theoretical framework for the interdependence between the cultural values and characteristics of the reward system. In the second section we present the context for the research, research method and research design, describe the main characteristics of the organisational culture of the selected company as well as the design of the new reward system introduced in the selected company. The third section contains the results of the research. The discussion of the results is also provided. Finally, we address some of the practical implications primarily for managers working in a collectivistic cultural context and potential limitations of this study, and identify some possible directions for further research.

2. Linking Collectivism to the Reward Preferences

As culture has many expressions and meanings, so many authors have proposed different definitions of culture. One of the most frequently cited and recognized as "a consensus of anthropological definitions" (Hofstede, 1980) is that "culture consists in patterned ways of thinking, feeling and reacting, acquired and transmitted mainly by symbols, constituting the distinctive achievements of human groups, including their embodiments in artefacts; the essential core of culture consists of traditional (i.e. historically derived and selected) ideas and especially their attached values" (Kluckhohn, 1951, p. 86). In the area of management studies, Hofstede's definition is also repeatedly cited, given that it covers what he was able to measure. According to Hofstede (1980), the culture is treated as "the collective programming of the mind which distinguishes the members of one human group to another", and as its building blocks includes "systems of values" (p. 21). As such, culture is conceptualized and measured through different value dimensions identified and measured by numerous scholars (Hofstede, 1980; House, Wright, & Aditya, 1997; House, Hanges, Javidan, Dorfman, & Gupta, 2004; Inglehart & Baker, 2000; Schwartz, 1994, 2006, 2008; Triandis, 1995; Trompenaars & Hampden-Turner, 1998).

Individualism vs. Collectivism describes the relationship between the individual and the collective that prevails in a given society (Hofstede, 1983). In individualistic societies the ties between individuals are very loose and individuals view themselves as independent of collectives (Triandis, 1995, p. 2). Everybody is supposed to look after his or her own self-interest and maybe the interest of his or her immediate family; this is made possible by the large amount of freedom that such a society leaves individuals (Hofstede, 1983). Involvement with an organisation is largely based on the contractual/market relationship, which is calculative and utilitarian (Glazer, Daniel, & Short, 2004). At the other end of the scale there are societies in which the ties between individuals are very tight. People are born into collectivities or in-groups that may be their extended family, co-workers, their tribe, or their village. Everybody is supposed to look after the interest of his or her in-group and to have no opinions and beliefs other than those in their in-group; in exchange, the in-group will protect them when they are in trouble (Hofstede, 1983; Triandis, 1995). Collectivists demonstrate a strong moral commitment and long-term relationship with their organisations (Shamir, 1990). According to Hofstede (1980) Individualism prevails in developed and Western countries, while Collectivism prevails in less developed and Eastern countries and Japan takes a middle position.

The relevant literature indicates that Individualism-Collectivism determines the extent to which individuals display cooperative versus competitive behaviours in work groups (Cox, Lobel, & McLeod, 1991), so individuals with a collectivistic orientation are more likely to prefer cooperation with peers (Mann, 1980) and shared responsibility (Earley, 1993). Within individualistic cultures the equity principle is preferred, meaning that rewards should be proportional to the individual contribution, whereas collectivistic cultures promote the equality principle, meaning that group members should receive equal rewards (Aycan, 2005; Bond, Leung, & Wan, 1982; Easterby-Smith et al., 1995; Hui, Triandis, & Yee, 1991; Huo & Van Glinov, 1995; Leung & Bond, 1984; Ramamoorthy & Carroll,

1998; Zhou & Martocchio, 2001). Within individualistic cultures people believe that reward allocation based on individual contributions will lead to the productivity and performance increase (Mowday, 1987). Collectivism supports the fear that increase of pay differences may motivate individuals to sacrifice group interests by pursuing their personal interests only and would be detrimental to employee moral (Baker, Jensen, & Murphy, 1988). Higher pay differences between organisational members may result either from greater span of pay range (the difference between the maximum and the minimum pay rates of a pay structure) or from higher share of contingent pay which may increase the pay difference between the employees who are performing the same job. Greater pay differences consequently increase status differences between group members (Reis, 1984), which may devastate the harmony within a specific group (Leung, 1988).

Collectivism emphasizes job security to promote employee commitment to the organisation (Ramamoorthy & Carroll, 1998, p. 575). Thus, as Ramamoorthy & Carroll (1998) suggested, the greater emphasis placed by Collectivism on internal equity (e.g. seniority based pay, pay based on hierarchical status) and lower emphasis on external equity are complemented by the greater job security (p. 575).

Some authors have focused their attention to the influence of the national culture on the employees' preferences regarding design and characteristics of the reward system. For example, Schuler & Rogovsky (1998) analyzed the impact of the national culture's dimensions on differences between various reward systems, by testing their hypothesis on three different databases (IBM - Towers Perin; ISSP - International Social Survey Programme; Price Waterhouse-Cranfield). According to them, and similarly to results reached by some other authors (Bond et al., 1982; Hui et al., 1991), Individualism favours the performance-based reward system, as well as individual bonuses and commissions. Individualists tend to view performance as primarily the outcome of an individual's effort (Staw, 1980), and therefore would prefer rewards based on individual contributions (Fiske, Kitayama, Markus, & Nisbett, 1998). On the other hand, collectivists view performance as context-specific (Hampden-Turner & Trompenaars, 1994), and therefore would prefer reward allocation based on non-performance factors (Leung, Smith, Wang, & Sun, 1996; Tower, Kelly, & Richards, 1997), such as seniority and skills. The «face» concept is built into all collectivistic cultures (Hofstede, 2001; Schneider, 1992; Schuler et al., 2001), so explicit and public evaluation of individual achievement could harm a group's harmony and social relationships, and therefore it is not well accepted. The collectivistic cultures more commonly prefer group or team incentives (Schuler & Rogovsky, 1998).

The relevant literature essentially describes the features of reward preferences in different cultural settings either in individualistic or in collectivistic ones. However, little empirical work is done about what may be expected when applying the reward system preferred in individualistic cultures, such as the performance-based reward system, within the collectivistic cultural context: Would it be rejected immediately as highly incompatible? Even if it is highly unfavourable, are there some prospects for its efficient implementation, and if so, under which conditions? We, therefore, expect that this study may contribute to the existing knowledge in shedding the light on the process of bringing together Collectivism and reward systems preferred in individualistic cultures in a successful manner. This may be of special importance for collectivistic transition countries, which are often externally pressured to adopt highly incompatible market-based management systems and tools preferred in individualistic developed Western economies.

3. Research Methodology

Context for the research. The transition of the ex-socialist countries towards a market economy assumes changes in the institutional and economic settings, and consequently changes in how firms operate and how managers and employees behave (Bogićević Milikić, 2007). This process has led Serbian companies to introduce management technologies and systems generally recognized and applied in developed market economies and successful companies worldwide (Bogićević Milikić et al., 2008). According to Hofstede (see Table 1) the Serbian national culture is characterized by high Power Distance Index, high Uncertainty Avoidance Index, Collectivism – low Individualism, and high to medium Femininity – low to medium Masculinity (Hofstede, 2001; Hofstede & Hofstede, 2005).

Major differences exist between Serbian and Anglo-Saxon cultures in all the mentioned dimensions (Hofstede, 2001), which makes Serbia quite incongruent cultural context for the implementation of Western (i.e. U.S.) management theories and practices.

Research method. We used a case study method of one Serbian company for which we believe it is matching with the research aim. Since the research aim is to contribute to theory building through an attempt to provide for better understanding of the relationship between cultural values and reward system, we select the case study method, which is considered as the most suitable for this type of research focused on new and relatively unknown phenomenon (Dyer & Wilkins, 1991; Glasser & Strauss, 1967; Yin, 1989).

To select a company, we followed three criteria. The first criterion was to have an access to the company. Secondly, we wanted to select a company with a rich background of so-

Table 1: Hofstede's dimensions of the Serbian national culture

DIMENSIONS OF NATIONAL CULTURE	Ex YUGOSLAVIA	SERBIA	
	Score	Score	Rank out of 74 countries
POWER DISTANCE INDEX	76	86	8
UNCERTAINTY AVOIDANCE INDEX	88	92	11-13
INDIVIDUALISM INDEX	27	25	53-54
MASCULINITY INDEX	21	43	47-50

Source: According to Hofstede, G., (2001), Culture's Consequences, 2nd ed., Thousand Oaks, CA: Sage Publications; see also Hofstede, G., Hofstede, G.J., (2005), Cultures and Organizations: Software of the Mind, revised and expanded 2nd edition, Mc Graw-Hill.

cial ownership that guaranteed the existence of the socialist values, especially the existence of Collectivism. Finally, we needed the company intended to introduce a performance-based reward system. The company "Sintelon" Bačka Palanka[1] fulfilled all mentioned requirements. It was a socially owned company producing and selling carpets and some other materials used in flats (stores, decorative materials). It was established in 1884. Development strategy of the company is focused on diversification of supply led by customer preferences with simultaneous expansion on selected market segments. At the time of research the company employed 1671 employees and achieved income of above 79 million US$. It was organized according to the divisional organisational model with six strategic business units (SBUs) and seven departments supporting the operations of SBUs.

Research design. Research aim and research method determined the qualitative and interpretative character of the research design. The focus was put on the original organisational context in the selected company. This research took place after the investigation and measurement of organisational culture and introduction of a new performance-based reward system, which had replaced the previous, seniority-based, reward system. The top management of the Company introduced the new reward system as a part of the overall process of organisational culture's change. Investigation and measurement of organisational culture and design of new reward system had been done by consultants contracted by the Company's top management team, so the author was not involved in selection of the methodology applied in these processes. Information provided by the HR Manager of the Company and from the "Act on the Organisational Culture of the Company" reveals that the cultural values of the employees were identified through interviews with the managers at different hierarchical levels and with selected employees from all organisational units. Representation of the identified values among the employees was then checked through the questionnaire. The strength of the culture was measured by using the consensus/intensity approach (Payne, 1990), which involves two dimensions: the degree of consensus between the organisational members and intensity of the feelings of the employees. However, in our research the focus was not on recognition of the cultural values. Our aim was to see how employees, who share Collectivism, would accept the new, performance-based reward system in the period of nine months after its introduction, and what the role of the cultural values in this process was.

In our analysis we used multiple data sources. We collected data through observations, interviews with the managers and employees, internal documents such as The Internal Act on the Compensation System. We first observed the reactions of the employees and managers after the introduction of the new reward system. At the same time we organized in total 38 semi-structured interviews with the CEO, six directors of the strategic business unit (SBU), HR manager and the other four employees in the HR department (Specialist for performance appraisal, Specialist for training and development, Specialist for recruitment and selection, and Specialist for HR information system), six middle managers

---

[1] Nowadays, the Sintelon Company became a part of international company Tarket.

and twenty employees from different SBUs. The interviewees were selected to represent all strategic business units and all staff categories involved: the managerial staff (having the role of the raters in the new system), the employees (the ratees) and the HR staff (which was in charge of the successful implementation of the new reward system). The aim of the interviews was to collect data from different employee groups about their expectations and perceptions regarding the new reward system. The new reward system is a performance-based system that includes as a formal component performance evaluation. Performance evaluation (or performance appraisal) is the process by which an employee's contribution to the organisational goals during a specified period of time is evaluated, thus tying it to "the creation of value for the organisation" (Lawler, Anderson, & Buckles, 1995, p. 630). It may also be defined as a formal, structured system for measuring, evaluating and influencing an employee's job-related attributes, behaviours and outcomes (Schuler & Jackson, 1996, p. 344). Therefore, the questions were focused on various issues related to the reward system and performance evaluation such as: managers' (employees') expectations regarding the new reward system, goals the managers want to achieve, problems arising during the implementation of the system (validity of the performance criteria, the quality of rater's and ratees' training, measurement scales, performance feedback interviews, quality of the participation of the employees, employees' reactions and equity perceptions regarding the new system, etc.). Apart from these issues, the interviews with HR staff were related to some additional issues associated with the implementation of the new system raised by both sides – the managers and the employees, and the role of the HR department in this process. In addition, it was particularly interesting to see, from the point of view of the HR department, how the managers accepted their role as the performance raters, whether they tried to devastate the whole system and to maintain the status quo in order to retain good communication with the employees, etc.

We have also analyzed secondary data from the following two reports based on two employees' surveys performed by the HR department in the Company: (1) Report on the employees' satisfaction with the new performance-based reward system and (2) Report on the employees' satisfaction with the performance evaluation system. In both surveys the employees' satisfaction with the new reward system (14 items) and performance evaluation (16 items) is measured by using a five-point scale from 1 (absolutely untrue) to 5 (absolutely true). Approximately hundred randomly selected employees filled in both questionnaires from all SBUs. We also analyzed data from the Report on how the employees value the working conditions done as part of organisational culture analysis in the Company. The selected sample for this report was 229 employees randomly selected from all SBUs to represent the whole Company. The employees rated 40 selected working conditions by using a five-point rating scale, from 1 ("it is not important for me at all") to 5 ("it is very important for me"). Finally, we analyzed data from the performance evaluation sheets within nine months after the implementation. In the analysis of data we used simple statistical techniques (descriptive statistics).

The research took place during nine months, after the introduction of the new reward system, and assumed personal involvement of the author who worked as a consultant for the company.

Company Characteristics Regarding Organisational Culture and Reward System

Organisational culture. Organisational culture of the Company (see Table 2) is characterized by seven cultural values – orientations (describing desirable state or aim) - and attitudes for each identified value (describing means to achieve a desirable state), as identified and described by the Company's Internal Act on Organisational Culture (see Table 2). Their relative strengths (at what extent employees accept identified values and attitudes) in the Company were identified through average marks from 1 (no acceptance) to 5 (total acceptance), as follows: < 3 = weak value (attitude); from 3 to 3.5 = medium strong value (attitude); from 3.5 to 4 = strong value (attitude); from 4 to 5 = very strong value (attitude).

The cultural values presented in Table 2 describe the cultural context in the Company, characterized, among other cultural values, by quite strong Collectivism (Value number V: "Orientation toward employee needs"), as defined by Hofstede (1980). Data in Table 2 shows that the employees in the Company highly value Collectivism (defined as the re-

Table 2: Strength of cultural values and attitudes in the company

CULTURAL VALUES AND ATTITUDES	Abbreviations	Means	Standard deviation
I Orientation toward flexibility	FLEX	3.5	1.5
II Orientation toward continuous development	DEV	3.9	1.3
III Orientation toward application of market-based business standards	MAR	3.5	1.4
IV Orientation toward customer preferences	CUST	3.3	1.4
V Orientation toward employee needs	EMPL	3.5	1.4
Secure employment	EMPL1	4.1	1.4
Collectivism	EMPL2	4.5	1.4
Nepotism	EMPL3	3.7	1.6
Egalitarism	EMPL4	3.5	1.7
Secure income	EMPL5	3.4	1.6
External locus of control	EMPL6	3.4	1.6
Good social relations	EMPL7	2.1	1.2
VI Orientation toward results	RES	3.7	1.4
VII Orientation toward privatization	PRIV	2.9	1.5
Organisational culture of the Company		**3.48**	

quirement that individuals take care about collective interests rather than about their own), Egalitarism in distribution, External locus of control, and Good social relations. These results support that the cultural context of this company is suitable to analyze the prospects of introducing performance-based reward system within a collectivistic cultural milieu.

Reward system. The Company decided to replace a seniority-based reward system with a performance-based reward system. In this way the Company replaced its "bureaucratic re-ward strategy", which rewards seniority, with an "organic reward strategy", which values individual and group contributions to organisational performance (Gomez-Mejia & Wel-bourne, 1988, p. 182).

The new reward system included indirect (non-monetary rewards or benefits and servic-es in accordance with the Serbian Labour Code) and direct (monetary) rewards. Mone-tary rewards included salary (determined traditionally through job evaluation by using four compensate factors: knowledge, problem solving, responsibility, working conditions) and pay for performance (individual and group short term incentives for the employees and managers, and some long-term incentives for managers such as options and phantom shares). Eight pay grades were established within the pay structure and the span of pay range was 1:14. As the formal part of the new reward system a performance evaluation system was introduced. The performances of all employees were appraised. Selected per-formance indicators included the following: (1) quality of performance, (2) quantity of performance, (3) following deadlines, (4) efficiency, (5) initiative, learning and develop-ment, and (6) interpersonal influence. The performance evaluation cycle for the blue-col-lar workers was one month, for the administrative staff three months, and for the rest of the employees one year. The immediate supervisors were given the role of raters. For meas-uring performance, the five-point scale was proposed ranging from -2 to +2. The incen-tives (negative and positive) consequently ranged from -20 percent (decrease) to +20 per-cent (increase) of the base salary.

The most important changes that took place by the introduction of the new reward sys-tem were the following: (1) the span of pay range was increased from 1:7 to 1:14, and consequently the job evaluation changed the ratio between the blue-collar and white-col-lar workers in favour of the blue-collar workers; (2) introducing performance-contingent bonuses based on both individual and group contributions, as important parts of the to-tal compensation package; (3) introducing performance evaluation system for measuring individual performance; (4) linking the compensation of employees and managers with group performance – financial performance of the organisational unit to which they be-long; (5) promotion based on achieved results and performance through ranks within pay grades and placement of young professionals on managerial positions, instead of promo-tions based on work experience.

4. Research Findings

The new reward system was implemented by formal CEO's decision and by enacting the Internal Act on Reward System in the Company. However, promptly after the official endorsement of the new reward system, the system was formally modified, by the CEO's decision. The interview with the CEO revealed the reasons behind his decision. As he said, the main reason for this modification was his wish to prevent the employees' resistance he expected to emerge. The CEO found out from the HR manager, but also from the line managers, that the employees were mostly dissatisfied with issues such as: too high span of pay range (extremely high pay differences between the lowest and highest salary, according to the equity perceptions of the employees, produced the feeling of strong pay inequity among the employees); too high salaries of young managers compared to the salaries of their senior colleagues; linking individual bonuses with the financial performance of the organisational units was perceived by the majority of the employees as unfair, because they are not responsible for their placement within the organisation and therefore they do not want to bear the risk of the whole unit (especially if they are located within the unit which is recognized as a poor performer), etc. The initial, partially negative, reactions of the employees to the new reward system motivated the CEO to decide to partially modify the reward system straight away in order to provide greater acceptance of the new system by the employees. Interviews with the top managers of the Company revealed that they feared that the whole reward system would fail if they did not modify it in some extent in order to make it more acceptable for the majority of the employees. The CEO's reaction is consistent with the values of Collectivism, as both managers and employees want to have good social relations, and with high Uncertainty Avoidance in Serbian national culture (Hofstede, 2001, 2005), which makes managers willing to avoid any uncertain situation and unnecessary conflict with the employees. The top management was willing to continue with the application of the performance-based reward system within the collectivistic milieu, even though this achievement required some modifications of the reward system at the early beginning. This shows that the top management of the Company is willing to implement the performance-based reward system within the collectivistic cultural context, regardless of some employees' dissatisfaction. However, the formal modifications of the reward system brought by the CEO actually reflect the perception of the top management about necessary modifications within the performance-based reward system in order to be applied within the Company. The formal modifications of the reward system took place through the formal, written changes of the Internal Act on Reward System. The formal modifications were as follows:

1. The span of pay range was decreased from 1:14 on app. 1:10, which consequently leads to the changes of salaries within pay grades;
2. Pay ratio between the base pay of blue-collar and base pay of white-collar workers increased compared to proposed ratio;
3. Perceived internal inequity of the new reward system decreased with the increase of the number of ranks within the 5th pay grade (from six to nine ranks), 6th pay grade (from six to eight ranks) and 7th pay grade (from seven to ten ranks);

4. Salaries of young managers with short work experience in the company decreased compared to their older and experienced colleagues at the same hierarchical level;
5. The link between the size of individual employee bonuses and financial success of the organisational unit to which they belonged were eliminated.

The interviews with the Managers of SBUs revealed an additional way of modifying the new reward system but quite informally: through discretionary placement of the employees within the seventh pay grade, they in fact established two additional pay ranks. They assigned ranks to certain entry jobs, originally not proposed to be ranked, thus raising the compensation of blue-collar workers performing these jobs. Moreover, the interviews with the employees in HR Department, the raters and the ratees focused our attention to one additional implicit modification of the new reward system: the raters tried to eliminate perceived internal inequities built in the new reward system through the process of performance evaluation, by making a lot of intentional rating errors. The raters openly said that they gave subjective, usually higher, ratings in order to eliminate inequalities built in the new reward system. This was tested through the analysis of the employees' ratings during four months after the implementation of the new reward system. This analysis suggests that the raters made numerous rating errors, namely restriction of range errors, since distribution of individual ratings shows that the highest number of ratings is placed within two intervals: (1) from 0 to +1 and (2) from +1 to +2 (see Table 3).

The analysis of average rating for each performance indicator in the same period shows that raters often made leniency errors, namely positive leniency, since average ratings in each month within the taken period are higher than the means of the interval, which is 0: in May 0.74, in June 0.72, in July 0.68, and in August 0.72. To see whether raters made also «halo» errors, it was not possible to get given ratings by each rater separately (Murphy & Balzer, 1989; Saal et al., 1980; Sulsky & Balzer, 1988). The only possibility to do this was the analysis of cumulative data, i.e. aggregated average ratings for each performance indicator, which significantly limits analytical value of the results. A correlation analysis shows that there is a high positive correlation between almost all performance indicators, except indicator "Quantity", which is not correlated with any other indicator (see Table 3a). This can be explained by the fact that this is a fully result-oriented indicator, which excludes the possibility for any subjective judgment. Since «halo» error is ap-

Table 3: Distribution of individual ratings during 4 months after the implementation of a new reward system

	May	June	July	August
From -2 to -1	2	31	62	24
From -1 to 0	100	166	206	231
From 0 to +1	619	642	661	620
From +1 to +2	304	451	379	417

Table 3a: Correlation analysis of the performance indicators

Pearson Correlation		Discipline	Efficiency	Initiative	Interpersonal influence	Quality
	Efficiency	0.70*				
	Initiative	0.76*	0.54*			
	Interpersonal influence	0.88**	0.83**	0.66		
	Quality	0.84**	0.66	0.92**	0.86**	
	Quantity	-0.26	0.39	-0.18	-0.05	-0.18

** = p < .01; * = p < .05

pearing only at the individual level, analysis of cumulative ratings can rather be used as an indicator of its potential existence.

However, presence of intentional rating errors is not something considered to be related to collectivistic cultures only, but to the individualistic societies, too. Rating errors are errors in judgment that are emerging in a systematic way whenever one individual observes and evaluates another person (Latham & Wexley, 1981, p. 100). Longencker, Sims, & Gioia (1987) and Ferris & Judge (1991) argue that many managers intentionally make rating errors for different, mainly political reasons. This is the reason why a number of studies, primarily in the US, have focused on the investigation of sources of rating errors as well as on ways to eliminate them to improve the quality of performance evaluation.

Nevertheless, previous research findings obtained from the analysis of internal acts, through the interviews with the CEO, HR staff, raters and the ratees, and through the analysis of the evaluation ratings confirmed that the new reward system was modified in both ways formally, by the CEO's formal decision, and informally, by the managers through assignment of ranks to the entry jobs and through making a lot of intentional rating errors.

In order to find out more about the employees' perceptions regarding the new reward system, we analyzed the data on employees' satisfaction with the new reward system and performance evaluation. This data is taken from the two Company's official reports and they are presented below.

Results from the "Questionnaire about employees' satisfaction with the performance evaluation system" (see Table 4, statement 14) show that almost half of the surveyed employees (45.1 percent) perceive that ratings do not make differences between their advantages and disadvantages, meaning that there is no difference between ratings at the individual level. Although almost 40 percent of the surveyed employees disagree with this statement, the percentage of those who agree is quite high.

The results of the Questionnaire give some indications about the existence of cognitive rating errors present in performance evaluation process, although they are in some extent

Table 4: Questionnaire about employees' satisfaction with the performance evaluation system

	STATEMENTS	No.*	Means	St.Dev.	Frequencies**				
					1	2	3	4	5
1	Performance ratings are objective.	102	3.17	1.43	23.5	10.8	3.9	49	12.7
2	It is often the case that my colleagues and I receive unjustified higher or lower ratings.	102	2.84	1.55	32.4	9.8	19.6	17.6	20.6
3	Raters are competent and able to evaluate employees' performances objectively and accurately.	102	3.34	1.48	21.6	8.8	6.9	39.2	23.5
4	Raters are subjective and do not follow defined rating g procedure.	101	3.13	1.47	22.8	9.9	21.8	22.8	22.8
5	I am aware of all aspects of job, which are subject to performance evaluation.	101	3.99	1.21	8.9	5	5	40.6	40.6
6	I think that performance indicators are misleading.	100	2.80	1.50	29	15	24	11	21
7	After evaluation, the rater always spends some time to explain me why I get such performance ratings.	101	2.99	1.75	37.6	7.9	4	18.8	31.7
8	We all get very similar performance ratings.	100	2.95	1.53	28	14	13	25	20
9	Raters give us almost same ratings each month.	101	2.59	1.58	42.6	5.9	18.8	14.9	17.8
10	Performance evaluation motivates me to put in more effort on job.	101	3.43	1.53	22.8	5.9	5.9	36.6	28.7
11	Whenever I get low performance rating I try to improve my performance next month.	101	3.29	1.65	28.7	5	7.9	25.7	32.7
12	Whenever I get low performance rating, I loose motivation for work.	101	3.02	1.71	35.6	6.9	6.9	20.8	29.7
13	I do not think that performance evaluation is so important.	99	2.20	1.58	55.6	13.1	3	12.1	16.2
14	Ratings do reflect my good and poor performances.	102	2.94	1.55	31.4	8.8	13.7	26.5	19.6
15	Performance evaluation system clearly indicates what behaviour is desirable in my organisational unit.	102	2.96	1.55	29.4	11.8	13.7	23.5	21.6
16	I have noticed that some of my colleagues have changed their behaviour after implementation of performance evaluation system.	102	2.85	1.63	38.2	3.9	13.7	22.5	21.6

* Number of surveyed employees
** 1 - absolutely untrue; 2 - partially untrue; 3 - I do not know; 4 - partially true; 5 - absolutely true

contradictory. On the one hand, employees, in general, consider that the raters in the Company give objective evaluations (see Table 4, statements 1, 2, and 3).

On the other hand, about 50 percent of the employees believe that their raters are subjective and do not follow the rating procedure that is determined in advance (see Table 4, Statement no. 4). Moreover, the results of the Questionnaire show that the performance evaluation system does not send clear signals about what behaviours are desirable and what behaviours are not (see Table 4, statements no. 14 and 15), which indirectly indicates that there are no clear differences between the performance ratings. In addition, the majority of employees (65 percent) believe that performance evaluation produced changes in behaviours (see Table 4, statement no. 16) and it motivated them to put some additional efforts in the workplace (see Table 4, Statement 10).

Almost bipolar distribution of answers for item 6 and 7 in Table 4 seems to indicate that the raters (the line managers) are not behaving in same manner throughout the Company. It seems that only some managers (app. 40 percent) explained the performance indicators well and gave useful performance feedback to their subordinates, which indicates that the performance evaluation system was not applied efficiently throughout the whole organisation, so there were some managers who did not appreciate the advantages of the performance evaluation system or were not trained well.

The results of another survey „Questionnaire about employees' satisfaction with the new reward system" presented in Table 5 suggest that the employees, in general, perceive reward system as unfair. 82 percent of surveyed employees perceive the reward system as internally unfair, i.e. that some jobs are intentionally underestimated during the job evaluation process.

The majority of employees (app. 83 percent) perceive the span of pay range as too large, that the CEO pay is too high (71 percent), that the reward system does not provide equal opportunities for earning to all employees, and that the size of individual performance-contingent incentive is not sufficient to motivate employees to make additional efforts.

On the other hand, the majority of employees express the attitude that the new reward system is easy to understand and that performance indicators are well known to all employees (app. 66 percent of surveyed employees).

Regarding the motivational potential of the new reward system, results are somehow divided: 46 percent of the surveyed employees think that its motivation potential is high, whereas the other half thinks it is low. Simultaneously, the majority of employees (more than 65 percent) consider the reward system differentiates between good and poor performers.

For this purpose we took data from the Company's database on cultural values, and performed one-way ANOVA to see if there are any statistically significant differences between the values and attitudes of top management and other employees. The obtained results of multi-group comparison (see Table 6) show that there are statistically significant differences between the attitudes of top management and other groups of employees for almost half of the attitudes, which suggest that the hierarchical position influences the differences in attitudes and values of employees (managers).

Table 5: Employees' satisfaction with the new reward system

	STATEMENTS	No*	Means	St.Dev.	Frequencies**				
					1	2	3	4	5
1	Reward system provides that results of the employee work are highly valued.	105	3.03	1.43	24.8	15.2	2.9	46.7	10.5
2	Reward system is simple and easy for understanding.	105	3.38	1.43	20	5.7	14.3	36.2	23.8
3	Reward system is objective and fair, since it provides all employees with equal opportunities for earning.	105	2.52	1.46	39	15.2	8.6	28.6	8.6
4	Reward system favours white-collar workers compared to blue-collar workers.	105	3.21	1.55	23.8	11.4	13.3	22.9	28.6
5	Reward system is fair since it provides each employee with an opportunity to earn more if he/she works more.	103	2.90	1.59	35.9	6.8	4.9	35.9	16.5
6	I am aware of how my compensation is determined.	105	3.86	1.25	7.6	6.7	20	23.8	41.9
7	Rewards and punishments are well balanced.	105	2.76	1.39	30.5	10.5	20	30.1	8.6
8	Reward system has a high motivation potential for me since I can earn more if I work more.	105	2.76	1.62	40	7.6	5.7	29.5	17.1
9	Reward system provides for extremely higher compensation for directors then for workers.	103	4.12	1.28	7.8	3.9	17.5	10.7	60.2
10	Some jobs are unfairly under evaluated.	104	4.36	1.13	4.8	4.8	8.7	13.5	68.3
11	Reward system provides for sufficient differences between good and poor performers.	104	3.42	1.59	25	5.8	3.8	32.7	32.7
12	Reward system produces inequalities between organisational units within the Company.	104	3.36	1.25	12.5	4.8	41.3	17.3	24
13	Pay range in company is too big.	105	4.41	1.01	3.8	1	12.4	16.2	66.7
14	Incentives based on performance ratings are not sufficient to motivate.	104	4.02	1.20	7.7	3.8	12.5	30.8	45.2

* Number of employees who filled in the questionnaire.
** 1 - absolutely untrue; 2 - partially untrue; 3 - I do not know; 4 - partially true; 5 - absolutely true.

Table 6: Identified significant differences between the attitudes of top management and other employees (results of the One-Way ANOVA)

ANOVA	Type of job	Sum of Squares	Df	Mean Square	F
FLEX4	Between Groups Within Groups Total	60.85 498.62 559.47	8 218 226	7.61 2.29	3.33**
FLEX5	Between Groups Within Groups Total	70.07 453.86 523.93	8 218 226	8.76 2.08	4.21**
EMPL1	Between Groups Within Groups Total	69.65 501.85 571.50	8 217 225	8.71 2.31	3.76**
EMPL2	Between Groups Within Groups Total	52.54 358.59 411.13	8 216 224	6.57 1.66	3.96**
EMPL3	Between Groups Within Groups Total	85.47 481.34 566.81	8 218 226	10.68 2.21	4.84**
EMPL4	Between Groups Within Groups Total	131.75 498.94 630.70	8 218 226	16.47 2.29	7.20**
CUST1	Between Groups Within Groups Total	42.62 525.38 568.00	8 217 225	5.33 2.42	2.20*
CUST3	Between Groups Within Groups Total	79.40 587.36 666.77	8 217 225	9.93 2.71	3.67**
PRIV1	Between Groups Within Groups Total	70.50 319.68 390.18	8 217 225	8.81 1.47	5.98**
PRIV2	Between Groups Within Groups Total	52.99 546.65 599.64	8 218 226	6.62 2.51	2.64**
PRIV3	Between Groups Within Groups Total	48.02 487.71 535.73	8 217 225	6.00 2.25	2.67**
DEV1	Between Groups Within Groups Total	28.63 347.51 376.14	8 218 226	3.58 1.59	2.24*
DEV2	Between Groups Within Groups Total	11.94 163.56 175.51	8 218 226	1.49 0.75	1.99*
DEV3	Between Groups Within Groups Total	89.45 368.10 457.54	8 218 226	11.18 1.69	6.62**

Table 6: Continuation

ANOVA	Type of job	Sum of Squares	Df	Mean Square	F
DEV4	Between Groups Within Groups Total	48.23 456.69 504.92	8 218 226	6.03 2.09	2.88**
RES1	Between Groups Within Groups Total	56.25 436.64 492.89	8 217 225	7.03 2.01	3.49**
RES5	Between Groups Within Groups Total	29.75 330.34 360.09	8 218 226	3.72 1.52	2.45**
MAR77	Between Groups Within Groups Total	62.68 541.30 603.98	8 216 224	7.84 2.51	3.13**

** = $p < .01$; * = $p < .05$

However, One-Way ANOVA shows that there are no statistically significant differences regarding Collectivism and External locus of control between the employees and the managers.

The analysis of means for all respective groups of employees and managers (see Table 6a) shows: (1) Egalitarism (EMPL4) is to a greater extent shared by employees on other than

Table 6a: Means for selected attitudes

Report	N	Selected attitudes			
Type of job		Egalitarism (EMPL4)		Reward system based on results (RES5)	
		Mean	SD	Mean	SD
Production worker	97	3.97	1.55	4.03	1.35
Administrative worker	37	4.00	1.35	4.14	1.46
Shift manager	15	3.20	1.93	4.73	1.03
Manager of the organi-sational unit	9	3	1.73	4.44	0.73
Professional	25	3.52	1.29	4.48	0.92
Salesman	16	3.19	1.68	3.63	1.50
Sales manager	2	2.5	0.71	4.50	0.71
Top manager	24	1.54	1.35	4.96	0.20
Total	227	3.52	1.67	4.23	1.26

managerial jobs, (2) the attitude of having a reward system based on results (RES5) is stronger among top managers.

In order to get more information on the employees' satisfaction with the new reward system we also used the data from the Report on how the employees value the working conditions, done by the HR Department in the Company (see Table 7). 250 employees randomly selected from eight strategic business units valued forty working conditions by using a five-point measurement scale (1 – I am not satisfied at all; 2 – I am little satisfied; 3 – I am satisfied moderately; 4 – I am satisfied; 5 – I am very satisfied).

Table 7: Report on how the employees value the working conditions: frequencies

FACTORS	Frequencies		
	1 & 2 (%)	3 (%)	4 & 5 (%)
1. Salary level	24.9	27.5	44.6
2. Clear criteria and pay equity	30.6	23.6	42.4
3. The job I enjoy	8.8	25.8	59.8
4. The company that is adapting to its environment	11.4	32.3	51.6
5. Efficient teamwork	11.8	25.8	59.9
6. Performing the job which is meaningful for the company	9.6	20.5	66.3
7. Security of employment	15.7	18.3	62
8. Regular and secure payments	4.4	8.3	83.8
9. The company that permanently invests in its growth	6.1	15.3	73.8
10. Good immediate supervisor	11.8	14.4	69.9
11. Respectable MD	6.1	6.6	83.9
12. Capable individuals on the top	5.7	15.3	75.9
13. Possibilities for career advancement	24.9	24	47.6
14. Company which operates by following the worldwide business standards	7.4	20.1	69.5
15. Professional and reliable colleagues	12.7	22.7	62
16. Good relationships with colleagues	5.2	15.7	76
17. Friendly atmosphere in the workplace	9.2	13.5	73.3
18. Colleagues as friends	8.3	29.7	59.1
19. Company that is adapting to the customers' needs	6.1	18.8	72.5
20. Absence of conflicts in the company	13.6	22.7	61.1

Table 7: Continuation

FACTORS	Frequencies		
	1 & 2 (%)	3 (%)	4 & 5 (%)
21. Possibilities for professional advancement	24	27.5	47.2
22. Objective ratings of individual performances	26.7	27.1	45
23. Informing employees about major news regarding the company	38.9	29.7	28.4
24. The carefulness of the company for the employees' needs	30.1	22.7	45.8
25. Job where I exactly know what is expected from me	13.5	18.8	65
26. Challenging job	14	29.7	53.7
27. Modern technology	14.4	25.8	58.1
28. Reasonable pay	26.2	25.3	45.8
29. Company where it is known how much everyone has to work	19.2	33.2	45
30. Possibilities for autonomous work	16.6	25.3	55.9
31. Supervisor who asks his subordinates for their opinion	23.6	22.3	52.4
32. Work load that does not require extra working hours	19.3	27.9	48.9
33. Privately-owned company	28.4	28.4	39.4
34. Absence of night shifts	17.9	31.4	47.6
35. Strong discipline	15.7	25.8	56.8
36. Good physical working conditions	24.9	24.9	48
37. Organized food, recreation and leisure for employees	28.8	24	45
38. Stipends for the employees' children	9.6	22.3	65.5
39. Help in housing	44.5	21	32.3
40. Absence of layoffs	30.1	33.6	34

* The sum of frequencies is not equal to 100% in all rows due to missing cases for some factors.

Results show that the majority of employees do not value salary level highly, but rather regular and secure payments. Among the selected employees in the company the following factors were identified as the most important motivators: leadership style, social relations, and relationship with the supervisor.

5. Discussion

Research findings suggest that there is a noteworthy effect of cultural values on the characteristics of the reward system, indicated by the formal and informal modifications of the new reward system almost immediately after its introduction. Formal modifications resulted from the CEO`s formal decision immediately after the introduction of the new reward system. One type of informal modifications by the line managers immediately after the introduction of the new reward system was done through assigning the ranks to employees rather than to the jobs. The second type of informal modification of the new reward system through subjective ratings was noted during the whole selected time frame of nine months. In an attempt to explain why the new reward system was modified so fast after its introduction, i.e., the influence of cultural values on the characteristics of the reward system, we carefully analyzed each modification of the reward system that was made. The first mentioned modification, the reduction of the span of pay range from 1:15 to approximately 1:10 resulting from the CEO's formal decision, aimed at preventing eventual employees' resistance and dissatisfaction. A large span of pay range is not compatible with high Egalitarism in distribution, which is an important characteristic of the organisational culture in the Company, as well as of the Serbian national culture. Egalitarism in distribution is directly related to high Collectivism, which alleviates the fear that pay differences increase the differences between group members (Reis, 1984), which may destroy group harmony (Leung, 1988). Egalitarism in distribution is based on the equality principle, which entails that equity in distribution is present when all employees, regardless of their inputs, are equally rewarded (Mueller, Iverson, & Jo, 1999). This means that if this principle is not accepted (if there is a difference between individual rewards), such a distribution, and consequently the reward system, is perceived by organisational members as unfair. However, regardless of the fact that the span of pay range has been decreased immediately after the introduction of the new reward system, results from the Report on the employee satisfaction with the new reward system suggest that the span of pay range continued to be an important source of employees' dissatisfaction and their perception that the whole reward system is unfair. According to equity theory (Adams, 1965) if individuals perceive they are undervalued, in order to eliminate the imbalance they will either decrease their inputs or increase their outcomes (rewards). Research findings in the Company show that employees doubled their outcome: through formal decrease of the span of pay range, and through increase of individual performance ratings made by the raters. The analysis of ratings suggests that raters in the Company make restriction of range error, actually positive leniency, in which way they allow the employees to earn higher variable pays. Interviews with the raters suggest that raters make those rating errors intentionally. This indicates that the performance evaluation process is seen as an informal tool for establishing the pay equity within the reward system. However, the fact is that even though the span of pay range was decreased employees continued to perceive the reward system as unfair, meaning that equity was not established within the whole time frame (see Table 5).

The second and third modifications, change of the ratio between base pay of blue-collar and white-collar workers, as well as increasing the number of ranks within pay grades, are also consequences of the CEO's formal decision made immediately after the introduction of the new reward system. This was done in order to prevent employees' resistance, primarily resistance of blue-collar workers who had a significant share in the total employment in the Company. After comparing base pay of different employee groups in the old and new reward system, it was obvious that all employees benefited from the new reward system through pay raise, but some employees benefited significantly more then others (the increase in base pay in the new system, compared with the old pay structure, was from 1 percent to 127 percent for secretaries). Similarly to the first modification, the employees' perception about internal inequity of the system also initiated the need for eliminating perceived inequity of the system through change of the span of pay range and through an increase of ranks within lower pay grades. These modifications may also be explained as the consequence of high Egalitarism in the organisational culture of the Company.

The fourth modification, decrease of base pay of young managers in relation to their older peers at the same hierarchical level, was also decided by the CEO's immediately after the introduction of the new system, in spite of the fact that the CEO was the major promoter of the idea that young professionals and managers should be encouraged. However, this idea simply is not compatible with the Collectivism, which facilitates slow promotions and loyalty to collective interests (Ramamoorthy & Carroll, 1998). Placing young professionals on higher managerial positions is perceived by the majority of employees as unfair, and according to the equity theory decrease of their outcome (reward) was the best way for establishing the right balance between their input-output ratios.

The fifth modification, the elimination of the direct link between individual variable pay and financial performance of organisational units, requires a more careful analysis. At first glance, it seems that Uncertainty Avoidance, as strong characteristic of the Serbian national culture (Hofstede, 2001; Hofstede & Hofstede, 2005), is responsible for this modification. Linking individual incentives to the organisational unit financial performance should provide that all employees share the risk and responsibility for the group outcome. High Uncertainty Avoidance may explain why employees in Serbia do not want to bear the risk, whereas high Collectivism further facilitates this behaviour, but also strongly encourages the process of transferring the whole risk to the elite at the top. However, we did not identify high Uncertainty Avoidance in the Company (in spite of the fact that this is an important characteristic of the Serbian national culture). On the contrary, the strength of the flexibility value shows that employees in the Company are positively oriented toward changes. Interviews with the employees suggested that the fifth modification in the system should be explained by some other factors. There are large differences between organisational units in the Company regarding their financial performances. If individual incentives are to be directly linked to the organisational unit's financial performance, this will significantly increase pay differences between peers working in different organisational units regardless of their individual performances. Interviews with the employees further suggest that employees compare their pay with the pay of their peers in other organisational units, and perceive any pay difference between them as unfair. Therefore, the fifth modification should be explained as the attempt of the CEO to avoid anticipated employees' dissatisfaction in advance. At the same time, bonuses for managers continued to be linked with financial performance of their organisational units, which may be explained by the fact that top managers in the Company share, in some extent, different cultural values. This was confirmed by the analysis of the differences between the values (and attitudes) of different groups of employees.

The results presented in tables 6 and 6a actually suggest that the new reward system, which values results and creates differences between poor and good performers is more compatible with cultural values of top management than with the attitudes of other groups of employees. This may be the reason why the introduction of a performance-based system in the Company was possible at all, since in high Power Distance cultures (such as Serbian national culture, according to Hofstede, 2001) all changes are almost always initiated and promoted from the top of the organisation. Moreover, different cultural values (attitudes) of top managers may also be the reason why the new reward system was not further changed or fully suspended.

All described modifications of the new reward system lead to the conclusion that, consistent with existing knowledge, culture is an important determinant of the employees' equity perceptions (Lind & Tyler, 1988; Tyler, 1987). Research suggests that both national culture (Mueller et al., 1999) and organisational culture (Leung & Bond, 1984) significantly influence employees' equity perceptions. Through equity perceptions, the culture makes a strong influence on employees' pay (dis)satisfaction and creates the need for its adjustment to the dominant cultural values. Our case research findings suggest that Collectivism and Egalitarism (rooted in Collectivism) significantly influence the employees' equity perceptions.

There is also one additional underlying question: Why did employees not express dissatisfaction with performance-based pay, based on different contributions to the organisational success? The large span of the pay range is seen as the main source of the employees' perception that the reward system is unfair, whereas performance-based pays which allow for 40 percent differences in total compensation at the same job did not produce any inequity perception. This is an unexpected result, since it is not compatible with the existing knowledge, which suggests that pay for performance is not compatible with high Collectivism at all (Hofstede, 1980; Spector, 1982). This is because the first component of expectancy theory, which is crucial for the motivating potential of pay for performance, that is, the expectancy of the individual that if he invests an effort he can achieve an outcome, is not compatible with Collectivism and External locus of control. However, in spite of strong Collectivism and External locus of control the employees' dissatisfaction with performance-based pay in the Company has not been identified. Furthermore, results of the "Questionnaire about employees' satisfaction with the performance evaluation system" (see Table 4) suggest that performance evaluation is seen as a good motivating force. How can this be explained? One possible explanation might be low base pay: Employees perceive variable pay as a means to increase their chance for higher total pay. Another possible explanation we may find in discrepancy theories of satisfaction, which introduce individual comparison standards to explain level of individual satisfaction with compensation (Goodman, 1974; Heneman, 1985; Lawler, 1971). Each employee compares his compensation with one or more comparison standards: what he/she believes he/she deserves, what he/she wants or what other employees receive. In this sense, individual satisfaction with compensation is determined by a discrepancy between individual compensation and the chosen comparison standard: lower discrepancy leads to greater satisfaction and the other way around. Results of our research (See statements 9 and 13 in Table 5) suggest that in cultures characterized by high Collectivism (and consequently by high Egalitarism in distribution) employees do not compare themselves with their peers, but rather with top managers. This can also explain the fact that employees in the Company see every span of the pay range as a huge one. Additionally, an important conclusion is that the personal comparison standard is not total compensation, but rather base pay resulting from the job evaluation process. Apparently the comparison standard is higher the higher is the discrepancy between pay and extent of pay dissatisfaction. One way to decrease employee pay dissatisfaction is through reduction of a discrepancy. However, to date there are no suggestions in the literature how to change personal comparison standards, or how these changes should be managed. A few authors suggest that if salaries are generally low, differences in satisfaction of employees with high and low personal comparison standards are lower and consequently in this case personal comparison standards are not valid in explaining satisfaction with compensation (Rice, Phillips, & McFarlin, 1990). In Serbia, salaries are generally at a very low level. Even salaries that are several times higher then the average salary are not sufficient to cover the costs of living. This is probably the reason why anyone who receives higher then average salary causes the employees' dissatisfaction, because this devastates the harmony within the collective. Also, the very low level of salaries, which does not allow for fulfilment of existential needs, might partially explain why employees in the Company choose salaries of top managers and CEO as their personal comparison standards instead of salaries of their peers. Of course, there is the question whether the increase of average salary level will contribute in any way to the decrease of employees' personal comparison standards. Perhaps it would be beneficial to enhance the employees' perception of justice in some other ways, for example, by comparing their salaries with employees with significantly lower salaries in other companies throughout Serbia, etc.

The next important question certainly is why the reward system has not been completely adjusted to dominant cultural values or simply rejected, since employees' dissatisfaction with the new reward system was present during the whole selected time frame. Furthermore, no employees left the Company during that period, although this may be the result of the fact that the employees of the Company did not have many opportunities for alternative employment in Backa Palanka or in Serbia. However, in Serbia it is very rare that employees leave the company even if they do not receive salary for months, as they expect that the government will solve the problems of insolvency of their companies. Therefore, we may perhaps explain this by a strong External locus of control, which is an important characteristic of the organisational culture in the Company, as well as of the Serbian national culture (Hofstede, 2001). According to some authors, prolonged continuation of misbalance between old and new cultural values is quite possible and, moreover, expected in cultures characterized by strong external locus of control (Spector, 1982). Externalists (people with external locus of control) stay in the company even when they are not satisfied, since they believe that they cannot influence the source of their dissatisfaction. Prolonged cognitive dissonance (the difference between individual values and behaviour) is characteristic of externalists, whereas internalists (individuals with internal locus of control) cannot stand cognitive dissonance, therefore adjusting their values and behaviour in a way that even when their behaviour differs from their values they will try to see their own behaviour from some other perspective as quite acceptable (Spector, 1982). Additional explanation for the eventual existence of prolonged dissatisfaction with some elements of the reward system may be found in the report on how the employees value the working conditions (see Table 7), which suggests that for the majority of employees salary level generally does not have high valence, but rather regular and secure payments. Among the selected employees in the Company the following factors were identified as the most important motivators: leadership style, social relations, and relationship with the supervisor. Measurement of the employees' satisfaction with these factors might be helpful in explaining the persistence of employees' dissatisfaction with some elements of the reward system without taking any further actions.

6. Conclusions from this Research

Aforementioned findings indicate the routes and the nature of the influence of culture on the reward system and lead us to four conclusions. First, research findings suggest that organisational culture makes a strong influence on the characteristics of the reward system in the short term. Immediately after the introduction of the new reward system it was formally and informally modified by the management of the Company to prevent the employees' resistance to the new reward system at the beginning of the implementation process. All identified modifications of the new reward system may be explained by the dominant cultural values in the Company. Therefore, based on the results of our investigation, we conclude:

Conclusion 1: Organisational culture has a strong impact on the reward system in short term.

Secondly, consistent with theory, research findings suggest that the culture is an important determinant of the employees' equity perceptions (Lind & Tyler, 1988; Tyler, 1987), including both national (Mueller et al., 1999) and organisational culture (Leung & Bond, 1984). Culture influences the reward system by affecting the employees' equity perceptions. Employees' equity perceptions actually show how they perceive organisational, i.e. distributive and procedural justice in their organisation (Greenberg, 1990). Distributive justice refers to the perceived fairness or equity of the manner in which rewards are distributed in organisations, while procedural justice refers to the perceived fairness or equity of the procedures used in making decisions regarding the distribution of rewards (Folger & Greenberg, 1985). Distributive justice predicts pay satisfaction, whereas procedural justice affects organisational commitment (Sweeney & McFarlin, 1993). Therefore, culture strongly influences the level of employees' (dis)satisfaction with a reward system and creates the need for its adaptation to dominant cultural values through its influence on employees' equity perceptions about distributive justice in organisation.

The most important role in creating employees' equity perception regarding the distributive justice seems to have the deepest level of culture-basic assumptions (Schein, 1985), which are "invented, discovered, or developed by a given group as it learns to cope with its problems of external adaptation and internal integration – that has worked well enough to be considered valid and, therefore, to be taught to new members as the correct way to perceive, think, and feel in relation to those problems" (p. 9). According to Schein (1985), basic assumptions are equated to Argyris & Schön's (1978) "theories-in-use". Basic assumptions may be so implicit, taken for granted, and unconscious that surfacing them can require intensive interviewing and observation (Schein, 1985, p. 21). As such, Schein's basic assumptions coincide with the Hofstede`s definition of culture as the mental program which is developed in the family in early childhood and reinforced in schools and organisations and contain a component of national culture (Hofstede, 1980).

If the equity perception of the distributive justice is in any way strongly devastated creating pay dissatisfaction among the majority of organisational members, the reward system will have to be changed in order to eliminate at least those inequity perceptions, which show to be comprehensively shared among the majority of the organisational members. This is consistent with the assumption suggested by Robert et al. (2000) and Joshi & Martocchio (2008) that the relationships between employees' attitudes and behaviours and various proximal events (i.e., the implementation of human resources practices such as an incentive pay system) are influenced by such distal contingency factors as national culture. Therefore, we conclude:

Conclusion 2: An efficient reward system has to comply with employees' perceptions regarding pay equity, which are affected by employees' basic assumptions contained within organisational culture and rooted in national culture.

Thirdly, research findings suggest that Collectivism, as an important national culture dimension (Hofstede, 1980), as well as Egalitarism, which is directly related to Collectivism, have a significant influence on employees' equity perceptions. Our research indicates that the main sources of employees' pay dissatisfaction include the following: large span of pay range causing large pay differences and fast promotion of young professionals and managers. Both changes are not consistent with the Collectivism. Large pay differences increase the differences between group members while fast promotions may devastate loyalty to collective interests. Therefore, we conclude:

Conclusion 3: Collectivism is an important determinant of the employees' perceptions regarding pay equity.

Fourthly, our research findings also suggest that employees in the Company did not express any dissatisfaction with performance-based pay, in spite of strong Collectivism and External locus of control, which is not consistent with earlier studies, which suggest that pay for performance is fully incongruent with both Collectivism and External locus of control, since they do not allow for fulfilment of the main element of the expectancy theory, which is the ground for performance-based reward systems (Bond et al., 1982; Chen et al., 1998; Leung & Bond, 1984; Ramamoorthy & Carroll, 1998; Reis, 1984). Our study found that employees expressed satisfaction and great level of acceptance of performance-based pay. Employees expressed dissatisfaction only with the size of individual incentives, in a way that they should be larger. The main source of the employees` pay dissatisfaction is the perceived internal inequity resulting from job evaluation and large span of base pay range. If span of base pay range is lower, and base pay differences are lower, findings indicate that the performance-based pay may be well accepted even within collectivistic contexts. Therefore, we conclude:

Conclusion 4: Collectivism and external locus of control are incompatible with large span of pay range resulting from job evaluation, but not necessarily with the performance-based reward system.

These conclusions give the answer to our research question "Is it possible to introduce the performance-based reward system within the collectivistic cultural context, and, if it is possible, how?" Our case study confirms that culture experts strong influence on the reward system, especially in short term. It also suggests that culture and, consequently, Collectivism influence the reward system by affecting the employees' equity perceptions. However, our evidence suggests that it is possible to introduce the performance-based reward system within collectivistic cultural context, but under specific conditions. These conditions are related to the requirement to avoid a large span of pay range resulting from job evaluation, because in this way the pay differences become less visible to the majority of employees. We believe that these conclusions, which are based on a case study, might serve as hypotheses for further studies to test their generralizability.

7. Limitations and Implications for Management and Further Research

Before jumping to implications we have to point out that this study has some important limitations, which need to be mentioned. First, the selected case study method, although suited to the research aim, does not allow for generalization of research findings. Therefore, further research should include a higher number of companies. Secondly, an important limitation of this study is related to the semi-archive character of this research, since secondary documents and survey results have been used. Thirdly, selected time frame of research is relatively short, so there is a question whether incompatibility between cultural values and characteristics of the new reward system could be resolved in a longer period of time either through further modification of the reward system or through the changes of organisational culture. However, timely limited access to the Company restricted our research. Fourthly, only 102 to 105 from 1,671 employees rated their satisfaction with the reward system and the performance evaluation. However, respondents were randomly selected from (all) different organisational units and various hierarchical levels, so the results may be taken as an indication of employees' satisfaction in the Company. Finally, perhaps the selected company is not a typical Serbian ex-socialist company due to its orientation to results and application of market-based business standards, which might cause doubts regarding broader implications for other ex-socialist countries and influence of national culture.

However, regardless of the mentioned limitations, we believe that these research findings have some important implications for management of the Company and other Serbian companies, as well as for further theoretical research. First, the top management of the Company should rethink further modifications of the reward system in a way to decrease the span of pay range through decrease of number of pay grades by increasing their range, since the research finding suggests that employees are dissatisfied with the span of pay range and not with introduction of performance-based pay. Additionally, employees see the size of the incentive of 20 percent above the average performance as insufficient, which means that valence of rewards is low and that it should be increased. Practically, it will mean that the share of variable pay (based on performance) within total compensation should be increased. In this way level of fixed pay will be lower, which is for the majority of employees the standard of comparison with each other. Secondly, top management should pay some attention to the ways for decreasing subjectivity in evaluating employee's performance, expressed through presence of «halo» and positive leniency errors, which deteriorates validity and reliability of performance ratings. Especially, because performance evaluation is a formal part of the new reward system and performance ratings notably influence individual compensation package. The objectivity of evaluation could be increased through various measures as follows: increasing the number of raters by introducing the employees as raters of their supervisors, systematic analysis of rating errors, further training of raters and more comprehensive definition of performance indicators used. However, there is still a risk that all these measures may be violated by the raters and might not be effective, since our case study suggests that rating errors are often made intentionally.

This study has also some important implications for the management of other Serbian companies, as well as for the management of companies in other transition economies with similar cultural characteristics. First, blind application of Western management theories, concepts and instruments in different cultural milieu may be damaging. Implementation of market-based reward systems requires that the original cultural context should be considered in advance in order to avoid negative consequences on employees' equity perceptions. Collectivism as an important national culture dimension has significant influence on employees' equity perceptions. Since Collectivism is rather a basic assumption – the deepest level of culture, there is the question whether the Collectivism is possible to change if it is likely to be quite resistant to convergence forces (Hofstede, 2001). Therefore, it seems that in collectivistic cultures the span of pay range may be the main source of the employees' pay dissatisfaction. It seems that a more appropriate solution might be to increase a difference between different contributions through status symbols and perks (Newman & Nollen, 1998). It is also possible to gradually increase the span of pay range. Secondly, when designing reward systems in collectivistic national cultures, management of decentralized companies should take into account the fact that the personal comparison standard of one employee is likely to be a fixed pay of CEO and/or a fixed pay of his peers in other organisational units. Linking the pay to organisational unit performance, in that sense, may be contra-productive. More suitable approach in this case may be to link individual variable pays with the company financial performance. Thirdly, research finding also suggests that the performance evaluation is used as informal mechanism for decreasing perceived inequity built in the reward system design. Research findings indicate that in collectivistic cultures raters (often, middle managers) frequently make intentionally restriction of range rating errors, due to their unwillingness to take on the responsibility to make the difference between good and poor performers, since it may increase the pay differences and devastate the group harmony. Therefore, perhaps, at the beginning, the forced distribution scale may be used as a performance evaluation instrument, regardless of it's recognized numerous disadvantages.

Finally, it should be noted that this study presents only the first step in deepening our understanding of relationship between Collectivism and reward system design. Many questions still remain to be dealt with in future. First, research findings suggest that Collectivism and External locus of control are not compulsory incompatible with performance-based pay, and consequently with the assumptions of Expectancy theory. Therefore, more research is needed to check the proposed hypothesis. This could contribute to better understanding of performance-based pay, especially with a focus on the further modification of expectancy theory in collectivistic national cultures. It might be that in collectivistic cultures other factors beyond the external locus of control (i.e. tendency to attribute personal experiences to powerful others, fate, chance, or luck) are influencing employees' expectations and behaviours. According to Expectancy theory, the employees make decisions among alternative behaviours on the basis of their perceptions (expectancies) of the degree to which a given behaviour will lead to desired outcomes. The basic mismatch between external locus of control and motivation described by the Expectancy theory is that employees with external locus of control will not put additional effort to receive the outcome, since they do not see a direct link between their own effort and outcomes. However, in collectivistic cultures, beyond the external locus of control other values are also quite present such as loyalty, good social relations and strong moral commitment and long-term relationship with their organisations (Shamir, 1990). Therefore, it may be argued that in collectivistic cultures the psychological contract between the employees and the organisation (i.e. what an individual expects to offer the organisation and what the organisation expects to receive from the individual) shapes the employee's expectancies, so the employee would show the commitment, loyalty, and enthusiasm for the organisation and its goals if there is (1) a high degree to which his own expectations of what the organisation will provide him with what he owes the organisation match with what the organisation's expectations are of what it will give and get; and (2) if there is agreement on expectations between the two parties what actually is to be exchanged (Schein, 1980, p.77). Secondly, the results of this research show that in ex-socialist countries, nowadays transition economies, the national culture presents an important limitation for application of Western theories and concepts. Therefore, further investigation is needed, especially within companies that experienced successful transformation in order to learn about new methods, which could be applied in other companies attempting to adapt to market requirements. The finding of some degree of convergence in employment practices across countries suggests there is room for culture – or country – atypical practices and that being unique may be effective (Katz & Darbishire, 2000), so the perseverance of differences may be seen as a desirable outcome (Brodbeck et al., 2000).

References

Adams, J.S. (1965). Inequity in Social Exchange. In L. Berkowitz (Ed.), Advances in Experimental Social Psychology, Vol. 2 (pp. 267-299). New York: Academic Press.

Alas, R. & Svetlik, I. (2004). Estonia and Slovenia: Building Modern HRM Using a Dualist Approach. In C. Brewster, W. Mayrhofer & M. Morley (Eds.), Human Resource Management in Europe: Evidence of Convergence (pp. 353-383)? Elsevier Butterworth-Heinemann.

Argyris, C. & Schon, D. (1978). Organisational learning: A theory of action perspective. Reading, Mass: Addison Wesley.

Aycan, Z. (2005). The interplay between cultural and institutional/structural contingencies in human resource management practices. International Journal of Human Resource Management, 16 (7), 1083-1119.

Aycan, Z., Kanungo, R.N. & Sinha, J.B.P. (1999). Organizational Culture and Human Resource Management Practices: The Model of Culture Fit. Journal of Cross-Cultural Psychology, 30, 501-526.

Baker, G.P., Jensen, M.C. & Murphy, K.J. (1988). Compensation and incentives: Practice vs. theory. The Journal of Finance, 43 (3), 593-616.

Bogićević Milikić, B. (2007). Role of the Reward System in Managing Changes of Organizational Culture. Economic Annals, 174-175, 9-27.

Bogićević Milikić, B., Janićijević, N. & Petković, M. (2008). HRM in Transition Economies: The Case of Serbia. South East European Journal of Economics and Business, 3 (2), 75-88.

Bond, M.H., Leung, K. & Wan, K.C. (1982). How does cultural collectivism operate? The impact of task and maintenance contributions on reward distribution. Journal of Cross-Cultural Psychology, 13, 186-200.

Brewster, C. (1993). Developing a 'European' model of human resource management. International Journal of Human Resource Management, 44, 765-784.

Brewster, C. (2006). Comparing HRM policies and practices across geographical borders. In G. K. Stahl & I. Bjorkman (Eds.), Handbook of Research in International Human Resource Management (pp. 68-90). Cheltenham, UK: Edward Elgar.

Briscoe, D. R., Schuller, R.S. & Claus, L. (2009). International Human Resource Management: Policies and Practices for Multinational Enterprises, third edition, Routledge.

Brodbeck, F. C., Frese, M., Akerblom, S., Audia, G., Bakacsi, G., Bendova, H., Bodega, D., Bodur, M., Booth, S., Brenk, K., Castel, P., Hartog, D. D., Donnelly-Cox, G., Gratchev, M.V., Holmberg, I., Jarmuz, S., Jesuino, J.C., Jorbenadse, R., Kabasakal, H. E. & Keating, M. (2000). Cultural variation of leadership prototypes across 22 European countries. Journal of Occupational and Organizational Psychology, 73 (1), 1-29.

Chen, C.C., Chen, X. & Meindl, J.R. (1998). How can cooperation be fostered? The cultural effects of indi-vidualism-collectivism. Academy of Management Review, 23 (2), 285-304.

Chiang, F.F.T. & Birtch, T. (2007). The transferability of management practices: Examining cross-national differences in reward preferences. Human Relations, 60, 1293-1330

Cox, T.H., Lobel, S.A. & McLeod, P.L. (1991). Effects of ethnic group cultural differences on cooperative versus competitive behavior on a group task. Academy of Management Journal, 34, 827-847.

Dyer, G.W. & Wilkins, A.L. (1991). Better stories and better constructs. Academy of Management Review, 16 (3), 612-619.

Earley, P.C. (1993). East meets West meets Mideast: Further explorations of collectivistic and individualistic work groups. Academy of Management Journal, 36, 319-348.

Easterby-Smith, M., Malina, D. & Yuan, L. (1995). How Culture Sensitive is HRM? A Comparative Analy-sis of Chinese and UK Companies. International Journal of Human Resource Management, 6 (1), 31-59.

Ferris, G.R. & Judge, T.A. (1991). Personnel/Human Resources Management: A Political Influence Perspec-tive. Journal of Management, 17 (2), 447-488.

Fiske, A.P., Kitayama, S., Markus, H.R. & Nisbett, R.E. (1998). The cultural matrix of social psychology. In D.T. Gilbert, S.T. Fiske & G. Lindzey (Eds.), Handbook of social psychology (pp. 915-981). New York: McGraw-Hill.

Folger, R. & Greenberg, J. (1985). Procedural justice: an interpretational analysis of personnel systems. Re-search in Personnel and Human Resources Management, 3, 141-183.

Glasser, B. & Strauss, A. (1967). The discovery of grounded theory: Strategies for qualitative research. Chica-go: Aldine.

Glazer, S. Daniel, S.C. & Short, K.M. (2004). A study of the relationship between organizational commit-ment and human values in four countries. Human Relations, 57 (3), 323-45.

Gomez-Mejia, L.R. & Welbourne, T.M. (1988). Compensation strategy: An overview and future steps. Hu-man Resource Planning, 11, 173-189.

Gomez-Mejia, L. R. & Welbourne, T. (1991). Compensation strategies in a global context. Human Resource Planning, 14, 29-41.

Goodman, P.S. (1974). An examination of referents used in the evaluation of pay. Organizational Behavior and Human Performance, 12, 170-195.

Greenberg, J. (1990). Organizational justice: yesterday, today and tomorrow. Journal of Management, 16 (2), 399-432.

Hampden-Turner, C. & Trompenaars, F. (1994). The Seven Cultures of Capitalism. London: Piatikus Book.

Heneman, H.G. III. (1985). Pay Satisfaction. In K.M. Rowland & G.R. Ferris (Eds.), Research in personnel and human resource management, Vol. 3 (pp. 115-140). Greenwich, CT: JAI Press.

Hofstede, G. (1980). Culture's consequences: International differences in work-related values. 2nd ed, Bever-ly Hills, Calif.: Sage.

Hofstede, G. (1983). The cultural relativity of organizational practices and theories. Journal of International Business Studies, 14 (1), 75-89.

Hofstede, G. (2001). Culture's Consequences. 2nd ed. Thousand Ouks, CA: Sage Publications.

Hofstede, G. & Hofstede, G.J. (2005). Cultures and Organizations: Software of the Mind. Revised and ex-panded 2nd edition. Mc Graw-Hill.

Holden, L. (2001). International human resource management. In I. Beardwell & L. Holden (Eds.), Human Resource Management: A Contemporary Approach (pp. 633-678). Third edition. Prentice Hall.

House, R.J., Wright, N.S. & Aditya, R.N. (1997). Cross-cultural research on organizational leadership: A crit-ical analysis and a proposed theory. In P.C. Earley & M. Erez (Eds.), New perspectives on international industrial and organizational psychology (pp. 535-625). San Francisco: Lexington Press.

House, R. J., Hanges, P. J., Javidan, M., Dorfman, P. W. & Gupta, V. (Eds.) (2004). Culture, leadership, and organizations: The GLOBE study of 62 societies. Thousand Oaks, CA: Sage.

Hui, C.H., Triandis, H.C. & Yee, C. (1991). Cultural differences in reward allocation: Is collectivism the ex-planation? British Journal of Social Psychology, 30, 145-157.

Huo, Y.P. & Von Glinov, M.A. (1995). On Transplanting Human Resource Practices to China: A Culture-Driven Approach. International Journal of Manpower, 16 (9), 3-11.

Inglehart, R. & Baker, W.E. (2000). Modernization, cultural change, and the persistence of traditional values. American Sociological Review, 65, 19-51.

Joshi, A. & Martocchio, J.J. (2008). Compensation and Reward system in a Multicultural Contect. In D. L. Stone & E. F. Stone-Romero (Eds.), The Influence of Culture on Human Resource Management Processes and Practices (pp. 181-205). Psychology Press & Lawrence Erlbaum Associates.

Katz, H. C. & Darbishire, O. (2000). Converging Divergences: Worldwide Changes in Employment Systems. Ithaca, NY: ILR Press/Comell University Press.

Kim, K.I., Park, H. & Suzuki, N. (1990). Reward allocations in the United States, Japan, and Korea: A comparison of individualistic and collectivistic cultures. Academy of Management Journal, 33 (1), 188-198.

Kluckhohn, C. (1951). Universal categories of culture. In D. Lerner & H.D. Lasswell (Eds.), The policy sciences. Stanford, CA: Stanford University Press.

Koubek, J. & Brewster, C. (1995). Human resource management in turbulent times: HRM in the Czech Republic. The International Journal of Human Resource Management, 6 (2), 223-47.

Koubek, J. & Vatchkova, E. (2004). Bulgaria and Czech Republic: Countries in Transition. In C. Brewster, W. Mayrhofer & M. Morley (Eds.), Human Resource Management in Europe: Evidence of Convergence (pp. 313-51)? Elsevier Butterworth-Heinemann.

Laurent, A. (1986). The cross-cultural puzzle of international human resource management. Human Resource Management, 25, 91-102.

Latham, G.P. & Wexley, K.N. (1981). Increasing Productivity Through Performance Appraisal. Addison-Wesley Publishing Company.

Lawler, E.E. (1971). Pay and organizational effectiveness: A psychological view. New York: McGraw-Hill.

Lawler, J.J., Anderson, W.R. & Buckles, R.J. (1995). Human Resource Management and Organizational Effectiveness. In Ferris, G.R., Rosen, S.D., & Barnum, D.T., (Eds.), Handbook of Human Resource Management (pp. 630-649). Blackwell Publishers.

Leung, K. & Bond, M.H. (1984). The impact of cultural collectivism on reward allocation. Journal of Personality and Social Psychology, 47, 793-804.

Leung, K. (1988). Theoretical advances in justice behavior: Some cross-cultural inputs. In M.H. Bond (Ed.), The cross-cultural chalenge to social psychology (pp. 218-229). Newbury Park, CA: Sage.

Leung, K., Smith, P.B., Wang, Z.M. & Sun, H.F. (1996). Job satisfaction in joint venture hotels in China: An organizational justice analysis. Journal of International Business Studies, 27, 947-962.

Li, J. & Karakowsky, L. (2001). Do we see eye to eye? Implications of cultural differences for cross-cultural management research and practice. The Journal of Psychology, 135, 501-517.

Lind, E.A. & Tyler, T.R. (1988). The social psychology of procedural justice. New York: Plenum Press.

Longenecker, C.O., Sims, H.P., Jr. & Gioia, D.A. (1987). Behind the Mask: The Politics of Employee Appraisal. The Academy of Management Executive, 1 (3), 183-193.

Mann, L. (1980). Cross-cultural studies of small groups. In H.C. Triandis & R.W. Brislin (Eds.), Handbook of cross-cultural psychology (pp. 77-109). Vol. 5. Boston: Allyn & Bacon.

Mowday, R.T. (1987). Equity theory predictions of behavior in organizations. In R.M. Steers & L.W. Porter (Eds.), Motivation and work behavior (pp. 89-100). New York: McGraw-Hill.

Mueller, C.W., Iverson, R.D. & Jo, D. (1999). Distributive Justice Evaluations in Two Cultural Contexts: A Comparison of U.S. and South Korean Teachers. Human Relations, 52 (7), 869-893.

Murphy, K.R. & Balzer, W.K. (1989). Rater errors and rating accuracy. Journal of Applied Psychology, 74, 619-624.

Newman, K.L. & Nollen, S.D. (1998). Managing Radical Organizational Change. Sage Publications.

Payne, R.L. (1990). The Concepts of Culture and Climate. Working paper 202, Manchester Business School.

Podsakoff, P.M., Dorfman, P.W., Howell, J.P. & Todor, W.D. (1986). Leader reward and punishment behaviors: A preliminary test of a culture-free style of leadership effectiveness. Advances in International Comparative Management, 2, 95-138.

Ramamoorthy, N. & Carroll, S.J. (1998). Individualism/Collectivism Orientations and Reactions Toward Alternative Human Resource Management Practices. Human Relations, 51 (5), 571-588.

Reis, H.T. (1984). The multidimensionality of justice. In R. Folger (Ed.), The sense of injustice (pp. 25-57). New York and London: Plenum.

Rice, R.W., Phillips, S.M. & McFarlin, D.B. (1990). Multiple Discrepancies and Pay Satisfaction. Journal of Applied Psychology, 75 (4), 386-393.

Robert, C., Probst, T., Martocchio, J.J., Drasgow, F. & Lawler, J.J. (2000). Empowerment and continuous improvement in the United States, Mexico, Poland, and India. Journal of Applied Psychology, 85, 643-658.

Rollinson, D. & Broadfield, A. (2002). Organisational Behaviour and Analysis. 2nd ed. Prentice Hall.

Saal, F.E., Downey, R.G. & Lahey, M.A. (1980). Rating the Ratings: Assessing the Psychometric Quality of Rating Data. Psychological Bulletin, 88 (2), 413-428.

Schein, E. H. (1980). Organizational psychology. New Jersey: Prentice-Hall.

Schein, E. (1985). How Culture Forms, Develops and Changes. In R.H. Kilmann, M.J. Saxton & R. Serpa et al. (Eds.), Gaining Control of the Corporate Culture (pp. 17-43). San Francisco, Calif: Jossey Bass.

Schneider, S.C. (1992). National vs. Corporate Culture: Implications for Human Resources Management. In V. Pucik, N. Tichy & C. Barnett (Eds.), Globalizing management (pp. 452-479). New York: John Wiley & Sons.

Schuler, R.S. & Jackson, S.E. (1996). Human Resource Management: Positioning for the 21st Century. Sixth edition. West Publishing Company.

Schuler, R.S. & Rogovsky, N. (1998). Understanding Compensation Practice Variations Across Firms: The Impact of National Culture. Journal of International Business Studies, 29 (1), 159-177.

Schuler R., Jackson S., Jackofsky E. & Slocum, J. (2001). Managing Human resource in Mexico: A Cultural Understanding. In Albrecht M. (Ed.), International HRM: Managing Diversity in the Workplace (pp.245-270). London: Blackwell.

Schwartz, S. H. (1994). Beyond individualism/collectivism: New cultural dimensions of values. In U. Kim, H. C. Triandis, C. Kagitçibasi, S.C. Choi & G. Yoon (Eds.), Individualism and collectivism: Theory, method and applications (pp. 85-119). Thousand Oaks, CA: Sage.

Schwartz, S. H. (2006). A Theory of Cultural Value Orientations: Explication and Applications. Comparative Sociology, 5, 136-182.

Schwartz, S. H. (2008). Cultural Value Orientations: Nature & Implications of National Differences. Unpublished manuscript, The Hebrew University of Jerusalem.

Schwartz, S. & Bilsky, W. (1987). Toward a Psychological Structure of Human Values. Journal of Personality and Social Psychology, 53 (3), 550-562.

Shamir, B. (1990). Calculations, values, and identities: The sources of collectivistic work motivation. Human Relations, 43 (4), 313-32.

Sparrow, P.R. & Wu, P. (1998). Does National Culture Really Matter? Predicting HRM Preferences of Taiwanese Employees. Employee Relations, 20 (1), 26-56.

Spector, P.E. (1982). Behavior in Organizations as a Function of Employee's Locus of Control. Psychological Bulletin, 91, 482-497.

Staw, B.M. (1980). Rationality and justification in organizational life. In B.M. Staw & L.L. Cummings (Eds.), Research in organizational behaviour (pp. 45-80). Greenwich, CT: JAI Press.

Sulsky, L.M. & Balzer, W.K. (1988). Meaning and Measurement of Performance rating Accuracy: Some Methodological and Theoretical Concerns. Journal of Applied Psychology, 73 (3), 497-506.

Sweeney, P.D. & McFarlin, D.B. (1993). Workers' evaluations of the 'ends' and the 'means': an examination of four models of distributive and procedural justice. Organizational Behavior and Human Decision Processes, 55, 23-40.

Tower, R.K., Kelly, C. & Richards, A. (1997). Individualism, collectivism and reward allocation: A cross-cultural study in Russia and Britain. The British Journal of Social Psychology, 36 (3), 331-45.

Triandis, H.C. (1995). Individualism and Collectivism. Boulder, CO: Westview Press.

Trompenaars, F. & Hampden-Turner, C. (1998). Riding the waves of culture: Understanding cultural diversity in global business. 2nd edition. New York: McGraw-Hill.

Tung, R. L. & Havlovic, S. J. (1996). Human resource management in transitional economies: the case of Poland and the Czech Republic. The International Journal of Human Resource Management, 7 (1), 1-19.

Tyler, T.R. (1987). Procedural justice research. Social Justice Research, 1, 41-65.

Von Glinov, M.A. (1985). Reward Strategies for Attracting, Evaluating, and Retaining Professionals. Human Resource Management, 24, 191-206.

Yin, R.K. (1989). Case study research: Design and methods. Newbury Park: Sage.

Zhou, J. & Martocchio, J.J. (2001). Chinese and American Managers' compensation award decisions: A comparative policy-capturing study. Personnel Psychology, 54, 15-145.

Zupan, N. & Kaše, R. (2005). Strategic human resource management in European transition economies: building a conceptual model on the case of Slovenia. International Journal of Human Resource Management, 16 (6), 882-906.

Motivation to Knowledge Transfer: Self- Determination Theory

Laurent Sié, Ali Yakhlef

With the increased interest in knowledge work, theorists have taken a keen interest in the factors that boost or diminish employees' motivation to share knowledge. Of crucial concern is: what are the effects of rewards on knowledge transfer? Why do rewards sometimes undermine and sometimes enhance employees' disposition to share their knowledge? Whereas most previous research concerned itself with the effects of formal, extrinsic rewards on knowledge transfer outcomes, the present paper uses the components of „Self-Determination Theory" – self-control, feeling of competence and social-relatedness – to investigate their effects on the transfer of tacit knowledge. To these ends we interviewed a number of scientific experts working in a large multinational oil company to find out what motivates them to share their expertise with newly-recruited engineers. Our findings seem to suggest that Self-Determination Theory provides a better explanation of experts' knowledge sharing behaviour than extrinsic rewards. Implications of the study are explored.

1. Introduction

It is conventionally held that firms can choose between two types of knowledge-based strategies: exploration vs. exploitation (March 1991). Both strategies require a great deal of knowledge transfer and knowledge sharing among organizational members. Whereas the sharing of explicit knowledge saves time, the sharing and transfer of tacit knowledge improves quality and increases innovation and signals competence to customers (Haas & Hansen 2007). Although tacit knowledge has come to be regarded as central to learning, innovation and competitiveness (Nonaka, 1994), transferring it is difficult, since as Polanyi (1996) asserts, we know tacitly more than we can tell in explicit terms. On the one hand, tacit knowledge is not easily accessible to our consciousness, while on the other it is difficult to articulate in explicit terms. Given the significance of knowledge sharing, in general, and of tacit knowledge, in particular, researchers have taken a keen interest in what motivates individuals to share their knowledge (Szulanski, 1996; Argote, McEvily & Reagans, 2003).

While there are many reasons why organizations are interested in motivating their employees to share their knowledge with their colleagues, it may not be clear why organizational members would be motivated to willingly do so if they are not rewarded for that. The logic of contribution-reward systems suggests that rewards are commonly regarded as a device to increase employees' motivation to transfer and share knowledge (Menon & Pfeffer, 2003). In general such rewards range from tangible benefits, such as money, to intangible ones, such as social recognition and acknowledgement (Gagné & Deci, 2005). By the same token, researchers make a distinction between a psychological type motivation referred to as 'intrinsic', and an economic one, referred to as extrinsic motivation (Deci 1975; Ryan, 1998). Motivation is intrinsic when an „activity is undertaken for one's immediate need satisfaction" (Osterloh & Frey, 2000, p.539). By contrast, motivation is extrinsic when it serves to satisfy indirect needs, for example money" (Osterloh, 2007, p.7). Furthermore, researchers assume that there is a tension between the two forms of motivation. If, with regard to intrinsic motivation, the ideal incentive system would lie in the meaningful work content itself (Osterloh & Frey, 2000), attempts at controlling intrinsically motivated behaviours (through, for instance the use of economic incentives and rewards) may have a negative, crowding-out' effect that may reduce performance (Osterloh & Frey, 2000), Deci, Koestner & Ryan's (1999) meta-analysis of 128 laboratory experiments tends to confirm the thesis that tangible rewards undermine intrinsic motivation (Deci , Koestner & Ryan, 1999). Using this the appropriate reward mechanism rests on the ability to distinguish between intrinsically and extrinsically driven activities and to strike a balance between them. For instance, Chesbrough and Teece (1996) sound the alarm that when the transfer of tacit knowledge is at stake, introducing market mechanisms is bad advice. The assumption is that tacit knowledge is based on intrinsic motivation and, therefore, requires other rewards than just extrinsic rewards.

The aim of the present paper is two-fold: 1) to examine the nature of tacit knowledge, suggesting that it is more associated with intrinsically-driven activity; and 2) explore the form of rewards that seems to apply to the transfer of tacit knowledge, assuming that Self-Determination Theory holds more promise in explaining the transfer of tacit knowledge. On this latter view, a feeling of competence, social relatedness and esteem, and autonomy are factors that impact positively on the motivation of individuals (Ryan & Deci, 2000) by increasing their intrinsic motivation. To understand this dynamic, we interviewed 28 knowledge workers within the field of geo-sciences who, among other tasks, are in charge of coaching newly recruited-engineers. Our study focuses on a group of experts because it is estimated that 30 per cent of them will retire in the next five years, and given that their expert knowledge involves a form of tacit and sticky (hard to transfer to others) knowledge (Szulanski, 1996), finding ways of promoting and facilitating the transfer process is of strategic importance for the company. Based on previous disappointing experience, the management was somewhat reluctant to just rely on extrinsic rewards as motivators. The argument in this paper will unfold in the following way. In the next section, we review previous accounts on expert knowledge and its links to tacit knowledge. Knowledge transfer literature tends to not discriminate between intrinsic and extrinsic motivation in the context of transfer of tacit knowledge. Self-Determination Theory is suggested as a possible framework for understanding the transfer of expert knowledge. Then, we present the method and the empirical material elicited from our respondents. Our analysis shows how the experts under consideration report on the motivation inspiring them in sharing their knowledge with newly recruited engineers. Finally, implications of the present study for the theory and practice of knowledge transfer are drawn.

2. Theoretical Background and Framework

2.1 On Expertise, Tacit Knowledge and Motivation

Polanyi's (1966) challenge that we "can know more than we can tell" lies at the heart of the difficulty of transferring this form of tacit knowledge that we may possess but cannot articulate. In these terms, tacit knowledge exists in the background of our consciousness helping our consciousness to focus on specific tasks and problems. Firstly, this implies that when a skilled performer attempts to describe or explain how to solve a certain problem to an unskilled person, they must first try to develop their own awareness of all the necessary components for the success of that performance before they can attempt to communicate these to their students (Gertler, 2003). This point is crucial for knowledge transfer, since the student plays a central role in prompting the master to become aware of how to solve the problem successfully. Were it not for the student, the master would not have reflected upon the successful outcome of the performance.

Secondly, even when s/he achieves full awareness of how to perform, there still remains the problem of expressing and communicating it because the codes of language are not well enough developed to allow clear explanation (Gertler, 2003). The best way to convey this form of knowledge is by demonstrating it: "since I cannot explain this very well, let me show you instead" (Gertler, 2003, p. 78). This is what happens in the classic master-apprentice relationship in which observation, imitation, correction and repetition are employed in the learning process (Polanyi 1966; Gertler, 2003).

In sum, the transfer of tacit knowledge assumes that 1) the master switches from the unconscious to the conscious when challenged to explain his or her skills, and that 2) the best way to prove those skills is by exhibiting and demonstrating them to an apprentice. Most important for the purpose of the present study is the point that making explicit tacit knowledge is a joint venture between master and apprentice. Furthermore, tacit knowledge can only be acquired through expertise and can only be produced in practice (Gertler, 2003).

As Ericsson and Lehman (1996) point out, experts acquire their expertise through extensive deliberate practice. Deliberate practice is defined „as the individualized training activities, especially designed by a coach or teacher to improve specific aspects of an individual's performance through repetition and successive refinement" (Ericsson & Lehman 1996, p. 278). It is not the capabilities of persons, which enable people to become experts, but it is the extended intense practice, which causes physiological, anatomical, and even neurological adaptations in the body (Ericsson & Lehman, 1996). The term „expert" is rooted in the Latin adjective „expertus", meaning experienced in and with something (Smith, 1991). In their study of the difference between expert and novice, Tanaka, Curran and Sheinberg (2005, p.145) consider that: „an obvious difference between an expert and a novice is that the former has greater exposure to objects from their domain of expertise than do novices". Hinds, Patterson and Pfeffer (2001, p.1236) add, „we consider experts to be those with both knowledge and experience in applying this knowledge to a variety of problems within the domain". Expertise involves using one's abilities to acquire, store, and utilize at least two kinds of knowledge: explicit knowledge of a domain and implicit or tacit knowledge of a field (Sternberg & Horvath 1999). The mode of acquiring expertise also becomes a crucial feature of what expertise is: in effect, experts learn by doing (Greeno & Simon, 1998). For Mieg (2001, p.2) „Experts in the literal sense are experimentalists: they know from active, reflexive experience". Foley and Hart (1992, p.234) summarize what they understand by expert in the following way: „someone who has attained a high level of performance in the domain as a result of years of experience". Since expertise comes with years of experience and since it is based on learning-by-doing, acquiring it requires a great deal of investment and interest in that domain.

2.2 Intrinsic-extrinsic Motivation

The term „motivation" in the knowledge management literature is generally used to refer to an individual's motives that energize him or her to achieve some benefits (e.g. extrinsic vs. intrinsic, Osterloh & Frey, 2000) and to achieve a certain degree of satisfaction. In the knowledge management literature, social and monetary rewards have been found as motives that facilitate and encourage knowledge transfer within organizational settings (Argote et al., 2003, Menon & Pfeffer, 2003). For instance, individuals may be primarily motivated to share information and knowledge because they want to accrue recognition and rewards or because of a desire to help their colleagues (Burgess 2005). The implication is that if the paid rewards and the perceived rewards are not in balance, the intended plans to transfer knowledge will most likely be doomed to failure (Osterloh, Frost & Frey, 2002). Correlatively, absence of motivation has negative effects on knowledge transfer (Burgess, 2005, Osterloh et al., 2002, Osterloh & Frey, 2000). Researchers have stated many reasons to explain why a person may not be willing to transfer and share their knowledge with others: „A source of knowledge may be reluctant to share crucial knowledge for fear of losing ownership, a position of privilege, superiority; it may resent not being adequately rewarded for hard-won success; or it may be unwilling to devote time and resources to support the transfer" (Szulanski, 1996, p.31). This view presumes that motivation is an explicit psychological state, which consciously guides people's behaviour. This may not always be the case since we do not sometimes know what really motivates different individuals (Burgess, 2005). Furthermore, research into knowledge-sharing behaviours is limited, for instance, we cannot explain the relationship between incentives to encourage knowledge transfer and their outcomes (Brown & Duguid, 1991; Quigley, Tesluk, Locke & Bartol, 2007).

In their study of the dynamics of motivation, Osterloh et al. (2002) emphasize two types of motivation: intrinsic and extrinsic motivation and the importance of balancing between them. Individuals are extrinsically motivated if they are able to satisfy their needs indirectly, especially through monetary compensation (Osterloh & Frey, 2000). „Money as such does not provide direct utility but serves to acquire desired goods and services, an assumption which is basic to all economic analysis" (Osterloh et al. 2002, p. 64). Extrinsically motivated coordination in firms is achieved by linking employees' monetary motives to the goals of the firm (Osterloh & Frey, 2000). Here the ideal incentive system is strictly pay-for-performance. Extrinsic rewards can take the form of recognition, increased responsibility, advancement, better supervisory relations, better peer relations, increased pay, or job security (Dermer, 1975). Extrinsic rewards are also a good signal that conveys the idea that the time experts spend sharing knowledge with newcomers is highly valued by the organization (Kogut & Zander, 1992; Pan & Scarbrough 1999), and that experts' efforts are appreciated.

In contrast to extrinsic rewards, intrinsic motives involve an activity that is undertaken for the immediate satisfaction of one's needs (Osterloh & Frey, 2000). Intrinsic motivation is „valued for its own sake and appears to be self-sustained" (Deci, 1975, p. 105, in Osterloh et al., 2002, p.64). Intrinsic motivation can be directed 1) to the activity's flow – for example reading a book, 2) to a self-defined goal – for example climbing a mountain, or 3) to the obligations of personal and social norms of their own sake, for example benevolence, identity, norms of distributive fairness and procedural fairness (Osterloh et al., 2002). Intrinsic motivation is fostered by commitment to the work itself, which must be both satisfactory and fulfilling to the employees (Dermer, 1975). Therefore, the ideal incentive system is in the meaningful work content itself (Osterloh & Frey, 2000).

As noted above, expert knowledge is acquired through years of experience and sustained interest in a certain knowledge domain. Such commitment to an area of expertise implies somehow that the expert derives a certain degree of satisfaction from his/her work. If we assume that expertise is a self-sustained professional pursuit, it is more responsive to intrinsic than extrinsic rewards. From a psychological perspective, experts are defined in terms of intrinsic characteristics because they invest time and interest in developing their expertise. But what type of intrinsic rewards would prove more appropriate to the transfer of expertise knowledge? The next section elaborates on the theory of self-determination pointing to its potential to help understand experts' motivation to share their hard-won tacit knowledge.

2.3 Self-determination Theory

Given the importance of intrinsic motivation, which is assumed to stimulate experts' commitment to their area of expertise (or tacit knowledge), it is instructive to inquire into the conditions that enhance, sustain or subdue and forestall the innate propensity that catalyses it. Theorists have developed what is called „Self-Determination Theory" (SDT) to define the factors that positively impact intrinsically motivated individuals (Ryan & Deci, 2000), propelling them to pursue their search for knowledge, which in the case of tacit knowledge means interacting with others and exhibiting their expertise in a social context consisting of peers and colleagues. The social nature of tacit knowledge transfer directs our attention to a number of social factors that enhance or impede that transfer. Among these factors, theorists have identified feeling of competence, autonomy and relatedness. As noted above, these three concepts constitute what is referred to as 'self-determination theory' (SDT).

SDT argues that the social, contextual events that are conducive to feelings of competence during an action or interaction could enhance intrinsic motivation for that interaction. Positive performance feedback from peers and superiors, for instance, was found to enhance intrinsic motivation, whereas negative feedback diminished it (Deci, 1975). Ryan (1982) added that feelings of competence would enhance intrinsically driven behaviour only if it is accompanied by a sense of autonomy, that is, by an internally perceived locus of causality (deCharms, 1968).

This amounts to saying that people must not only experience feelings of competence, but also feel that their behaviour is self-determined and caused by themselves, and not dictated from the outside. It is in this connection that some researchers hold that extrinsic rewards can undermine intrinsic motivation (Deci, 1975) because people feel that an external influence is a loss of internal control and reduction in autonomy (Lepper, Greene & Nisbett, 1973). Additionally, several studies have shown that not only tangible rewards, but also threats (Deci & Cascio, 1972), deadlines (Amabile, DeJong & Lepper, 1976), directives (Koestner, Ryan, Bernieri & Holt, 1984), competition pressure (Reeve & Deci, 1996) diminish intrinsic motivation, because they lead toward an externally perceived locus of causality (Deci et al., 1999). In contrast, choice, acknowledgement of feelings, and opportunities for self-direction were found to enhance intrinsic behaviour, confirming a sense of autonomy (Ryan & Deci, 2000). On this count, an autonomy-supporting context, in contrast to a controlling one, would incite more intrinsic motivation, encourage initiative, curiosity and a desire for challenge.

Over and above autonomy and competence, intrinsic motivation requires a third factor, namely feelings of social relatedness. Accordingly, satisfaction of the need for relatedness implies an increase in intrinsic motivation (Ryan & Deci, 2000). Because our sense of self grows in part out of our relations and interactions with others, a sense of belonging and a feeling of being part of, and appreciated by other members of the community supports intrinsically motivated action. Normally, people will be more inclined to pursue a certain type of behaviour if they feel that their social network supports and approves that. For example, students are more intrinsically motivated to learn when they experience their teachers as warm and caring. In the main, a secure, relational base appears to provide some support for intrinsic motivation.

Most research in this area tends to suggest that the social context plays an important role in facilitating or thwarting intrinsic motivation. Of crucial importance is the point that the activity itself is inherently interesting for its own sake, involving creativity and exploration. As noted above, intrinsic motivation is vulnerable to the negative impact of external control and management through the use of extrinsic rewards. Research suggests that if people are rewarded for doing what they would have done out of interest in the activity itself, they will be less likely to do it in the future if they are paid (Deci et al., 1999).

This transfer of power or control from the inside of the individual to the person who externally controls and manages the rewards will diminish intrinsic motivation. When extrinsic rewards are used to harness for some purpose that is not in harmony with the interest of the individual, it will be experienced as a loss of control and of freedom, a sense of not being the origins of their action. In contradiction, when the rewards are intrinsic to the person's self-understanding and purposeful fulfilment, when perceived as providing supporting evidence relevant to the individual's sense of freedom, of responsibility and of competence, such rewards would have positive effects.

Translated into the context of tacit knowledge transfer, we obtain the following: an organizational context that promotes experts' feeling of competence, enhances their sense of autonomy and strengthens their social ties with their colleagues and peers will encourage them to put more teeth in what they intrinsically like to do, namely share their tacit knowledge through interacting with others – a process which, as noted above, involves efforts to reflect consciously, articulate and exhibit their skills in concrete problem-solving situations. Hence, based on the assumption that intrinsic motivation is related to self-determination, the remainder of the paper explores how the experts under consideration regard the process of sharing their expertise. How is their behaviour affected by the degree of perceived autonomy in defining and deciding on their tasks, the degree to which they perceive themselves (and are perceived by their peers) as competent, and the degree to which they feel part of a social network?

Our framework (figure 1) seeks to show that in the context of expertise knowledge transfer, which is largely an intrinsic practice, rewards that are perceived as promoting self-causality, self-competence and the social status of individuals would have a positive, re-enforcing effect on the motivation to transfer knowledge. By contrast, if rewards were perceived as impairing these conditions, they would have discouraging and inhibiting effects on individuals' motivation to transfer their knowledge. This framework will guide us in generating and interpreting the information underlying this study.

As figure 1 seeks to capture, the three elements underlying self-determination theory are facilitators of tacit knowledge transfer, as tentatively illustrated in the case presented in the following section.

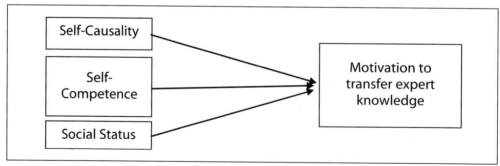

Figure 1: The effects of self-determination on the motivation to transfer tacit knowledge

3. Oilexplore: A Case Illustration

As noted above, our empirical site involves an international oil company, Oilexplore (a fictitious name), which is one of the four largest international oil companies in the world. With operations in more than 130 countries, Oilexplore engages in all aspects of the petroleum industry, including upstream operations (oil and gas exploration, development and production, LNG) and downstream operations (refining, marketing and the trading and shipping of crude oil and petroleum products). The company also produces base chemicals (petrochemicals and fertilizers) and specialty chemicals for the industrial and consumer markets (rubber processing, adhesives, resins and electroplating). In addition, Oilexplore has interests in the coal mining and power generation sectors. It is also developing renewable energies, such as wind and solar power, and alternative fuels. The company employs 96 000 people. In 2006, its sales were about 154 billion Euros. The net income was about 12.6 billion Euros for the same year, the larger part of it coming from its „upstream" activities (Oilexplore's Annual Report 2006). Oilexplore is determined to remain one of the most dynamic and successful energy groups in the world today by:
– Paying careful attention to safety and environmental protection, which allows the group to improve the reliability of its industrial plant;
– Pursuing an investment strategy aimed at profitable organic growth, leveraging its top expertise in high-growth sectors (deep offshore, LNG, heavy crudes) and implementing a wide-ranging human-resources program with the emphasis on diversity at the managerial level;
– And by maintaining good geographic diversity of both reserves and production.

One of its competitive advantages is based on its geoscientists' ability to discover new reserves in an as efficient a manner as possible (Oilexplore's Annual Report 2006). Consequently, the company is very dependent on the long-term knowledge of its experts, i.e., the tacit knowledge that is internally accumulated through years of experience. The life cycle of this expertise is fairly stable over a time span of about 30 years or even more. Within the strategic geosciences division, which is the focus of the present study, geophysicists, geologists and reservoirs engineers are regarded as knowledge workers. Their work can be described in the following way. Geophysicists derive and interpret underground images of the earth. Geologists analyse how the petroleum system is formed and what the features of the underground look like. The reservoir engineers determine the dynamic properties of the reservoir to predict the behaviour of a petroleum field, to optimize its production and to compute its reserves. If the wrong decision is made – such as drilling a well that proves unproductive –, the company will incur a very large financial loss, of approximately several million Euros. Given the high stakes involved in these decisions – decisions that can only be processed by the experts of the company – transfer of expertise is a central issue in the company. Added to this is the fact that most of those scientific experts will retire in the next 10 years. Their average age is over 50. In this field, expertise is acquired through decades of practice and learning by doing. In the face of this imminent mass retirement, the company is undertaking a number of training programs.

Training does not solve the whole problem given that the knowledge in question is tacit and thus cannot be easily transferred to newly recruited novices overnight. To these ends, the geo-science division organizes work processes in project-based and cross-age teams. In their concerted efforts to transfer knowledge to newly trained engineers and scientists, experts are taking a leading role, assuming the responsibility for teaching, transferring their expertise and guiding the novices. Our focus is thus on a number of experts in order to determine what encourages or discourages them to share their knowledge with newly recruited engineers.

As noted above, the approach used in this paper is case study. A case study is a research methodology, which focuses on understanding the dynamics within single settings (Eisenhardt, 1989). Case studies can be used for many purposes, such as to provide description, to test theory or to generate theory. The aim of the present case is to suggest a different approach to the transfer of tacit knowledge in the context of expertise. Because the concern is with testing the application of this framework the sampling is theoretical and not random. Given the unique, non-random nature of a case study, it has been a matter of some debate as to whether generalization is an appropriate requirement to demand of case study research. Of course, generalization is central, since it enables us to avoid continual repetition of the same experiences. It is in this sense that a case study is thought of mostly as a preliminary stage of an investigation to generate hypotheses.

However, researchers, mainly working from an interpretive perspective reply that an interest in generalization stems from a belief that theoretical knowledge is more valuable than practical knowledge, suggesting that one can generalize on the basis of a single case, and the case study may be central to scientific development via generalization as a supplement to other methods (Flyvbjerg, 2001, p. 425). The implication is that people can learn much that is general from a single case. Individuals are familiar with other cases through personal engagement or vicarious experience and as they add new cases, thus making a slightly new group from which to generalize, there is a new opportunity to strengthen, modify or reject old generalizations (Patton & Appelbaum, 2003). Yin (2003), for instance, points out, however, that the goal of a case study can expand and generalize theories (analytic generalization) and not to enumerate frequencies (statistical generalization). Consistent with this line of thinking, the present study aims for analytic generalizability, hopefully triggering researchers' interest in testing the utility of the present model in different contexts. The empirical material is elicited from 28 geo-scientists at Oilexplore's geosciences division. We interviewed: five experts with more than 20 years of experience, two experts retired but still working on research projects, 8 specialists, senior researchers, future experts, with more than 15 years of experience; three technical managers who managed technical teams with experts and specialists; and finally 10 less experienced scientists with less than 5 years of experience, who interact with experts. The latter are interviewed mainly in order to provide a view of how they perceive the process of transfer. The informants feature 12 different nationalities: Algerian, Angolan, Dutch, British, French, Iranian, Israeli, Lebanese, Nigerian, Norwegian, Russian, and Spanish. Interview time ranged from 50 to 120 minutes: average time was 70 minutes. During these interactions with the experts and specialists, we focused our questions on how they see their field of expertise and what motivates them to readily and willingly transfer it to younger generation. In order to know about the perspective of the novices and technical managers, our questions to them revolved around how they experience the transfer process and what, according to them, are the requirements for an effective knowledge transfer process. In order to protect the identity of the interviewees, we have used fictive names. Most of the interviews were conducted in French; the material was subsequently translated into English.

The analysis proceeded in the following way. As a first step, the verbatim transcripts from the interviews were read through to obtain a sense of the whole. Themes, i.e., threads of meaning running through the descriptions were abstracted. The material was then analysed in the light of the suggested framework and identifying emergent themes regarding the nature of expertise and the factors that amplify or reduce its transfer (Creswell, 2003, Denzin & Lincoln, 2000). As a second step, the analysis became an iterative process between the theoretical assumptions and the empirical material each informing the other.

4. Findings

4.1 The Intrinsic Nature of Expertise

The majority of the experts we interviewed consider their work as inherently interesting. Novices as well as experts emphasize the importance of curiosity and exploration as prerequisites for conducting being an expert. Nicholas summarizes his understanding of what he is doing: „When you are an expert, in general it is because you invested many years into your work, and for that you need to be curious about learning new things the whole time. To become an expert, curiosity is necessary because it enables you to develop an inquisitive and investigative mind". Adam, one of the informants we interviewed, describes why he has chosen to be a geo-scientist in the following way: „I had this 'sweet' taste for discovery and exploration: I always wanted to find out the solutions that others couldn't... I just like discovering". One is motivated in one's work as long as one is curious about one's field of interest. Frederich supports this viewpoint: „The willingness to actualize one's self and the curiosity towards one's job are hallmarks of what it is to be an expert. Of course, we should not forget social recognition and job satisfaction as further factors that determined my decision". Vincent defines job satisfaction in terms of satisfaction of his curiosity to learn: „I take pleasure in learning in order to satisfy my curiosity; if I cannot satisfy my curiosity to learn I am not happy with doing my job". What motivates John – a geo-statistician – in his work is the „Curiosity to learn, to understand and to think, it is an inner drive that sustains [his] thirst for learning". Kadder adds, „When I was a kid I liked to disassemble my toys because I was so curious about what was inside them and how they worked ... this is why I became an engineer". John said more or less the same thing: „My wife is often complaining that I cannot take my mind off my work, because even when we are on holiday, such as when climbing a mountain, I would stop and examine the stones and rocks that look unfamiliar to me". For Patrick, a former geophysical research manager: „The ideal expert has more than curiosity. S/he also needs to be passionate about the objects of their knowledge. Because this form of knowledge can only be learned by doing and through many years, one needs curiosity, enthusiasm, passion and humour". John adds that: „A true geologist has a certain relation, a physical, but not a sexual one, with stones: s/he would touch it, feel it, smell it and sometimes lick it in order to come closer to it".

In this sense, expertise is related to the emotional commitment experts invest in their knowledge. They regard enthusiasm, curiosity and passion as intrinsically bounded elements of expertise. Becoming an expert is a lengthy and painstaking process, which cannot be sustained without emotional investment and passion. In order to understand the perspective of the novices who are coached by the experts, we have asked the former about their views of what defines a good expert and the factors facilitating knowledge transfer. CB had the following to say: "The fundamental features of an expert are passion and patience. An expert needs to be passionate about what they do otherwise they will not be able to cope with the challenges that confront them. An expert has to be patient if he is to coach others and help them solve problems, learn and improve themselves". For MB "An expert needs curiosity and a willingness to help others especially in connection with challenging and complicated issues. When an expert is interested in a certain question he will willingly talk about it without even you asking him". HB, speaking specifically from his position as a learner, he says: "Personally, if I have to choose between two experts, I will prefer the one who is passionate because I know he will be more interested in my questions and consequently I will learn more from him". CM is of the opinion that "A good expert has to have pedagogical skills if he is to be able to share his knowledge". Finally, RA notes "a sign of a good expert is that his door is always open – which encourages and invites us to come in and talk to him whenever we have a question".

4.2 Autonomy

With regard to autonomy, experts have emphasized the significance of being self-determining, as GH says: "If one's role is reduced to that of implementer and executor of what others have planned and devised, it will not be interesting in the long run. One needs to have the leeway to take and to shape the thrust of what is one doing". More daringly, JLR states the following: "I am known for doing what I want; my boss used to say to me: "you always find ways of doing what you want to do; even when you are supposed to keep to operative tasks you manage to get involved in conducting research"... In truth, I would have left this company if I were not given some degree of freedom. One has to have the chance of going one's way and to decide on what one does. It is in the nature of our work to think and act differently sometime...and if I think that something is ok I do not have to wait for permission from my superior". In this vein, GM2 adds "To a certain extent we enjoy a degree of autonomy; but when we feel that we do not have enough of it we always manage to create it ... autonomy is for me a motivator; motivation is also autonomy". Conscious of what autonomy and freedom mean to experts, a manager says that "an expert cannot be managed; there is no point in being directive, the best way to deal with experts is to leave them alone; try to understand, help them realize their ideas. Most of the time, their ideas bear so much fruit that it is worth while taking the risk of giving ample freedom" (BS). This same manager believes that he succeeded to retain his experts largely because he has accorded them more freedom than competitors.

4.3 Feeling of Competence

Furthermore, what emerged as significant is the feeling of being competent; as put by Frederich: „I personally feel that public acknowledgement is a strong motivator for an expert like me … I get a feeling of satisfaction when I see that people recognize my competence in these conferences and that they really listen to what I have got to say". Another relevant statement was made by the same informant: "Doing your job well is a fundamental issue of expertise. This links expertise to the feeling of belonging to a community I previously talked about. The feeling of contributing to the collective performance is a very strong motivator to transfer knowledge" (Frederich). Finally, John who is about to retire, put it in the following way: „The fact that I am not going to stay here for long, and because I am not going to need my expertise anymore, it is crucial for me to see it lives on after I am gone...For me, money is not the issue anymore".

4.4 Social Relatedness and Expertise

Experts have emphasized the nature of expertise, implying that it is self-sustained, driven by an insatiable thirst to learn and explore new things. In this section, we discuss the role of the social context in which expertise is embedded, develops and grows. The descriptive evidence underscores the significance of the social context in creating and strengthening a feeling of self-esteem and self-confidence. David, a specialist in uncertainty assessment says that: „To have expertise without transferring it is nonsense." Because expertise is an attribute bestowed on experts by others, it can only manifest itself in social acts of sharing and helping others solve concrete problems. In the absence of sharing and transferring of knowledge, an expert would not be recognized as such. When we asked the experts about what motivates them to share their expertise and how they view the process of transferring it to younger colleagues we were surprised to learn that for them transferring knowledge is a process of learning, or rather, of co-learning. For Nicholas there is no distinction between knowledge transfer and knowledge creation: „You are neither a source only, nor just a recipient, you are both, that is, a knowledge creator. (...) it is when you are discussing with somebody that you are engaged more in a process of knowledge creation process rather than just in a transfer process. (...) You cannot learn alone, it makes no sense". Maria seconds that view: „when you work with someone else, you always learn something". John maintains that „when learners are curious and highly motivated we feel that our efforts are meaningful and thus more motivated to work with them". Adam adds that „If you are curious, if you like to discover new issues and solutions, to share your knowledge with others ... then you are able to discover new knowledge".

The upshot of these brief statements is that expertise is a social phenomenon that is nurtured in a social context. Experts justify their expertise through deploying it and it is on that basis that the status of being expert – and of being esteemed and recognized as such – is attributed to them.

4.5 The Effects of Rewards

The claim that expertise presupposes a set of intrinsic motivators, such as curiosity, enthusiasm and passion may not be consistent with external intervention: any such effort to intervene would be regarded as an intrusion into the experts' natural élan, reducing their sense of self-control. More specifically, when we asked questions about whether extrinsic rewards such as bonuses, or social recognition would impact what they intrinsically do, we received the following two types of information.

With regard to the straightforward question of whether monetary rewards would enhance their motivation to transfer/co-create knowledge, their answers are very subtle. Monetary incentives have a positive effect if they are meant to signal management's appreciation of their work in general, but not if they are regarded as a mode of intervention, aiming at changing their behaviour. Their reasoning is that, as experts, „money is not a problem for them, a bonus here or a bonus there will not make us more interested in our work. For if it were the case, we [experts] would not be where we are today" (Adam). To that, Nicholas adds: „monetary rewards will neither affect experts' curiosity to explore and search, nor their interest in their jobs". Frederich expressed himself in more explicit terms: „money is a reward for job performance but not for transferring what one knows and the extent to which one wants to know". It seems as though most experts would still transfer their knowledge if they were not paid for it, just because they are interested in their field of competence. „When one expert transfers his/her knowledge, s/he is enriching his/her field of expertise, in however small way that may be" (Nicholas). Since being interested and passion cannot be manipulated in a transactional manner, offering money as a way of manipulating them would be interpreted as a potential loss of control, with the risk of exerting a de-motivating, crowding out effect. (For more detailed descriptive evidence see appendix).

5. Discussion

It is conventionally held that rewards can be used to increase the motivation to transfer knowledge (Alavi & Leidner, 2001; Argote & Ingram, 2000; Argote et al., 2003; Cabrera & Cabrera, 2002; Cabrera et al., 2006; Goodman & Darr 1998; Hansen 1999; Hansen et al. 2005; Quigley et al., 2007; Menon & Pfeffer 2003; Spender & Grant, 1996; Szulanski, 1996). However, in the light of our findings, we need to adopt a more sophisticated approach to understand this dynamic between intrinsic and extrinsic rewards, given this context of transfer of tacit knowledge which is a body of knowledge learned through years of practice, and which is assumed to be sustained by intrinsic motivation. In line with Osterloh and Frey (2000), for intrinsically motivated individuals, the ideal incentive system would be a meaningful content of work. According to our informants, if there are to be extrinsic rewards, they should not be understood as exerting a causal effect on the experts' behaviour, but rather as a result of work well done in general terms. That is, experts do not want to account for their willingness to share their knowledge in terms of rewards – for that would affect their sense of pride and probably crowd out their intrinsic motivation; rather they try to project an image of experts who are self-controlled, and who like to be appreciated as competent and autonomous individuals. Being aware of experts' aspirations, managers place more weight on issues of freedom and social esteem than extrinsic motivation.

These intrinsically driven experts work mainly in various projects, where sharing knowledge is the basis of teamwork. For instance, when an operational geoscientist has a measurement problem that he discusses with an expert, this problem is one further case for the expert to think about, and a learning opportunity, which enriches his experience. Transferring and sharing expert knowledge is part of the expert's daily work. As noted above, the dominant logic underlying intrinsic motivation is not understood in terms of exchange value; 'in terms of only prices for work, but it is also in terms of prizes'. In this regard, experts emphasized the importance of linking rewards to organizational goals but not to individual objectives. For them, rewards should be paid only if these overall goals are achieved. The informants warned against the risk that rewards might imply: changing a culture of sharing into a culture of bargaining and transactional exchange. It was argued that the function of monetary rewards is merely a sign of recognition of experts' intellectual superiority. In this case, money is itself not a means to an end but it is a symbol of high social esteem. It stands for (or is a symbol of) something that is more coveted by the experts – namely that their bosses and colleagues hold them in high esteem. This is what explains why monetary rewards were not seen as the only motivating factor in the sharing of expertise. Experts are expecting recognition for their status as experts, not for sharing their expertise since the latter is part and parcel of being an expert. Their attachment to their field of expertise is not only a means to an end, but it is largely an end in itself – performing an activity for the pleasure and the pride of performing it and enjoying a degree of discretion while doing it. This is so because, in our case, extrinsic rewards, such as money and promotion, noted above, cannot be regarded as the causes of experts' behaviour, but as a result of a good performance. In terms of social rewards, peer recognition of an individual expert is regarded as paramount. These raise their perceived status inside the organizations, and sense of competence, affording them more credibility (Thomas-Hunt, Ogden & Neale, 2003) among their peers. Peers value experts' knowledge and afford them the status as experts. This social recognition is assumed to be highly motivating by most of the experts under consideration. Of course, as we have noted, extrinsic rewards can modify positively or negatively the relation between rewards and sharing expertise. When extrinsic rewards amplify the sense of competence, control and relational esteem, experts' motivation to share their knowledge (which is also a process of knowledge acqui-sition) is augmented. The reason is that such extrinsic rewards are not perceived by the ex-perts as attempts to displace the locus of control from the inside of experts to some oth-er external agents and to reduce their sense of autonomy. In this context, even monetary rewards would be themselves understood as a symbol of acknowledgement of their com-petence, and their social status – which are two factors that reinforce and encourage them to share their expertise and thus learn more.

Concluding Remarks

The aim of the paper was to investigate what motivates experts to transfer their knowl-edge. By first identifying expertise as a form of tacit knowledge we were then led to sug-gest „Self-Determination Theory" as a possible framework for understanding its transfer. Our main finding was that expertise is based on individual, psychological features (in that it draws on the motivation and commitment of the individual), but it is also social and relational in that it is a quality that is bestowed upon someone who discloses and practices it during problem-solving interactions with peers. Such interactions are not only oppor-tunities for experts to transfer their knowledge, but also occasions for them to learn from each particular case they encounter. It is nurtured and fostered in dialogues among groups, rather than within the innermost of an individual. Assuming its dialogical nature, expertise is a form of knowledge where learning and transferring knowledge are two processes that co-configure each other. Expertise knowledge transfer highlights an in-stance of transfer where knowledge processes (transfer and acquisition), the transmitter (expert) and the recipient are intrinsically bounded up. To the extent that there is a strong link between expertise knowledge, the source and the target, the role of external incen-tives and motivation becomes delicate. In particular, these could impact negatively if they undermine this triadic relationship, that is: a) if the expert's competence in the object of their passion is questioned, b) if its status is not recognized by peers, and, finally, c) if the expert does not feel as a sovereign source of their transfer/learning initiatives. However, extrinsic rewards will have a positive effect if they contribute to the cohesion of these three aspects of expertise knowledge transfer: (passion-driven) knowledge, (self-regulated) sources and (encouraging and supporting) feedback from recipients.

Further empirical research may investigate more explicitly the role of extrinsic motivation on this triadic relationship of this expertise knowledge transfer/acquisition process. The present study has put forward passion and curiosity as a strong predictor of tacit knowl-edge, which is intrinsically driven, and those feelings of competence, of autonomy and of self-esteem impact positively on the knowledge transfer process. The overall contribution of the paper is to suggest that acquiring (expert) knowledge is a process, which is embed-ded in social practices. It is not a private, cognitive feature of individual inwardness, but rather a practice that takes place in the public domain. Being so, its sharing and acquisi-tion are only two faces of the same coin. The passion for learning and sharing knowledge, the feeling of competence, autonomy and self-esteem cast some doubt on our conventional understanding of the effects of extrinsic motivation on knowledge transfer.

References

Alavi, M. & Leidner, D. (2001). Knowledge Management and Knowledge Management Systems: Conceptual Foundations and Research Issues. MIS Quarterly, 25 (1), 107-176.

Amabile, T. M., DeJong, W. & Lepper, M. R. (1976). Effects of externally imposed deadlines on subsequent intrinsic motivation. Journal of Personality and Social Psychology, 34, 92-98.

Argote, L. & Ingram, P. (2000). Knowledge transfer: A basis for competitive advantage of firms. Organ. Behavior Human Decision Processes, 82, 150-169.

Argote, L., McEvily, B. & Reagans, R. (2003). Managing Knowledge in Organizations: An Integrative Framework and Review of Emerging Themes. Management Science, 49 (4), 571-582.

Brown, J. S. & Duguid, P. (1991). Organizational learning and communities of practice. Organization Science, 2, 40-57.

Burgess, D. (2005). What Motivates Employees to Transfer Knowledge Outside Their Work Unit? Journal of Business Communication, 42 (4), 324-348.

Cabrera, A. & Cabrera, E.F. (2002). Knowledge Sharing Dilemmas. Organization Studies, 23 (5), 687-710.

Cabrera, A., Collins, W. C. & Salgado, J. F. (2006). Determinants of individual engagement in knowledge sharing. International Journal of Human Resource Management, 17 (2), 245-264.

Chesbrough, H. & Teece, W. D. (1996). When is Virtual Virtuous: Organizing for Innovation. Harvard Business Review, 65-73.

Creswell, J. (2003). Research design: Qualitative, quantitative, and mixed method approaches. Thousand Oaks, CA: Sage.

de Charms, R. (1968). Personal causation. New York: Academic Press

Deci, E.L. (1975). Intrinsic Motivation. New York: Plenum Press.

Deci, E.L. & Cascio, W. F. (1972). Changes in intrinsic motivation as a function of negative feedback and threats. Presented at the meeting of the Eastern Psychological Association, Boston.

Deci, E. L., Koestner, R. & Ryan, R. M. (1999). A meta-analytic review of experiments examining the effects of extrinsic rewards on intrinsic motivation. Psychological Bulletin, 125, 627-668.

Denzin, N. & Lincoln, Y. (2000). Handbook of qualitative research. Thousand Oaks, CA: Sage.

Dermer, J. (1975). The Interrelationship of Intrinsic and Extrinsic Motivation. Academy of Management Journal, 18 (1), 125-129.

Eisenhardt, K. M. (1989). Building theories from case study research. Academy of Management Review, 1 4(4), 532-550.

Ericsson, K. A. & Lehmann, A. C. (1996). Expert and exceptional performance: evidence on maximal adaptations on task constraints. Annual Review of Psychology, 47, 273-305.

Flyvbjerg, B. (2001). Making social science matter: Why social inquiry fails and how it can succeed again. Cambridge University Press.

Foley, M. & Hart, A. (1992). Expert Novice Differences and Knowledge Elicitation. In R. R. Hoffman (Ed.), The Psychology of Expertise: Cognitive Research and Empirical AI (pp. 233-269). Mahwah NJ: Springer-Verlag.

Gagné, M. & Deci, E. L. (2005). Self-Determination Theory and work motivation. Journal of Organizational Behavior, 26, 331-362.

Gertler, M. S. (2003). Tacit knowledge and the economic geography of context, or The undefinable tacitness of being (there). Journal of Economic Geography, 3, 75-99.

Goodman, P. S. & Darr, E. D. (1998). Computer-aided systems and communities: mechanisms for organizational learning in distributed environments. MIS Quarterly, 22 (4), 417-441.

Greeno, J. S. & Simon, H. A. (1988). Problem solving and reasoning. In R. C. Atkinson (Ed.), Steven's handbook of experimental psychology (2nd ed., pp. 589-639). New York: Wiley.

Haas, M. & Hansen, M.T. (2007). Different Knowledge, Different Benefits: Toward a Productivity Perspective on Knowledge Sharing in Organizations. Strategic Management Journal, 28, 1133-1153.

Hansen, M.T. (1999). The Search-Transfer Problem: The Role of Weak Ties in Sharing Knowledge across Organization Subunits. Administrative Science Quarterly, 44 (1), 82-111.

Hansen, M. T., Mors, L. & Lovas, B. (2005). Knowledge Sharing in Organizations: Multiple Networks, Multiple Phases. Academy of Management Journal, 48 (5), 776-793.

Hinds, P. J., Patterson, M. & Pfeffer, J. (2001). Bothered by Abstraction: The Effect of Expertise on Knowledge Transfer and Subsequent Novice Performance. Journal of Applied Psychology, 86 (6), 1232-1243.

Koestner, R., Ryan, R. M., Bernieri, F. & Holt, K. (1984). Setting limits on children's behavior: The differential effects of controlling versus informational styles on intrinsic motivation and creativity. Journal of Personality, 52, 233-248.

Kogut, B. & Zander, U. (1992). Knowledge of the firm combinative capabilities, and the replication of technology. Organization Science, 3 (3), 383-397.

Lepper, M. R., Greene, D. & Nisbett, R. E. (1973). Undermining children's intrinsic interest with extrinsic rewards: A test of the overjustification hypothesis. Journal of Personality and Social Psychology, 28, 129-137.

March, J. J. (1991). Exploration and exploitation in organizational learning. Organization Science, 2, 71-87.

Menon, T. & Pfeffer, J. (2003). Valuing Internal vs. External knowledge: Explaining the Preference for Outsiders. Management Science, 49 (4), 497-513.

Mieg, H. A. (2001). The Social Psychology of Expertise: Case Studies in Research, Professional Domains, and Expert Roles. Lawrence Earlbaum Associates.

Nonaka, I. (1994). A dynamic theory of organizational knowledge creation. Organization Science, 5 (1), 14-37.

Osterloh, M. (2007). Human Resources Management and Knowledge Creation. In I. Kazuo & I. Nonaka (Eds.), Knowledge Creation and Management: New Challenges for Managers. Oxford University Press, (retrieved the 2007/03/07 from http://www.iou.uzh.ch/orga/downloads/publikationen/OsterlohHRM_4.pdf).

Osterloh, M. & Frey, B. (2000). Motivation, Knowledge Transfer, and Organizational Forms. Organization Science, 11 (5), 538-550.

Osterloh, M., Frost, J. & Frey, B. (2002). The Dynamics of Motivation in Organizational Forms. International Journal of the Economics of Business, 9 (1), 61-77.

Pan, S.L. & Scarbrough, H. (1999). Knowledge Management in Practice: An Exploratory Case Study of Buckman Labs. Technology Analysis and Strategic Management, 11 (3), 359-74.

Patton, E. & Appelbaum, S. (2003). The case for case studies in management research. Management Research News, 26 (5), 60-72.

Polanyi, M. (1966). The tacit dimension. New York: Doubleday.

Quigley, N. R., Tesluk, P. E., Locke, E. A. & Bartol, K. M. (2007). A Multilevel Investigation of the Motivational Mechanisms Underlying Knowledge Sharing and Performance. Organization Science, 18 (1), 71-88.

Reeve, J. & Deci, E.L. (1996). Elements of the competitive situation that affect intrinsic motivation. Personality and Social Psychology Bulletin, 22, 24-33.

Ryan, R.M. (1982). Control and information in the intrapersonal sphere: An extension of cognitive evaluation theory. Journal of Personality and Social Psychology, 43, 450-461.

Ryan, R.M. (1998). Human psychological needs and the issues of volition, control and regulatory focus. In J. Heckhausen & C. Dweck (Eds.), Motivation and self-determination across the life span. New York: Cambridge University Press.

Ryan, R.M. & Deci, E.L. (2000). Intrinsic and extrinsic motivations: Classic definitions and new directions. Contemporary Educational Psychology, 25, 54-67.

Smith, J.A. (1991). The Idea of Brokers. Think tanks and the rise of the new policy elite. New York: Free press.

Spender, J.-C. & Grant, R.M. (1996). Knowledge and the Firm: Overview. Strategic Management Journal, 17, 5-9.

Sternberg, R.J. & Horvath, J.A. (1999). Tacit Knowledge in Professional Practice researcher and practitioner perspectives. Lawrence Earlbaum Associates.

Szulanski, G. (1996). Exploring Internal Stickiness: Impediments to the Transfer of Best Practice Within the Firm. Strategic Management Journal, 17, 27-43.

Tanaka, J. W., Curran, T. & Sheinberg, D. L. (2005). The Training and Transfer of Real-World Perceptual Expertise. Psychological Science, 16 (2), 145-151.

Thomas-Hunt, M., Ogden, T. & Neale, M. (2003). Who's really sharing? Effects of social and expert status on knowledge exchange within groups. Management Science, 49 (4), 464-477.

Yin, R.K. (2003). Case Study Research: Design & Methods (3 ed.). California: Sage Publications.

Attachment

Descriptive evidence and statements by the experts who are still working as well as 2 retired but still devoted to their work.

Experts

Curiosity and passion

«When one becomes an expert it means that one has invested a lot of time and attention in the area of expertise (…) it is a proof that one has enough curiosity to explore a large number of cases, no case can be rejected, all cases are interesting» (NK)

«Curiosity enables individuals to nourish this inquisitive sense which is necessary in order to become an expert … to be able to tackle so many cases, to resolve and draw the parallels between different cases» (NK)

«Curiosity provides you with the energy for enduring, working, coaching and sharing one's interest with others … commitment is central, I think» (NK)

«Although coaching and helping others take a lot of one's time – time that one would have devoted to tasks that are sometime very urgent, I enjoy doing it and I always give priority to coaching» (GM).

«An expert's relation to their expertise is comparable to a relationship between a couple, it is a long-term attachment and it needs to be nourished the whole time» (GH).

«Being an expert means a long-term investment, which brings satisfaction and disappointment ... you cannot claim that you know everything, for you often come across things you do not know. This may make you feel disappointed and tired; that is why one needs a lot of motivation for this kind of work» (JLR)

Autonomy

«If one's role is reduced to that of implementer and executor of what others have planned and devised it will not be interesting in the long run. One needs to have the leeway to take and to shape the thrust of what is one doing» (GH)

«I am known for doing what I want; my boss used to say to me: 'you always find ways of doing what you want to do; even when you are supposed to operate tasks you manage to get involved in conducting research'» (JLR)

«I would have left this company if I was not given some degree of freedom. One has to have the chance of going one's way and to decide on what one does» (JLR).

«An expert has to know when to say no. It is in the nature of our work to think and act differently sometime ... and if I think that something is ok I do not have to wait for a permission from my superior» (JLR)

«To a certain extent we enjoy a degree of autonomy; but when we feel that we do not have enough we manage to create it ... autonomy is for me a motivator; motivation is also autonomy» (GM2)

Competence

«When I feel that others have respect for me because of my competence, I tend to be more open and interact with others more comfortably. This is why I would not venture into a discussion with another about a certain issue when I know that I am not competent enough. Feeling competent is feeling self-confident, which makes me interact and share what I know more comfortably» (GH)

«The more competent you feel the more you likely want to reveal it to others. You do not want to show that you are incompetent because that will damage your reputation. It is a question of image too» (JLR)

Social relatedness

«I cannot isolate myself by sitting in from of my computer screen because that will not help me position myself with regard to others ... I need to interact with my colleagues in order to know what is going on, to discuss whether it is better this or that and what for. What each individual knows makes sense only when combined with that of others». (Bo)

«Our expertise increases as a result from our social networks; being appreciated by our peers is a motivator to share our views and the better the relationship with others the easier it is to interact with them» (Bo)

«It would be hard for me to stay at this company if I do not feel that I am recognized and appreciated by my colleagues. I do not only look for recognition of my peers inside the organization but also of external peers» (GH).

«Friendship relationships count a great deal; it is important to see people and to entertain those contacts to keep abreast of the ideas that circulate» (GH).

Effects of rewards

«Of course monetary rewards are necessary in a society like ours, but I derive a great deal of satisfaction from my work. This pleasure in my professional life is an indispensable element for me. The ideal is if I can strike a balance between satisfaction of doing something well and the monetary rewards ensuing from that, in other words, I would like to reach an equilibrium between personal pleasure and formal rewards» (GH).

«Formal rewards are not everything for me; if money is the main motivator I can double my salary by going to another company, given that there is a shortage in geo-scientists I can get a job anywhere I want» (JLR)

«The satisfaction I derive from work is more significant for me than financial rewards.»

«As long as I've got enough ... I was fed up because my salary was lower than that of the others; so after having grumbled for many years, the company has adjusted it up to the level of my peers» (JLR).

«To be honest, I have managed to make a good living. Although life would have been more comfortable with a higher salary, I did not care about that; what I cared for, however, was to be in par with my scientific area of interest.» (GM2)

Retired Experts

Curiosity and Passion

«A good expert is someone who has the curiosity to look into other domains in order to see whether he can make analogies and look at things from different perspectives. Although this may sound unscientific an expert must be curious. In general when one has a passion, one would like to share it with others. It seems to me paradoxical to be an expert without being committed to one's domain of expertise. What I really hope is to transmit part of my expertise to the younger generation» (B)

«An expert is someone who is systematically curious, who has an insatiable thirst to learn new things all the time» (M)

«If I now continue working, although officially retired, I only do it for the pleasure» (M)

Autonomy

«It is not the money that interests me. At the same time I do not want to have any pressure on me; I do not want to be a constraint» (B).

«Sometimes I keep on working until 3 o'clock in the morning from my own free will; nobody is asking me to do it. I organize and plan my work as I please. At other times I do not feel like working. I want to be in command of my own life. I appreciate this freedom to work and practice my expertise» (B)

«Exercising my expertise has become a basic need for me, I cannot do without it» (M)

Competence

«We should not forget that an expert is very sensitive to feedback; there is a need to get assurance that one is recognised and appreciated by others» (B).

«It is always flattering to help somebody who needs our expertise; it is a sign that we have a good reputation» (M)

Social relatedness

«It is when interacting with others that I become aware of new things, such as when young engineers ask questions that on the surface would sound naive but which in fact are thought-provoking, which is a learning opportunity for me (laughter). Being retired means that I now have less of this contact and these relationships with others» (B).

«I think that in my age, one has to share with others what one has learned over the years; this is why teaching and giving seminars are one of my greatest joys these days». (M)

Effects of rewards

«I enjoy working and I work more when there are no control constraints hanging over me. I think that too much intervention in our work would kill our natural inclination to our domain; one cannot work under pressure» B.

Work-life Balance Accounts and Total Compensation –
An Analysis of the Regulation of Work-life Balance Accounts in Collective Agreements in Germany

Lars W. Mitlacher

Although there is a voluminous literature on the determination of the amount paid to employees and on selected components of total compensation systems like pay for performance programs, surprisingly little research has been conducted on work-life balance accounts as a part of a total compensation approach. As the promotion of pay components as well as the design of total compensation systems is prominently influenced by evolving and existing regulation in collective agreements it is important to analyze the different objectives that the actors of the employment relations system address during the bargaining process. By analyzing two collective agreements on work-life balance accounts, the paper aims at examining the goals that the actors in the employment relations system follow with regard to work-life balance accounts and consequently how work-life balance accounts fit as a part of a total compensation system.

Introduction –
Work-life Balance Accounts and Total Compensation

The demographic development in industrialized countries is characterized by two trends (Staudinger, 2006): Low fertility rates and a rising life expectancy lead to shrinking populations and an increasing average age of the population. The demographic change will have several consequences for societies and companies as well. First, a decrease of effective labor supply is expected, as many workers from the baby-boomer generation will reach retirement age in the upcoming years (Staudinger, 2006). Challenges of this demographic change are securing a steady labour supply as well as finding new ways for a transition into retirement (Flynn, 2010; Henkens et al., 2008). The labour market will shift from a demand-driven market, in which companies are in a leading position, to a more supply-driven market, with employees having more bargaining power. Consequently, many employers will be struggling to cope with this structural shortage of labour (Börsch-Supan, 2002).

Thus companies are forced to develop more sophisticated HR instruments to attract and retain the needed workers. Traditionally compensation issues have played an important role in attracting and retaining employees. It is important that pay components create and maintain a competitive advantage on the labour market (Mathis & Jackson, 2009). Especially in firms with more highly educated employees indirect pay components or employee benefits make up a higher proportion of total compensation (Long & Shields, 2009) and have been in the focus of companies when designing pay systems. Work-life balance accounts represent one option for indirect pay. However, as benefits are costly for employers it is important that new employee benefits fit with the existing total compensation strategy and can be integrated into the existing total compensation system as well as support the strategic goals of the employer. As issues of pay and working time are at the heart of the bargaining process between employers and unions, an interesting question is how organized labour, most notably trade unions, copes with this new challenge. The aim of the paper is thus to discuss the different goals that the actors in the employment relations system follow with regard to work-life balance accounts and how work-life balance accounts fit as a part of a total compensation system.

The paper is structured as follows. After this introduction, a short discussion on total compensation systems, union influence and how work-life balance accounts work is given followed by an overview of the current legal regulation on work-life balance accounts. In a next step an overview and critical assessment of the current debate on total compensation systems and work-life balance accounts in the literature is given. Based on the results a conceptual framework is developed to assess the goals of the different actors in the employment relations system with regard to work-life balance accounts. Then, two collective agreements on work-life balance accounts and demographic change are analysed in order to address the question how the collective agreements support the goals of the different actors and if they shore up work-life balance accounts as a component of total compensation systems. A summary of the key results and further avenues for research conclude the paper.

Work-life Balance Accounts, Unions and Total Compensation Systems

Companies have to decide on two main types of questions when designing total compensation systems. First of all, companies have to determine the total amount of pay that they offer different groups of employees. The second aspect concerns the pay mix and the weighting of the different components of the remuneration system. It is surprising that this second aspect of the design of pay systems has not been extensively researched so far (Long & Shields, 2009). Especially unionized companies have little freedom in deciding about the amount of pay they offer but have more choice when it comes to settle the components included in their pay mix (Gerhart & Milkovich, 1990). It is not unexpected though that many companies follow a total compensation approach to have more freedom in determining the total amount of pay offered. At this point it is important to note that the concept of total compensation does not include all the rewards offered to employees (Vandenberghe et al., 2008) but only comprises the financial rewards provided by the company or the components that can be very easily provided with a financial equivalent. Therefore a company pension plan – whether it is fully employer or employee financed or even financed by contributions from both parties – would be a part of the total compensation concept. On the other hand a recreation room would not be part of the total compensation concept but would be included in the wider approach of total rewards (Mathis & Jackson, 2009), which is not the scope of the paper. Following this definition, work-life balance accounts can be considered as a part of a total compensation system, as they can be either employer financed, employee financed or have mixed contributions.

Four different components of a total compensation system can be considered. This includes a base salary, pay-for-performance components, employee share or stock option ownership plans and forms of indirect pay or employee benefits (Mathis & Jackson, 2009) such as pension plans or work-life balance accounts.

The first component, the fixed base pay, is guaranteed on an hourly, weekly, monthly or annual basis and based on the job requirements (Mathis & Jackson, 2009).

The second element, performance based pay, can either focus on the individual performance or the performance of a group (Brown & Heywood, 2005). Additionally, as individual contributions in many jobs are difficult to identify, many companies increasingly supplement individual performance measures with group, (business) unit or company-wide performance indicators (Rynes et al., 2005). Trade unions have not been very supportive of pay for performance plans to be included in their collective agreements. For instance there is evidence that the deployment of profit sharing plans is negatively associated with union presence in companies (e.g. Jones & Pliskin, 1997; Kruse, 1996; Cooke, 1994). Other studies show a negative relationship between individual performance based pay and unionized companies (e.g. Geddes & Heywood, 2003). This is not surprising as unions have traditionally preferred less pay differentiation between their members to increase member solidarity (Heery, 1997). However, in Germany there have been some collective agreements that have introduced small components of performance related pay lately (e.g. the ERA or the TVÖD).

Third, employee share plans or stock option plans grant employees' shares or stock options of the employing organization or offer these at a specific discount (Voß, 2003). Again, in unionized companies, at least in North America, employee stock plans are less common than in non-unionized firms (Kruse, 1996; Jones & Pliskin, 1997).

Finally, indirect pay components include a variety of benefits, which are not considered direct cash compensation but contribute significantly to a companies' compensation expenditure (Long & Shields, 2009). Studies show that in unionized companies indirect pay components constitute a higher proportion of total compensation than in non-union settings (Renaud 1998; Milkovich & Newman, 2002) indicating that employers use these components as an alternative strategy to influence the total amount of pay offered while at the same time unions also have a focus on these benefits as they are preferred by their members and support the acquisition of new ones. Therefore it can be expected that employers and unions will have a large interest in reaching an agreement on the regulation of work-life balance accounts for different reasons.

In most of the existing models of work-life balance accounts, employees are able to deposit different rewards into their account (Kümmerle et al,. 2006). For example, it is possible to deposit overtime hours, not used vacations, variable pay components or even parts of the fixed salaries into a work-life balance account (Kümmerle, 2007). The time contributions are converted into monetary values based on the current salary of an employee. That means if someone contributes one hour of overtime work into the work-life balance account and earns 20 € per hour, then 20 € are deposited to his account. This clearly shows that work-life balance accounts are regarded as a part of the total compensation system. Some employers subsides the deposits of their employees for example, if an employee deposits 100 € the employer might pay an additional 50 € as a bonus into the work-life balance account. This incentive has the intention to increase the number of participants (Kümmerle et al., 2006). The deposits of the accounts are then invested on the capital market, either in bonds or shares, whereas the proportion of shares is restricted to a maximum of 20% by law but changes can be made if a collective agreement is in place (Bothe, 2009b). The earned interests are then redistributed to the employees' accounts and the employees can deploy the amount saved for different purposes.

Legal Regulation of Work-life Balance Accounts

The deployment of work-life balance accounts in Germany is regulated in different laws. First of all there are taxation rules that have to be considered. The most important rule is that during the deposit phase there is no taxation. Taxes have to be paid if the money is withdrawn from the account (Moog & Wellisch, 2005). The same rule applies to paying social security contributions (Wonnenberger, 1999). Besides these general rules, a special regulation for work-life-balance accounts exists in Germany. The so-called Flexi-II regulation has altered the former Flexi regulation in several ways. What has been unchanged is that in the savings period the contribution to the work-life balance account is tax-free and no social security contributions have to be paid (Moog & Wellisch, 2005). However, there are new rules in place that improved the protection of the accounts in the case of insolvency of the employer (Kümmerle et al., 2006). If the employee wants to use the money of his work-life balance account he or she has several legal claims against the employer. According to Flexi II the employee is entitled to use the work-life balance account for part-time work, an earlier retirement, a longer maternity leave and for elderly care (§ 7 SGB IV). Exceptions to this rule are possible if a collective agreement allows it and hence company specific models could also include exceptions. In the case that the employment relationship is terminated before the employee claims his work-life balance account, the balance can either be transferred to the new employer or to the German public retirement insurance. Additionally, the employee has the right to get the amount paid out at the time

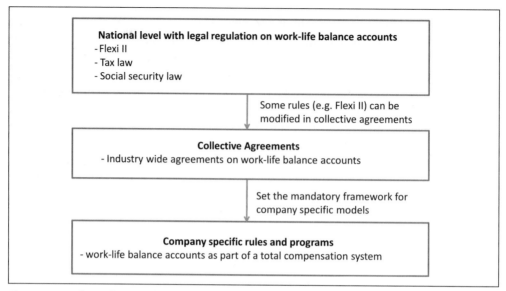

Figure 1: Legal regulation of work-life balance accounts

he leaves the company, but has to pay taxes as well as social security contributions (Kümmerle et al., 2006).

In the German system of industrial relations, regulation concerning pay components can mainly be found at the level of collective agreements. With regard to work-life balance accounts it can be stated that today only a few collective agreements on this topic have been closed. As work-life balance accounts are not very widespread yet in the German economy, collective agreements play a special role in promoting work-life balance accounts in specific industries as they set the frame for company specific regulations and models. Therefore the focus of (empirical) analysis will be on regulation concerning work-life balance accounts in collective agreements and their impact on the design of these accounts as a component of a total compensation system. Figure one summarizes the different levels of regulation for work-life balance accounts.

Literature Review on Work-life balance Accounts

In order to examine the research question, the relevant levels of employment relations' activities with regard to work-life balance accounts have to be analysed. To facilitate an understanding of the strategies of the different actors involved, existing and current research on work-life balance accounts was analysed. The literature was probed for articles focusing on the topic of work-life balance accounts in the context of total compensation systems and union influence. The research focused on the years 2008 until 2010 as the regulation on work-life balance accounts has seen many changes in this period and many companies just recently have considered introducing such accounts. Three primary search processes were deployed. The initial search began with searching in leading German academic journals of business administration and HRM for articles related to work-life balance accounts and total compensation. The journals included in the search are ZfBF, Die Betriebswirtschaft, Zeitschrift für Personalforschung, Industrielle Beziehungen and BFuP. The search did not lead to any significant results. Articles focusing on work-life balance accounts (here the natural language term "Zeitwertkonten" was used as a search item) have so far not been published in these journals and the search term total compensation just led to three articles in the period analysed. A combination of the search terms with union influence did also not lead to any studies available. In a second step the research was extended to leading academic journals of business administration and HRM that are published in English. Here the Academy of Management Journal, Academy of Management Review, International Journal on Human Resource Management, HRM Review, Administrative Science Quarterly and Industrial Relations were included in the search. Again the search terms work-life balance accounts and total compensation were applied independently and in combination with union influence. Once more the search did not generate any results on work-life balance accounts and only one article dealt with total compensation and focused on the influence of unions on the pay mix. As the topic has not been addressed in the academic literature so far, the search was extended to include practitioner-oriented journals. Here the WISO database was used which includes many German practitioner oriented HRM journals. As the regulation of work-life balance accounts is also in the focus of the article, journals that relate to labour law topics were also included in the search. Again the term "Zeitwertkonten" was used. The search identified twenty-two studies, which mainly focus on the change in regulation on work-life balance accounts. This hints at the rising importance of the topic in the German corporate community. Table one summarizes the identified studies on work-life balance accounts and total compensation systems.

As the analysis shows, studies that focus on the role of work-life balance accounts as a component of a total compensation system and the role that trade unions and the regulation in collective agreements play in supporting work-life balance accounts are missing so far in the literature. Thus in the following sections the paper focuses on the regulation of work-life balance accounts and analyses two collective agreements in order to find out how these agreements support the goals of the different actors in the employment relations system with regard to work-life balance accounts. In order to analyse this question a conceptual framework will be developed to serve as guidance for the remainder of the analysis.

Table 1: Results of the literature review

Author	Year	Journal & focus of journal	Focus of paper	Results
Ars et al.	2009	Betriebs-Berater/p	Theoretical/WLBA	Rules and legal regulation on WLBA
Aubert	2008	ZfP/a	Empirical (Best Practice)/TC and employee share purchase plan	Implementation of a ESPP (Best Practice)
Bothe	2009 a	Vermögen & Steuern/p	Theoretical/WLBA	Accounting rules for WLBA
Bothe	2009 b	Personalwirtschaft/p	Theoretical/WLBA	Legal discussion on new regulation of WLBA
Cisch/Ulbrich	2009	Betriebs-Berater/p	Theoretical/WLBA	Legal discussion on new regulation of WLBA
Duber	2009	Personalwirtschaft/p	Theoretical/WLBA	WLBA as a supplement for company pension plans
Gillekirch	2008	BFuP/a	Theoretical/Best Practice examples TC	Pay systems for managers
Hamisch	2008	Arbeit und Arbeitsrecht/p	Theoretical/WLBA	Legal regulation and rules on WLBA
Hasebrook/Maurer	2009	Bank & Markt/p	Theoretical/WLBA	Work-life balance accounts as instrument for pay flexibility
Heidemann	2010	Versicherungspraxis/p	Theoretical/WLBA	Description of WLBA and legal regulation
Kast	2009	Wirtschaftspsychologie/p	Theoretical/WLBA	WLBA as part of personnel development programs
Katheder/Kast	2010	Kreditwesen/p	Theoretical/WLBA	Best practice examples of WLBA
Klemm	2009	Personalmagazin/p	Theoretical/WLBA	Rules and legal regulation on WLBA
Klemm	2010	Personalmagazin/p	Theoretical/WLBA	Rules and legal regulation on WLBA
Long/Shields	2009	Industrial Relations/a	Empirical/TC	Union influence on mix of compensation methods used by employers
Reich	2008	Arbeit und Arbeitsrecht/p	Theoretical/WLBA	Rules and legal regulation on WLBA
Reichel/Köcheritz	2009	Arbeit und Arbeitsrecht/p	Theoretical/WLBA	Rules and legal regulation on WLBA

Table 1: Continuation

Author	Year	Journal & focus of journal	Focus of paper	Results
Steger/Hartz	2008	ZfP/a	Empirical/TC & employee ownership	Influence of the introduction of employee ownership components on the power relations in companies
Steinhaus/ Uckermann	2010	Vermögen & Steuern/p	Theoretical/WLBA	Rules and legal regulation on WLBA
Timmermann	2010	Vermögen & Steuern/p	Theoretical/WLBA	Examples of WLBA
Uckermann	2008	Betriebs-Berater/p	Theoretical/WLBA	Rules and regulation on WLBA
Vom Feld	2009	Personalwirtschaft/p	Theoretical/WLBA	Legal rules and regulation on WLBA
Wellisch	2008	Personalmagazin/p	Theoretical/WLBA	Accounting rules on WLBA
Wellisch/Machill	2008	KoR/p	Theoretical/WLBA	Accounting rules on WLBA
Wellisch/Machill	2009	Betriebs-Berater/p	Theoretical/WLBA	Accounting rules for WLBA
Wellisch et al.	2010	Personalwirtschaft/p	Empirical/WLBA	Study on deployment of WLBA in Germany

TC = Total compensation; WLBA = work-life balance accounts; p = practitioner focus; a = academic focus; ESPP = employee share purchase plan

Strategic Human Resource Management, Strategic Choices and Work-life Balance Accounts

In many companies, Human Resource Management (HRM) has often not been included into the strategic management process (Tichy et al., 1982). Instead the focus has been on operative tools and procedures that lead to neglecting strategic issues in the field of Human Resource Management. However, as strategy deals with the different choices that companies have to create competitive advantage, HR issues have come on the agenda of strategic management. Many studies have addressed the question how organizational and external factors shape HRM strategies and instruments (Schuler & Jackson, 1989). A vast number of variables have been identified that influence the design of HRM instruments, for example the business strategy, demographic developments, union activities, leadership style, technological and economic trends, political and legal regulation or the structure of the internal labour market (Hambrick & Snow, 1987; Galbraith, 1983; Kochan, McKersie, & Cappelli, 1984; Schuler, 1992; Delery & Doty, 1996). With regard to company performance, studies indicate that a coordinated practice across all HR instruments is necessary as well as the interaction between business and HR strategy (Youndt et al., 1996, Wright & Snell, 1991). This means that companies have to achieve an "internal fit" (Wright & McMahan, 1992) between HR instruments and the HR and business strategy as well as an "external fit" between their strategy, HR instruments and external factors that influence their business. In the external environment there is a vast variety of factors that influence the business of organizations and subsequently their business success. For example, the volatility of markets, technological developments, changes in regulation or the demographic change (Miller, 1988; Streb et al., 2009) have an impact on organizational effectiveness. These factors also influence the development of the business und HR strategy. Based on the strategic decisions the HRM instruments are chosen that are contributing to the organizations strategic goals and performance (Delery & Doty, 1996). These are for example training and development, profit sharing, employee ownership, job design and appraisal measures (Youndt et al., 1996; Delaney & Huselid, 1996). This means that the total compensation system of a company must also include strategic components to contribute to a companies' effectiveness (Boyd & Salamin, 2001), e.g. by supporting cost flexibility. The effectiveness of total compensation systems also depends on situational factors and strategic choices of different actors in the industrial relations system.

Therefore the strategic HRM approaches have to be extended by an industrial relations perspective. For that reason the strategic choice approach developed by Kochan, Katz and McKersie (1994) will be used to analyse the role of the social partners and the strategic choices associated with using work-life balance accounts as parts of total compensation systems. The basis for the strategic choice approach is the input-conversion-output model developed by Dunlop (1958). Based on the general assumptions of Dunlop's approach the framework incorporates besides this traditional theory of industrial relations, insights from corporate strategy research, institutional factors and structures as well as research concerning decision making (see for the following Kochan et al., 1994). Figure two shows the modified version for analysing activities of different actors in the employment relations system with regard to work-life balance accounts.

The approach starts with considering the relevant external forces that influence the employment relationship. These factors lead companies to make adjustments in their business strategy. The number of possible options is constrained by the values prevailing in the organisation as well as by historical decisions and structures. A key premise of the approach is that the system of employment relations is affected by the choice of management, employees and government (Kochan et al., 1994). This choice takes place in an institutional structure in which employee-management interactions occur. While other theories like neoclassic economics or behavioural or social science theories regard institutional factors as a black box, the suggested framework tries to identify these institutional forces that influence activities in the employment relations system (Kochan et al., 1994). The activities of the actors (management, employees or their representatives and the government) are divided into three tiers: long-term strategic activities (policy making), collective

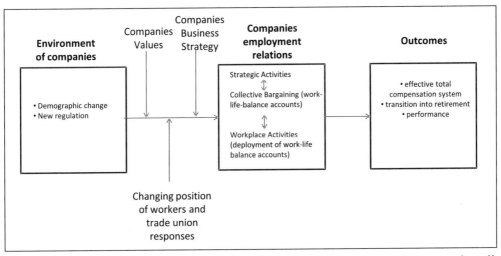

Figure 2: Modified framework for analysis (Modified from Kochan, Katz and McKersie (1994))

bargaining (personnel policy) and workplace relationships (individual-organization relationship) (Kochan et al., 1994). This is shown in table two.

With regard to work-life balance accounts the actors involved in the employment relations
system follow different strategies and try to accomplish different objectives on different
levels of the employment relations system through bargaining. The results of this bargaining process are collective agreements, which are the focus of analysis in the empirical part
of this paper.

Table 2: Strategic choices (Modified from Kochan et al. (1994))

Level	Employers & their associations	Unions	Government
Strategic	Business strategy, negotiation strate-gies	Political strategies	Social policies, labour law, transition into retirement
Collective bargaining	HR policies, negotia-tion strategies	Collective bargaining strategies	Collective bargaining regulation
Workplace	HR instruments (work-life-balance accounts)	Job quality, worker participation and representation	Job quality, labour standards, worker participation rights

Goals of Employers and their Associations

Strategic Level

One of the central concerns is that the applied HR instruments support the overall business strategy and ensure competitive advantages (Tichy et al., 1982). As a consequence of the demographic development, globalization processes and technological developments the demand for skilled employees will increase (Backes-Gellner, 2004). Historically, in Germany a demographic structure that was known as the age pyramid has prevailed for a long time (Statistisches Bundesamt, 2009). However, in the early 1970s the data from the German Federal Statistic Office showed the beginning of an imbalance of the age pyramid. As the number of births declined rapidly the pyramid began to change, with the bottom melting away and the peak becoming wider as life expectancy rose as a consequence of rising living standards, better health care and nutrition as well as advances in hygiene (Statistisches Bundesamt, 2009). Today this trend continues with the proportion of younger people declining and the number of old people increasing at the same time (Statistisches Bundesamt, 2009). Consequently, skilled workers have become critically scarce or are expected to become scarce in the upcoming years (Kalinowski & Quinke, 2010; Hummel et al., 2010). The need for motivated and skilled employees has become crucial for achieving competitive advantage (Brewster & Suutari, 2005; Thom & Zaugg, 2004). As studies show, companies are already competing strongly for talent (Ng & Burke, 2005). Therefore companies are looking for new strategic ways to deal with the problems associated with demographic change. One approach has been to start negotiations with the social partners to reach an overall agreement on dealing with this problem, including new instruments like work-life balance accounts in these agreements.

Level of Collective Bargaining

On the level of collective bargaining the strategic goals have to be specified. Most companies claim to deploy sophisticated pay components like pay-for-performance systems as part of their compensation strategy (Rynes et al., 2005). Total compensation systems should motivate employees to a better performance through either variable pay components or more individual choices concerning the composition of their pay. According to principal agent theory, performance based pay is one way to reduce agency problems (Gibbons, 1998). The idea behind this assumption is that although money does not provide direct utility it can be used to acquire desirable goods or services and is thus regarded as extrinsic motivation. On the contrary, intrinsic motivation emerges if an activity is undertaken for immediate satisfaction (Calder & Staw, 1975) and even though intrinsic motivation seems to be self-sustained it can be directed to social norms like for example aspects of distributive or procedural fairness (Fehr & Gachter, 2000; Tyler, 1994). As Herzberg has shown, intrinsic motivation is enhanced by commitment to work itself so it is necessary to give people a satisfying job with choices and autonomy (Kohn, 1999).

However, both forms of motivation are not additive as standard economic theory would suppose (Milgrom & Roberts, 1992) but studies have shown (Deci & Flaste, 1995; Frey & Oberholzer-Gee, 1997) that both types of motivation are rather endogenous variables. Crowding out effects that are based on cognitive evaluation theory (Deci, 1975) and psychological contract theory (Rousseau, 1995) lead to a weakening of intrinsic motivation if organization members perceive external incentives like flexible pay as controlling (Osterloh et al., 2002). Thus, variable pay components should try to achieve a balance between intrinsic and extrinsic motivation. Work-life balance accounts offer one possibility of combining both aspects. On the one hand employees are able to contribute variable pay components like bonus payments into the account while on the other hand they have a certain degree of autonomy of how to use the account later on. While the first contributes to enhancing the extrinsic motivation, the choices associated with the deployment of work-life balance accounts aims at intrinsic aspects of motivation.

Another challenge is to secure that employees have the necessary skills to fulfil their tasks. As personnel development programs have been identified as a leading driver of competitive advantage (Aragon-Sanchez et al., 2003), developing talent and retaining core employees are central tasks of HR (Brewster & Suutari, 2005). Therefore collective agreements on work-life balance accounts should regulate that employers and employees can deploy the money saved in the accounts for educational purposes. Work-life balance accounts can be installed as an instrument to enhance the employability of workers if the employees can use their accounts to take time off for instance for study purposes.

Besides motivational aspects, employers deploy total compensation systems to be more flexible to react to external changes such as the demographic development. Especially many German companies have in the past tried to send elder workers into earlier retirement with the goal of creating a younger workforce age structure and to reduce their workforce over all (Voelpel et al., 2007). As the mandatory retirement age will rise in the future and workers have to stay on their jobs for a longer time, flexible instruments are needed for allowing a smooth and individual transition into retirement for every single employee. A smooth and flexible transition into retirement does not only improve the employer branding and image but also reduces a loss of know-how, recruitment costs and allows for a better knowledge transfer (Nägele & Frerichs, 2004). Work-life balance accounts can be used as an instrument to give employees flexibility with regard to a transition into retirement. For example the accounts can be used to finance a longer period of part-time work before retirement without a pay reduction. Or they enable employees to quit working before reaching the mandatory retirement age by financing their additional time off through the savings in their work-life balance accounts.

Workplace Level

On the workplace level companies are interested in having flexibility to alter the rules of collective agreements to fit their company specific situation. With regard to total compensation systems companies are especially interested in achieving a fit of their current pay system and the new regulation on work-life balance accounts. A central question here is how work-life balance accounts can be combined with other components of the pay system – like for example pay-for-performance components – and how these components can be deployed as a basis for deposits into the work-life balance accounts.

Unions' Goals

Strategic Level

There are multiple reasons for skilled labour shortage in industrialized countries. One central concern of unions is of course the emerging new understanding of the employment relationship. As employment relationships have become more contractual, atypical employment relationships like temporary agency work have been rising in OECD countries (Mitlacher, 2008). In this context employability becomes a major aspect, as employees need skills that are usable with different employers. The significance of continuous learning in the workplace has become more important as technological developments as well as a permanent changing environment are shifting qualification needs enduringly (Morschhäuser et al., 2003). As studies show, when it comes to personnel development programs, the participation rate especially of elder workers is significantly lower than that of younger workers (Kuwan et al., 2003). As demographic change requires older workers to stay longer in the workforce, it is necessary to improve their participation in training measures. As already discussed, work-life balance accounts are one instrument to support this development as they allow workers in different phases of their working life cycle to take time off for study purposes, for instance going back to university to study for a post-graduate degree.

Another concern for unions is the transition into retirement. As social security systems have been reformed and government subsidized early retirement and Altersteilzeit (part-time retirement) have been abolished, unions are looking for new ways to enable their members an early retirement. This is especially important for workers in physically demanding jobs associated with high risks for their health and well-being. As empirical studies for Germany show, most workers would prefer a flexible and smooth transition into retirement that fits with their own personal needs (e.g. Deller et al., 2008). This shows that employees prefer in some cases to continue working even beyond the mandatory retirement age if flexible working arrangements are available (Hertel et al., 2003). A study by Dielmann (2007) shows, that 44% of the surveyed employees would like to continue working after reaching the mandatory retirement age. Work-life balance accounts offer one possible way to meet the demands of employees for either an earlier retirement or for staying in the job longer with a flexible transition into retirement still being possible.

Level of Collective Bargaining

With regard to total compensation systems, two essential questions have to be answered. The first is the determination of the total amount of pay that employees receive; the second is which components the pay system contains. As the total amount of pay has traditionally been the central concern of the unions (Mathis & Jackson, 2009), the pay mix has often been neglected. Thus a fundamental concern on the level of collective agreements is the regulation of the new pay component work-life balance accounts. That these indirect pay components are a focus of union strategies is also shown by results of studies on fringe benefits. Studies indicate for the US and Canada that indirect pay components constitute a higher share of total compensation in unionized than in non-unionized companies (Milkovich & Newman, 2002; Renaud, 1998). With regard to work-life balance accounts as a new indirect pay component several aspects are important from an employee's perspective. First, as work-life balance accounts are a new method of pay, it is important for unions to bargain for a high level of this new pay component. In an ideal world there would be a high proportion of employer-financed contributions to the accounts. As unions traditionally focus on the security of the income of their members (Long & Shields, 2009) it is important that work-life balance accounts are protected against insolvency and bankruptcy of the employers in order to avoid that workers bear the risk of losing their job and their retirement benefits. Another aspect is the deployment of the amount saved in the accounts. As noted earlier, transition into retirement is one major aspect as the average union member tends to be older (Renaud, 1998) but – as a consequence of demographic change and changing employment relationships – the deployment of the saved amounts for a sabbatical or for educational purposes is also a goal that unions try to achieve with work-life balance accounts.

Workplace Level

On the workplace level the union's main role is the support of the works councils as the work councils negotiate the workplace agreements with the employers. Here the focus of employee representatives will be to bargain company specific agreements with specific regulation for special groups of employees (e.g. workers on rotating shifts). In this case the bargaining strategy depends on the business model and for example on the production methods applied. Therefore the collective agreement should provide some flexibility to allow for company specific agreements.

Government and its Goals

As the government is not directly involved in the collective bargaining process in the German system of employment relations, a detailed analysis will not be the scope of the paper. However, the government sets the rules and regulation for work-life balance accounts.

Thus, it influences bargaining processes as it sets a mandatory legal framework for the actors. With regard to work-life balance accounts, the government's central goal is to provide an alternative instrument for a smooth transition into retirement (Deutscher Bundestag, 2002) while at the same time allowing the social partners to reach industry and company specific agreements. The introduction of the new Flexi II law clearly follows this approach. Thus in the following section is has to be analysed if the collective agreements support this goal.

The following table summarizes the goals that the different actors of the German system of employment relations have with regard to the installation of work-life balance accounts.

Table 3: Goals of the different actors concerning work-life balance accounts (WLBA) (Modified from Kochan et al. (1994))

Level	Employers and their associations	Unions	Government
Strategic	Dealing with demographic change WLBA as part of HR and compensation strategy	Dealing with demographic change WLBA as an alternative way for early retirement and enhancing employability	Dealing with demographic change Transition into retirement Framework for regulation on WLBA
Collective bargaining	WLBA as an instrument for transition into retirement, personnel development, motivation of employees and performance enhancement	High employer contributions to WLBA, protection against insolvency, different options of deployment of saved amounts	Specific rules in the WLBA regulation that can be disposed off by social partners
Workplace	Specific workplace agreements on WLBA to increase company specific flexibility and ensure fit with existing pay system	Specific workplace agreements on WLBA with regard to special groups of employees (e.g. workers on rotating shifts)	Regulation to ensure job quality, labour standards, protection of special groups

Analysis of Collective Agreements on Work-life Balance Accounts

Methodology and Sample

The literature review reveals that work-life balance accounts in connection with total compensation systems and the different goals that the diverse actors of the employment relations system pursue have not been comprehensively addressed in the academic literature. In order to close that gap the paper undertakes a detailed document and content analysis (Yin, 2003; Preuss et al., 2006) of two German collective agreements on work-life balance accounts, serving as exemplary cases for regulation of work-life balance accounts.

Regulation concerning work-life balance accounts can be found on different levels in the German system of industrial relations. There are three possible forms of regulation. Besides the regulation on a national level e.g. labour law regulations, agreements on the workplace level, most regulation concerning total compensation systems can be found in collective agreements as the unions and employer's associations have the right to negotiate wages which are then laid down in collective agreements. Applying the criteria suggested by Scott (1990) for judging evidence retrieved from documents – authenticity, representativeness, clarity, credibility and comprehensibility of meaning – collective agreements in general and collective agreements on work-life balance accounts in particular meet these criteria. As collective agreements are official documents signed by employer's associations and unions there is no reason to distrust their authenticity and credibility. However, the criteria representativeness may be challenged but as this study is explorative in nature and only a few specific collective agreements on work-life balance accounts exist so far, the size and selection of the sample is reasonable. Additionally, to alleviate this, the collective agreements are supplemented with data from other available sources, e.g. studies and articles on work-life balance accounts. However, the content analysis is limited to the intended meaning of the collective agreements and the paper does not include an analysis of how the documents may be perceived by different actors in different social settings (Scott, 1990). Nonetheless, one might argue that collective agreements on work-life balance accounts contain – like all publicly available documents (Preuss et al., 2006) – some degree of strategic positioning, but this is not problematic for the analysis as the focus is to identify the goals of the different actors associated with work-life balance accounts. In this context it can be expected that the analysed collective agreements on work-life balance accounts contain necessarily some strategic positioning. As this is an explorative study, one collective agreement from the service sector and one from the production sector have been selected to gain insight into regulation in different sectors of the economy.[1]

---

[1] In other industries similar collective agreements exist e.g. in the banking and the metal and steel industry. These could be included in future studies together with a larger sample of companies in these industries that have found company specific regulations. The collective agreements are available at www.boeckler.de and www.zds-seehafen.de.

The collective agreement of the chemical industry on "Lebensarbeitszeit und Demografie" has been closed in 2008 between the employer's association of the chemical industry (BAVC) and the IGBCE (the trade union for the chemical industry). It consists of fourteen sections and it is binding for chemical companies that are members of the employers' association in Germany and it covers all employees in the chemical industry that are members of the IGBCE. It is valid until the end of the year 2015 and cannot be terminated before. The fourteen sections have different focuses. Besides general rules on the application of the collective agreement (§1; 13; 14) the sections two and three focus on the demographic analysis and make suggestions which areas should be included. Sections four and five are concerned with issues of health care management and job engineering. The issues of qualification and different qualification measures are discussed in section six. The heart of the collective agreement is section seven that regulates the mandatory installation of a "demography fond" and the contribution of 300 € per year and employee that has to be paid by the employers. It also refers to the sections eight to twelve as these following sections regulate the possibilities for using the resources of the "demography fond". If no agreement between the partners on the workplace level can be reached then it is mandatory to introduce work-life balance accounts.[2] Section eight contains the detailed rules on work-life balance accounts while section nine regulates part-time retirement. Section ten is about part-time retirement pay ("Teilrente"), section eleven contains rules on closing a collective occupational disability insurance for all employees of the company and finally section twelve deals with aspects of company specific pension systems.

The collective agreement of the sea harbour industry has been closed in 2005 for five years between ver.di (union for service sector) and the employer's association in the sea harbour industry (Zentralverband der deutschen Seehafenbetriebe) and consists of eight sections. It is shorter than the collective agreement of the chemical industry and more focused on work-life balance accounts. Section one regulates who is entitled to participate. Sections two to five are the core of the collective agreement and deal with questions of the deployment of the saved amounts as well as with the different options that can be deposited in the accounts. Section six is concerned with the possibilities of transferability of the accounts in the case of employees leaving a company. The topic of insolvency protection of the accounts is addressed in section seven. Section eight contains general rules on the application and termination of the collective agreement.

Applying the developed conceptual framework, the collective agreements will be analysed with regard to the objectives of the involved actors on the different levels of the employment relations concerning work-life balance accounts.

---

[2] Mandatory for all companies with more than 200 employees (§ 7).

Analysis of the Collective Agreements

Strategic Level

In the theoretical discussion one of the central goals identified on the strategic level was that the collective agreement should also contain rules and regulation on dealing with the broader issue of demographic change. The collective agreement of the chemical industry accomplishes this goal, as it requires a demographic analysis including the age structure, skills and qualifications for different units or production sites (§ 2). The collective agreement in the sea harbour industry does not require a demographic analysis of companies that takes into account different qualifications and skills. With regard to the employer's goal of integrating work-life balance accounts into their existing total compensation system the collective agreement of the chemical company offers different options (time and pay components) for contribution into the accounts. Employees can be entitled – if a company agreement specifies it – to deposit parts of their vacation days, overtime hours or overtime pay, up to 10% of their yearly base pay as well as bonus payments (§ 8 No. 2). The collective agreement of the sea harbour industry also allows different components for contribution (e.g. bonus payments; § 3). On the strategic level one of the goals of the union and the government is to offer alternative ways for an early retirement. Both collective agreements explicitly regard work-life balance accounts as such an instrument (§ 8 No.1 & No.7 chemical industry; Präambel sea harbour industry).

Level of Collective Bargaining

One of the major concerns of the unions on the level of collective bargaining is financing and protecting the work-life balance accounts. In the chemical industry, the employers pay 300 € per year per employee into a "demography fond" and this money can be used for deposit into the work-life balance account (§ 7). Besides these mandatory contributions, employees can deposit parts of their vacation days, overtime hours or overtime pay, up to 10% of their yearly base pay as well as bonus payments (§ 8 No. 2). The collective agreement of the sea harbour industry regulates that besides pay components also time components like overtime can be deposited into the accounts (§ 3). Both collective agreements require that the capital in the work-life balance accounts is protected against insolvency. Another focus of the actors is the question for what purposes the amounts saved can be deployed. Employers and unions are interested in offering alternative instruments for transition into retirement as the government subsidies for "Altersteilzeit" (part-time retirement) have been abolished (Frank, 2008). Besides using the saved amounts for an early retirement the employees in the chemical industry are entitled – if a company specific agreement exists – to use their savings for sabbaticals for educational purposes, for part-time work or for elderly or child care (§ 8 No. 6).

Workplace Level

As has been discussed earlier, unionized companies offer more indirect pay components than non-unionized companies. As employers aim at increasing their leeway in compensation issues through indirect pay components, it is important that collective agreements offer a wide range of options. Besides work-life balance accounts companies can also choose to invest in additional company retirement plans, part-time retirement, part-time employment before retirement and insurance against vocational disability (§ 7 collective agreement in the chemical industry). However, the collective agreement restricts the flexibility of the actors, as they have to reach an agreement. If they do not reach an agreement on the deployment of the 300 € of the "demography fond" then work-life balance accounts have to be installed (§ 7). This mandatory rule however restricts the contribution to the work-life balance account to 300 € per year and the amount saved can only be used for early retirement. The collective agreement in the sea harbour industry gives the employers and works councils much freedom in deciding about additional components that can be used for a deposit into the account (§ 3). With regard to the options for using the saved money, the collective agreement delegates all specific regulation on the workplace level giving companies a high degree of flexibility. Both collective agreements do not explicitly focus on special groups of employees. However, the actors on the workplace level will have the freedom to reach agreements for special groups.

Summary of the Results and Avenues for Further Research

Given the different goals of the actors of the employment relations system with regard to work-life balance accounts, the question arises if the collective agreements support the deployment of work-life balance accounts as part of total compensation systems. Unions play an important role in affecting the components of a company's pay system. They can exercise their influence via collective agreements and to some extent by influencing the works councils that bargain with the employers on a local level. Employers turn to indirect pay components such as work-life balance accounts for a number of reasons, one being flexibility in the structure and total amount of pay offered as the base pay is rather fixed in unionized companies as a result of collective bargaining. Therefore it can be expected that employers will only introduce work-life balance accounts if the collective agreement gives them some flexibility in the design of this component. Both collective agreements offer enough flexibility and room for companies to negotiate company-specific regulations on the workplace level and to integrate work-life balance accounts into an existing total compensation system. Especially the rules in the collective agreement of the chemical industry that enable employees to deposit parts of their base pay or performance related bonuses in the work-life balance accounts offers plenty of opportunities for companies to combine different components of their total compensation system with work-life balance accounts. Besides allowing a wide range of resources for the accounts, it is important from a motivational point of view that the amounts saved can be deployed for different options – not only for early retirement as younger workers might prefer additional time off for educational purposes or child-care. Here again the collective agreements offer a wide range of possibilities. For instance, the collective agreement of the chemical industry explicitly states that the savings can be used for sabbaticals for educational purposes, for part-time work or for elderly or child care (§ 8 No. 6). The collective agreement in the sea harbour industry delegates the decision on the use of the saved amounts completely to the workplace level. This enables companies to bargain workplace level agreements on work-life balance accounts according to their needs and existing total compensation system.

Unions and employees accept indirect pay components as they contribute to satisfying their needs for security. The collective agreements take up this issue by requiring protecting of the accounts against insolvency of the employer to avoid that employees bear the risk of losing their savings and jobs at the same time. Another aspect of security is that the employer pays the contribution to the work-life balance accounts. Here the collective agreement of the chemical industry accomplishes this goal as the employers pay 300 € per year and employee in a "demography fond". The amount will rise in future with every pay increase of the employees, providing additional security. A further concern for unions is that many groups of employees will not be able to work until the mandatory retirement age due to health concerns. Thus it is important to install instruments that allow employees to enter retirement at an earlier stage without losing too much income. Work-life balance accounts offer one solution for this task and as part of a total compensation system they allow specific groups of employees to put more money into their accounts if they for example work in physically demanding jobs.

Concerning the government, the regulation for work-life balance accounts has set a framework in which industry and company specific agreements can be reached. It remains to be seen if more industries will follow and close collective agreements on work-life balance accounts.

Summarizing, the results of the analysis show that the regulations in the collective agreements allow companies to meet the expectations of a total compensation approach when using work-life balance accounts as part of their pay system. Additionally this preliminary study gives important hints on research topics in this area. To gain insight into the company specific problems with implementing work-life balance accounts as a part of a total compensation system, a more detailed analysis of company-level agreements is needed. This would allow to analyse the specific design of work-life balance accounts of individual companies and to judge them against the framework set in the collective agreement (e.g. how extensively was the framework used?) as well as to make comparisons between companies and industries concerning goals, components allowed for contribution and possibilities of using the accounts. In a next step surveys within companies should be conducted to analyse the acceptance of work-life balance accounts among employees, to evaluate why employees participate, how much they contribute and save, why it is attractive to participate and for which purpose they are planning to use their accounts. Another field of research concerns demographic change and the question if work-life balance accounts have supported companies by dealing with demographic problems such as reducing a loss of know-how or finding ways of a smooth transition into retirement. Future research should also address important effects on the link between work-life balance accounts and the total compensation system. Has the introduction of this new indirect pay component influence on the overall pay mix of companies, on individual and organizational performance, on motivational issues and aspects such as retention and employer attractiveness. As this short summary shows this field of research is just at its beginning with many open questions to answer for researchers and practitioners alike.

References

Aragon-Sanchez, A., Barba-Aragon, I. & Sanz-Valle, R. (2003). Effects of training on business results. International Journal of Human Resource Management, 14, 956-980.

Ars, V., Blümke, A. & Scheithauer, C. (2009)*. Nach dem Flexi II – Neue Spielregeln für Zeitwertkonten II. Betriebs-Berater, 42, 2252-2263.

Aubert, N. (2008)*. Developing an Ownership Culture with Employee Share Purchase Plans: Evidence from France. ZfP, 22, 130-151.

Backes-Gellner, U. (2004). Personnel Economics, Management Revue, 15, 215-227.

Becker, F.G. (1990). Anreizsysteme für Führungskräfte. Stuttgart.

Beier, M.E. & Ackerman, P.L. (2005). Age, Ability and the role of prior knowledge on the acquisition of new domain knowledge. Psychology and Aging, 20, 341-355.

Birkner, G. (2008). Zeitwertkonten im Mittelstand. Erwartungen und Erfahrungen mit Zeitwertkonten – eine Studie. F.A.Z.-Institut für Management-, Markt- und Medieninformationen GmbH/HDI Gerling Leben Serviceholding AG (Eds.), Frankfurt/Main.

Börsch-Supan, A. (2002). Labor Market Effects of Population Aging, Mannheim Research Institute for the Economics of Aging (MEA). University of Mannheim.

Bothe, A. (2009a)*. „Flexi II" und BMF-Schreiben schaffen erhöhten Beratungsbedarf. Vermögen & Steuern, 1, 26-27.

Bothe, A. (2009b)*. Zeit ist Geld. Personalwirtschaft, 36, 58-59.

Boyd, B.K. & Salamin, A. (2001). Strategic Reward Systems: a Contingency Model of Pay System Design. Strategic Management Journal, 22, 777-792.

Brewster, C. & Suutari, V. (2005). Guest Editorial. Global HRM: aspects of a research agenda. Personnel Review, 43, 5-21.

Bröckermann, R. (2007). Personalwirtschaft: Lehr- und Übungsbuch für Human Resource Management. 4. Auflage. Stuttgart.

Brown, M. & Heywood, J. (2005). Performance Appraisal Systems. Journal of Industrial Relations, 43, 659-679.

Calder, B.J. & Staw, B.M. (1975). The self-perception of intrinsic and extrinsic motivation. Journal of Personality and Social Psychology, 31, 599-605.

Chui, W.C.K., Chan, A.W., Snape, E. & Redman, T. (2001). Age Stereotypes and Discriminatory Attitudes towards older workers. Human Relations, 54, 629-661.

Cisch, T.B. & Ulbrich, M. (2009)*. Flexi-Gesetz II: Licht und Schatten. Betriebs-Berater, 11, 550-558.

Cooke, W.N. (1994). Employee Participation Programs, Group-Based Incentives and Company Performance. Industrial and Labor Relations Review, 47, 594-609.

Deci, E.L. (1975). Intrinsic Motivation. Plenum Press.

Deci, E.L. & Flaste, R. (1995). Why We Do What We Do: The Dynamics of Personal Autonomy. Putnam.

Delaney, J.T. & Huselid, M.A. (1996). The impact of human resource management practices on perceptions of organizational performance. Academy of Management Journal, 39, 949-969.

Delery, J.E. & Doty, D.H. (1996). Modes of theorizing in strategic human resource management: Tests of universalistic, contingency, and configurational performance predictions. Academy of Management Journal, 39, 802-835.

Deller, J. (2008). Personalmanagement im demografischen Wandel. Ein Handbuch für den Veränderungsprozess. Heidelberg 2008.

DeLong, D. (2004). Lost Knowledge. Oxford.

Deutscher Bundestag (2002). Schlussbericht der Enquete-Kommission „Demographischer Wandel". Drucksache 14/880, Berlin.

Dielmann, K. (2007). Von wegen „altes Eisen". Personalführung, 40, 60-63.

Duben, R. (2008)*. Vieles möglich, wenig genutzt. Personalwirtschaft, 12, 48-50.

Dychtwald, K., Erickson, T. & Morison, B. (2004). It's time to retire retirement. Harvard Business Review, 82, 48-57.

Dychtwald, K., Erickson, T. & Morison, R. (2006). Workforce Crisis. New York.

Fehr, E. & Gachter, S. (2000). Fairness and retaliation. The economics of reciprocity. Journal of Economic Perspectives, 14, 159-181.

Flynn, M. (2010). Who would delay retirement? Typologies of older workers. Personnel Review, 39, 308-324.

Frank, T. (2008). Sozialrechtliche Absicherung flexible Arbeitszeitregelungen. ZRP, 8, 255-258.

Freudenthal, D. (2001). The Role of Age, Foreknowledge and Complexity in Learning to Operate a Complex Device. Behaviour & Information Technology, 20, 23-35.

Frey, B.S. & Oberholzer-Gee, F. (1997). The cost of price incentives: an empirical analysis of motivation crowding-out. American Economic Review, 87, 746-755.

Galbraith, J.R. (1983). Strategy and organization planning. Human Resource Management, 22, 63-77.

Garhammer, M. (1994). Balanceakt Zeit. Auswirkungen flexibler Arbeitszeiten auf Alltag, Freizeit und Familie. Berlin.

Geddes, L.A. & Heywood, J. (2003). Gender and Piece Rates, Commissions and Bonuses. Industrial Relations, 42, 419-444.

Gerhart, B. & Milkovich, G. (1990). Organizational Differences in Managerial Compensation and Financial Performance. Academy of Management Journal, 33, 663-691.

Gibbons, R. (1998). Incentives in organizations. Journal of Economic Perspectives, 12, 115-132.

Gillenkirchen, R.M. (2008)*. Entwicklungslinien in der Managementvergütung. BFuP, 60, 1-17.

Gomez-Mejia, L.R. (1992). Structure and process of diversification, compensation strategy, and firm performance. Strategic Management Journal, 13, 381-397.

Grawert, A. (1995). Flexibilisierung und Individualisierung der Arbeitszeit aus Sicht der Mitarbeiter. In D. Wagner (Hrsg.), Arbeitszeitmodelle (S. 111-124).Göttingen.

Hambrick, D.C. & Snow, C.C. (1987). Strategic reward systems. In C.C. Snow (Ed.), Strategy, organization design, and human resource management (pp. 68-96). Greenwich.

Hamisch, A.-C. (2008)*. Neue Spielregeln für externe Kapitalanlage. Arbeit und Arbeitsrecht, 12, 746-747.

Hasebrook, J. & Maurer, M. (2009)*. Flexibel werden und bleiben – Ansätze im Personalmanagement. Bank und Markt, 8, 20-23.

Heery, E. (1997). Performance-Related Pay and Trade Union Membership. Employee Relations, 19, 430-442.

Heidemann, J. (2010)*. Betriebliche Zeitwertkonten. Versicherungspraxis, 8, 145-152.

Henkens, K., Remery, C. & Schippers, J. (2008). Shortages in an ageing labour market. International Journal of Human Resource Management, 19, 1314-1329.

Hentze, J. & Graf, A. (2005). Personalwirtschaftslehre 2. Bern.

Hertel, I., Wojtysiak, C. & Lorentz, R. (2003). Lebensarbeitszeitmodell als Alternative. Personalwirtschaft, 30, 19-22.

Hoff, A. & Priemuth, T. (2001). Langzeitkonten heute und morgen: Ergebnisse einer Betriebsumfrage. Personalführung, 34, 50-53.

Hoff, A. (2009). Zeitkonten in der Krise. Personalführung, 42, 58-64.

Hummel, M., Thein, A. & Zika, G. (2010). Der Arbeitskräftebedarf nach Wirtschaftszweigen, Berufen und Qualifikationen. In R. Helmrich & G. Zika (Hrsg.), Beruf und Qualifikation in der Zukunft (S. 81-102). Bielefeld.

Jones, D. & Pliskin, J. (1997). Determinants of the Incidence of Group Incentives. Canadian Journal of Economics, 30, 1027-1045.

Kalinowski, M. & Quinke, H. (2010). Projektion des Arbeitskräfteangebotes bis 2025 nach Qualifikationsstufen und Berufsfeldern. In R. Helmrich & G. Zika (Hrsg.), Beruf und Qualifikation in der Zukunft (S. 103-123). Bielefeld.

Kanfer, R. & Ackerman, P. (2004). Aging, Adult Development and Work Motivation. Academy of Management Review, 29, 440-458.

Kast, R. (2009)*. Personalentwicklung im Vorfeld des demografischen Wandels. Wirtschaftspsychologie, 3, 87-96.

Katheder, M. & Kast, R. (2010)*. Passgenauigkeit und Flexibilität als Anforderungen an moderne Zeitwertkontensysteme. Kreditwesen, 16, 862-864.

Kessler, I. & Purcell, J. (1995). Individualism and Collectivism in Theory and Practice: Management Style and the Design of Pay Systems. In P.K. Edwards (Ed.), Industrial Relations, Oxford.

Klemm, B. (2009)*. Neue Regelungen zu Wertguthaben. Personalmagazin, 4, 70-72.

Klemm, B. (2010)*. Wertguthaben bei Gutverdienern. Personalmagazin, 4, 72-73.

Kochan, T.A., Katz, H.C. & McKersie R.B. (1994). The transformation of American Industrial Relations. Ithaca.

Kochan, T.A., McKersie, R. B. & Cappelli, P. (1984). Strategic choice and industrial relations theory. Industrial Relations, 23, 16-39.

Kohn, A. (1999). Punished by Reward: The Trouble with Gold Stars, Incentive Plans, A's, Praise, and Other Bribes. Houghton Mifflin.

Krugman, P.R. (1995). Peddling Prosperity. New York.

Kruse, D. (1996). Why do Firms Adopt Profit-Sharing and Employee Ownership Plans? British Journal of Industrial Relations, 34, 515-538.

Kümmerle, K. (2006). Zeitwertkonten. Kompaktwissen für das Personalbüro. Heidelberg u. a.

Kümmerle, K. (2007). Zeit und Geld für später sammeln. Personalwirtschaft, 34, 36-39.

Kümmerle, K., Buttler, A. & Keller, M. (2006). Betriebliche Zeitwertkonten. Einführung und Gestaltung in der Praxis. Heidelberg u. a.

Kuwan, H., Thebis, F., Gnahs, D., Sandau, E. & Seidel, S. (2003). Berichtssystem Weiterbildung VIII. Bonn.

Long, R.L. & Shields, J.L. (2009)*. Do unions affect pay methods of Canadian firms? A longitudinal study. Industrial Relations, 64, 442-465.

Lüdenbach, W. (2008). Ein Sparpaket, das sich auszahlt, Personalwirtschaft. 35, 38-40.

Mathis, R.L. & Jackson, J.H. (2009). Human Resource Management: Essential Perspectives, Mason.

McEvoy, G. & Cascio, W. (1989). Cumulative Evidence on the Relationship between Employee Age and Job performance. Journal of Applied Psychology, 74, 11-16.

Milgrom, P.R. & Roberts, J. (1992). Economics, Organisation and Management. Englewood Cliffs, NJ: Prentice-Hall.

Milkovich, G. & Newman, J. (2002). Compensation. New York.

Miller, D. (1988). Relating Porter's business strategies to environment and structure: Analysis and performance implications. Academy of Management Journal, 31, 280-308.

Mitlacher, L.W. (2008). Job quality and temporary agency work. International Journal of Human Resource Management, 19, 448-462.

Moog, M. & Wellisch, D. (2005). Arbeitszeitkonten und Portabilität. Betriebs-Berater, 60, 1790-1795.

Morschhäuser, M., Huber, A. & Ochs, P. (2003). Erfolgreich mit älteren Arbeitnehmern. Strategien und Beispiele für die betriebliche Praxis. Gütersloh.

Naegele, G. & Frerichs, F. (2004). Arbeitnehmer, ältere. In E. Gaugler (Hrsg.), Handwörterbuch des Personalwesens (S. 85-93). 3. Aufl. Stuttgart.

Ng, E.S.W. & Burke, R.J. (2005). Person-Organization fit and the war for talent. International Journal of Human Resource Management, 16, 1195-1210.

Osterloh, M., Frost, J. & Frey, B.S. (2002). The dynamics of motivation in new organizational forms. International Journal of the Economics of Business, 9, 61-77.

Paul, R. & Townsend, J. (1993). Managing the older worker. Academy of Management Executive, 7, 67-74.

Preuss, L., Haunschild, A. & Matten, D. (2006). Trade Unions and CSR: a European research agenda. Journal of Public Affairs, 6, 256-268.

Reed, K., Doty, H. & May, D. (2005). The impact of aging on self-efficiency and computer skill acquisition. Journal of Managerial Issues, 17, 221-228.

Reich, T. (2008)*. Änderungen bei Zeitwertkonten. Arbeit und Arbeitsrecht, 10, 620.

Reichel, C. & Köckeritz, H. (2009)*. Mehr Flexibilität – auch bei Altguthaben? Arbeit und Arbeitsrecht, 7, 426-429.

Renaud, S. (1998). Unions, Wages, and Total Compensation in Canada. Industrial Relations, 53, 710-729.

Rousseau, D.M. (1995). Psychological Contracts in Organizations: Understanding Written and Unwritten Agreements. Sage Publications.

Rynes, S.L., Gerhart, B. & Parks, L. (2005). Personnel Psychology: Performance Evaluation and Pay for Performance. Annual Review of Psychology, 56, 571-600.

Schuler, R.S. (1992). Linking the people with the strategic needs of the business. Organizational Dynamics, Summer, 8-32.

Schuler, R.S. & Jackson, S.E. (1989). Determinants of human resource management priorities and implications for industrial relations. Journal of Management, 15, 89-99.

Scott, J. (1990). A Matter of Record: Documentary Sources in Social Research. Cambridge.

Statistisches Bundesamt (Hrsg.) (2009). Bevölkerung Deutschlands bis 2060. Wiesbaden.

Staudinger, U. (2006). Konsequenzen des demografischen Wandels für betriebliche Handlungsfelder: eine interdisziplinäre Perspektive. ZfBF, 58, 690-698.

Steger, T. & Hartz, R. (2008)*. The power of participation? Power relations and processes in employee-owned companies. ZfP, 22, 152-170.

Steinhaus, R. & Uckermann, S. (2010)*. BMF präzisiert die Rahmenbedingungen. Vermögen & Steuern, 1, 44-48.

Streb, C., Voelpel, S. & Leibold, M. (2009). Aging Workforce Management in the Automobile Industry: Defining the Concept and its Constituting Elements. Zeitschrift für Personalforschung, 23, 8-27.

Thom, N. & Zaugg, R.J. (2004). Nachhaltiges und innovatives Personalmanagement. In Schwarz, E.J. (Hrsg.), Nachhaltiges Innovationsmanagement (S. 215-245). Wiesbaden.

Tichy, N.M., Fombrun, C.J. & Devanna, M.A. (1982). Strategic human resource management. Sloan Management Review, Winter, 47-61.

Tyler, T.R. (1994). Psychological models of the justice motive: antecedents of distributive and procedural justice. Journal of Personality and Social Psychology, 64, 850-863.

Uckermann, S. (2008). Änderung der gesetzlichen Rahmenbedingungen von Zeitwertkonten. Betriebs-Berater, 63, 1281-1290.

Vandenberghe, C., St-Onge, S. & Robineau, E. (2008). An Analysis of the Relation between Personality and the Attractiveness of Total Rewards Components. Industrial Relations, 63, 425-453.

Voelpel, S., Leibold, M. & Fürchtenicht, J. (2007). Herausforderung 50plus. Erlangen.

Vom Feld, I. (2009)*. Wenn Gutes gestärkt wird. Personalwirtschaft, 4, 58-60.

Voß, E. (2003). Mitarbeiterbeteiligung in deutschen Unternehmen. Wiesbaden.

Wellisch, D. & Machill, M. (2008)*. Bilanzierung von Lebensarbeitszeitkonten nach IFRS. KoR, 12, 748-754.

Wellisch, D. & Machill, M. (2009)*. Bilanzierung von Wertkonten nach dem BilMoG. Betriebs-Berater, 25, 1351-1356.

Wellisch, D. (2005a). Der lange geplante Ausstieg. Personalwirtschaft, 32, 53-55.

Wellisch, D. (2005b). Mehr Flexibilität mit Lebensarbeitszeitkonten. Personalwirtschaft, 32, 48-50.

Wellisch, D. (2008)*. Vielfalt bei Arbeitszeitkonten. Personalmagazin, 12, 78-79.

Wellisch, D., Kroll, K. & Lenz, S.-O. (2010)*. Bitte nochmals nachbessern. Personalwirtschaft, 7, 20-23.

Winter, S. (1997). Möglichkeiten der Gestaltung von Anreizsystemen für Führungskräfte. DBW, 63, 615-629.

Wonnenberger, W. (1999). Der rechtliche Rahmen für flexible Arbeitszeitregelungen mit Arbeitszeitkonten. In J. Gutmann (Hrsg.), Arbeitszeitmodelle. Die neue Zeit der Arbeit: Erfahrungen mit Konzepten der Flexibilisierung (S. 79-93). Stuttgart.

Wotschack, P., Scheier, F. & Hildebrandt, E. (2009). Keine Zeit für die Auszeit. Langzeitkonten schaffen im Erwerbsverlauf bisher kaum Entlastungen. WZB Mitteilungen, 123, 12-15.

Wright, P.M. & McMahan, G.C. (1992). Alternative theoretical perspectives for strategic human resource management. Journal of Management, 18, 295-320.

Wright, P.M. & Snell, S.A. (1991). Toward an integrative view of Strategic Human Resource Management. Human Resource Management Review, 1, 203-225.

Yin, R. (2003). Case Study Research: Design and Methods. Thousand Oaks, CA.

Youndt, M.A., Snell, S.A., Dean, J.W. & Lepak, D.P. (1996). Human resource management, manufacturing strategy, and firm performance. Academy of Management Journal, 39, 836-866.

*=included in the literature review

List of Contributors

Conny Antoni
University of Trier, Work and Organizational Psychology, Universitätsring 15, D-54286 Trier, Germany, tel. +49 (0) 651 201 2030, antoni@uni-trier.de

Xavier Baeten
Vlerick Leuven Gent Management School, Reward Management Centre, Reep 1, 9000, Gent, Belgium, tel. +32 9 210 9897, xavier.baeten@vlerick.be

Biljana Bogićević Milikić
Faculty of Economics, University of Belgrade, Kamenićka 6, Belgrade, Serbia, tel. +381 (11) 3670 154, bbiljana@Eunet.rs

Marco Celentani
Departamento de Economía, Universidad Carlos III, Calle Madrid 126, Getafe (Madrid) 28903, Spain, tel. +34 91 624 9546, marco.celentani@uc3m.es

Jonathan Chapman
Cranfield School of Management, Bedford, England, MK43 0AL, tel. +44 (0) 1234 751122, Jonathan.chapman@cranfield.ac.uk

Clare Kelliher
Cranfield School of Management, Bedford, England, MK43 0AL, tel. +44 (0) 1234 751122, clare.kelliher@cranfield.ac.uk

Rosa Mª Loveira-Pazó
Departamento de Fundamentos del Análisis Económico e Historia e Instituciones Económicas, Universidade de Vigo, Campus Lagoas Marcosende, Vigo, 36310, Spain; fax: +34 986 812401, rloveira@uvigo.es.

Rosemary Lucas
Professor of Employment Relations, Manchester Metropolitan University, Business School, Manchester Metropolitan University, Aytoun St, Manchester M1 3GH, UK, tel. +44 (0) 161 247 3868, r.lucas@mmu.ac.uk

Lars W. Mitlacher
Baden-Württemberg Cooperative State University at Villingen-Schwenningen, Friedrich Ebert Str. 30, 78054 Villingen-Schwenningen, Germany, tel. +49 (0) 7720 3906 517, mitlacher@dhbw-vs.de.

Stephen J. Perkins
Professor of Strategy and HRM, Director, Business & Management Research Institute, University of Bedfordshire, Park Square, Luton, Bedfordshire LU1 3JU, UK, stephen.perkins@beds.ac.uk

Laurent Sié
IRMAPE Laboratory, Groupe ESC PAU, 3 rue Saint-John Perse , B.P. 7512 - 64075 PAU, Cedex , France, tel +33 5 59 92 33 06, laurent.sie@esc-pau.fr

Christelle Tornikoski
University of Vaasa, Department of Management, P.O.Box 700, FI-65101 Vaasa, Finland, ctorni@uwasa.fi / EMLYON Business School, Department of Law, Management & Human Resources, 23 Avenue Guy de Collongue, 69134 Ecully cedex, France, c-tornikoski@em-lyon.com

Matti Vartiainen
Aalto University, Department of Industrial Engineering and Management, Work Psychology and Leadership, P.O.Box 5500, 02015 TKK, Finland, tel. +358 50 555 3380, matti.vartiainen@tkk.fi

Ali Yakhlef
Stockholm University School of Business Roslagsvägen 101, Kräftriket Stockholm tel. +46 8 16 39 48, aya@fek.su.se

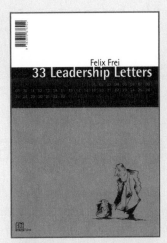

288 pages, Price: 25,- Euro
ISBN 978-3-89967-640-2

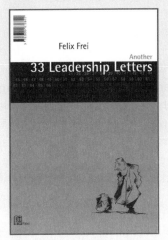

288 pages, Price: 25,- Euro
ISBN 978-3-89967-682-2

PABST SCIENCE PUBLISHERS
Eichengrund 28
D-49525 Lengerich
Tel. ++ 49 (0) 5484-308
Fax ++ 49 (0) 5484-550
pabst.publishers@t-online.de
www.psychologie-aktuell.com
www.pabst-publishers.de

Leadership Letters without managerial babble

Leading is not everything a manager does. In a narrow sense, leading people incorporates all the things the manager is personally held responsible for.

Leadership development primarily depends on self-critical reflection. That, however, requires a certain openness and readiness to learn – and self-reflection is not always easy.

With his 66 Leadership-Letters Dr. Felix Frei has developed a tool that may not be able to replace critical self-reflection, but can certainly contribute to it by stimulating thought.

The author is not promoting subversion, but he emphasizes: "The very core is p e r s o n a l leadership. What you will get is standing, more respect and a distinctive image. You will be perceived as an individual with his/her own leadership style. Master the modern work and management tools at your disposal - but don´t let them master you ..."

Felix Frei – Psychologist and Consultant in Zürich – writes in his own language and leaves it to his colleagues to try to impress people with ´management speak´...

Silvio Erni´s cartoons don´t only entertain, but they help to keep the topics and the user´s personal thoughts about them in mind.

Felix Frei: 33 Leadership Letters (English + German), Silvio L. Erni: 33 Cartoons. Pabst, Lengerich/Berlin 2010

Felix Frei: Another 33 Leadership Letters (English + German), Silvio L. Erni: 33 Cartoons. Pabst, Lengerich/Berlin 2011